Hunting Evil

Hunting Evil

Inside the Ipswich Serial Murders

PAUL HARRISON
and DAVID WILSON

SPHERE

First published in Great Britain as a paperback original
in 2008 by Sphere

Map © Russ Billington www.vector-redraw.co.uk

A CIP catalogue record for this book is
available from the British Library.

ISBN 978-0-7515-4024-6

Typeset in Sabon by M Rules
Printed and bound in Great Britain by
Clays Ltd, St Ives plc

Sphere
An Imprint of
Little, Brown Book Group
100 Victoria Embankment
London EC4Y 0DY

An Hachette Livre UK Company
www.hachettelivre.co.uk

www.littlebrown.co.uk

Contents

Timeline
Ipswich Murders

MONDAY 30 OCTOBER 2006. Tania Nicol goes missing from the red-light area of Ipswich, and on Thursday 2 NOVEMBER 2006 a public appeal is issued to the media asking for help to find the missing teenager.

TUESDAY 7 NOVEMBER 2006. Kerry Nicol – Tania's mother – gives an interview to the press asking for anyone with information about Tania's whereabouts to come forward. Leaflets are handed out on the bus route that Tania may have taken.

WEDNESDAY 15 NOVEMBER 2006. Gemma Adams is reported missing by her partner, and the police launch a further appeal for information. Four days later on Sunday 19 NOVEMBER 2006 the police hand out leaflets appealing for help to find the missing women at the Ipswich v Norwich football derby taking place at Portman Road, in the red-light district.

SATURDAY 2 DECEMBER 2006. A member of the public finds a naked body in a brook at Hintlesham, and the following day the body is formally identified as being that of Gemma Adams.

SUNDAY 3 DECEMBER 2006. Anneli Alderton disappears..

MONDAY 4 DECEMBER 2006. A murder inquiry is formally launched and a fourth woman, Annette Nicholls, is reported missing.

TUESDAY 5 DECEMBER 2006. Paula Clennell gives an interview saying that she knows the dangers involved but is prepared to go back on the streets.

FRIDAY 8 DECEMBER 2006. A second body is found by police divers at Copdock Mill and Paul Harrison does his first live broadcast for Sky about the case. The following day – Saturday 9 DECEMBER 2006 – the police confirm that the body is that of Tania Nicol and admit that there are 'obvious similarities' between the two cases.

SUNDAY 10 DECEMBER 2006. Paul Harrison and David Wilson make their first joint Sky broadcast. Wilson says, given his knowledge of the roads, that the killer 'lived or worked in the local area', was 'comfortable around prostitutes', and had 'killed before'. Later that day the police announce that the body of a third woman – Anneli Alderton – has been found in woodland near Nacton, although they do not confirm her identity until two days later. Detectives say it is too early to link this death to the deaths of Tania and Gemma.

MONDAY 11 DECEMBER 2006. Police announce that they are concerned about the disappearances of two other missing women – Paula Clennell and Annette Nicholls. Assistant Chief Constable Jacqui Cheer warns prostitutes to 'stay off the streets'.

TUESDAY 12 DECEMBER 2006. Police find two bodies near the village of Levington, some five miles south of Ipswich. Detective Chief Superintendent Stewart Gull states 'Sadly, I fear that these may be the bodies of Paula Clennell and Annette Nicholls.'

WEDNESDAY 13 DECEMBER 2006. Paula Clennell's body, which had been found at Levington, is removed for detailed forensic examination, and police confirm that the women did not die at the site where their bodies had been dumped. Annette Nicholls' body is removed the following day when police confirm that Paula had died as a result of 'compression to the neck'.

SATURDAY 16 DECEMBER 2006. CCTV footage of Anneli Alderton on a train shortly before she disappeared is released to the media. A minute's silence is held at Portman Road where Ipswich are playing Leeds United.

MONDAY 18 DECEMBER 2006. Police arrest Tom Stephens after he has given an interview to a Sunday newspaper.

TUESDAY 19 DECEMBER 2006. Steve Wright is arrested by detectives. Wright lives in London Road, Ipswich, in the heart of the red-light district.

WEDNESDAY 20 DECEMBER 2006. Inquests into the deaths of the women are opened and adjourned at Ipswich Coroner's Court.

THURSDAY 21 DECEMBER 2006. Steve Wright is charged with the murder of all five women and Tom Stephens is released on police bail.

FRIDAY 22 DECEMBER 2006. Wright appears before Ipswich magistrates and is remanded in custody.

TUESDAY 6 FEBRUARY 2007. Funeral of Annette Nicholls.

THURSDAY 8 FEBRUARY 2007. Funeral of Paula Clennell is held in her home town of Berwick.

MONDAY 12 FEBRUARY 2007. Funeral of Tania Nicol.

THURSDAY 15 FEBRUARY 2007. Funeral of Gemma Adams.

FRIDAY 23 FEBRUARY 2007. Funeral of Anneli Alderton.

WEDNESDAY 21 MARCH 2007. Wright appears before Ipswich Crown Court and pleads 'not guilty'.

MONDAY 14 JANUARY 2008. Trial begins at Ipswich Crown Court.

THURSDAY 21 FEBRUARY 2008. Wright found guilty of all five murders.

FRIDAY 22 FEBRUARY 2008. Wright sentenced to life imprisonment and a 'whole life tariff'.

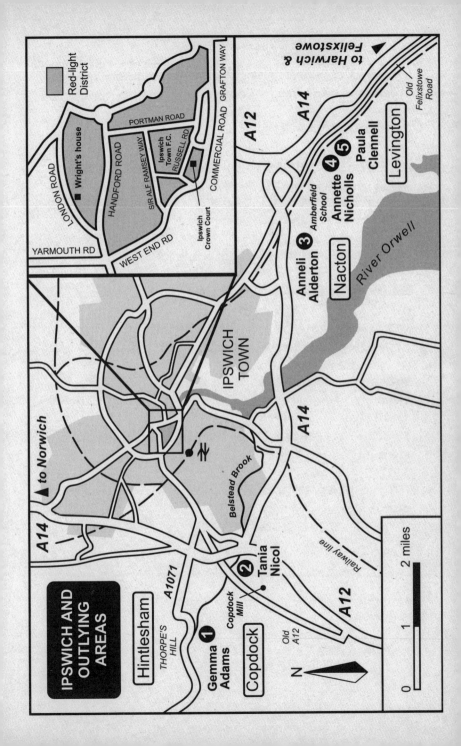

Hunting Evil

Prologue

The sign read: 'Diversion'. It might as well have said: 'Crime scene this way'.

Ignoring the bollard in the middle of the road, I mounted the kerb and drove on. Fifteen miles per hour in second gear, hazard lights flashing and windscreen wipers at half speed.

The macabre image of what I'd come to report on – though clearly formed by those I'd seen in television dramas – was nonetheless fixed and real in my mind. The two-hour drive had helped bring some focus to my thoughts.

The sudden urgency in the voice of the radio presenter brought my attention back to the dark and dreary evening, but the news headlines told me little more than I knew already. With no oncoming traffic the white lines in the middle of the road guided me towards the blurred, distant, blue flashing lights. It was only a matter of a few hundred metres before I was waved down by a sodden policewoman.

'And how did you manage to get here?' she asked, peering in, knowing full well I'd chosen to ignore the police's attempt to divert traffic.

'Here' was badly lit. It was cold, innocuous, and on this dark December evening it was damp too – heavy drizzle, the enemy of the forensic officer. And 'here' would also be the place where Suffolk Police would eventually realise that they were hunting a serial murderer. This was Copdock, and I would get to know it well.

'You'll have to park over there, sir,' said the officer as she helpfully kicked aside two traffic cones to let me pass.

Five p.m. was drawing close – three hours earlier the news desk had called.

'Paul, they've found a second body; what time do you think you can get there?'

'Ipswich? Probably two, two and a half hours at most, though it is Friday and you know what the M25 is like,' I said, suddenly feeling the pressure to get there in time for Sky News' main early evening show – *Live at Five*.

I had been preparing to head to Ipswich anyway – Sky News' managing editor and home news editor had seen the potential of the story a few days before, even though at that stage only the body of Gemma Adams had been discovered. But her nineteen-year-old friend Tania Nicol, who also earned her living as a prostitute, had been reported missing as well. Their journalistic instincts were to be proved right.

The brief had been to spend the night filming in the red-light district for a report for Saturday. The aim had been to talk to some of the girls working the streets about their fears now that one woman had been found dead on the outskirts of Ipswich, and see how they were protecting themselves from a potential serial killer.

Now that a second body had been discovered in Copdock, this 'pre-shoot' immediately became a live story.

'Hi, Paul, can you hear the programme OK?' asked the sound technician through my earpiece. A thumbs-up down the barrel of the camera answered his question. 'OK, I'll pass you on to the producer.'

'Is there anything you can show us, Paul?' asked the

gallery producer. The truth was we'd been purposely corralled a good hundred metres away from the area police had floodlit – so the answer was 'no'. 'We're coming to you in thirty seconds.'

Then came the voice of presenter Jeremy Thompson in my right ear. 'Now police in Ipswich investigating the murder of prostitute Gemma Adams have discovered a second body in the nearby village of Copdock. It's feared it could be that of missing nineteen-year-old Tania Nicol, who also worked in the town's red-light district. Sky's Paul Harrison is in Copdock. Paul, what more are police telling you?'

It would be the first of more than one hundred live 'two-ways' to come. My overnight bag in the boot would soon prove woefully inadequate – my 'overnight' in Ipswich would in fact last for what seemed like a lifetime.

It didn't, however, take me a lifetime to realise that I was no criminologist and the coverage of events that began to unfold needed the brain of someone tuned in to the complex minds of serial killers. So I was somewhat relieved when the news desk phoned to say that someone else was on the way. But there was a catch.

'You'll have to pay the taxi driver cash in hand; he'll have waiting time, too, and remember it is the weekend,' explained Mark Evans, manning the news desk.

It was to be a £250 fare worth every penny.

Two hours later a black Mercedes pulled up at the Elizabeth Hotel in Copdock and Professor David Wilson emerged from the back of the car. He was younger than I'd expected – 'Professor' always seems to suggest an older person – and he was well groomed, too.

'You must be Paul,' he said. I concurred with a firm handshake, an early seal of our friendship. We then moved off without further ado – what he really wanted to see was where the bodies of Gemma and Tania had been discovered.

Little did I know that, from that moment on, together we would be hunting evil.

Introduction

The Return of the English Murder

'. . . let me try to define what it is that the readers of Sunday papers mean when they say fretfully that "you never seem to get a good murder nowadays".'

George Orwell, 'Decline of the English Murder' (1946)

For three weeks in December 2006 the whole world seemed to descend on Ipswich, the county town of Suffolk. Described on the homepage of the local Borough Council as being 'in the heart of East Anglia and the heart of Europe', Ipswich is England's oldest continuously settled Anglo-Saxon town, with some 140,000 inhabitants. Located on the River Orwell – from which George Orwell took half of his pseudonym – the town's inhabitants found themselves gripped by a police investigation into the murders of five young women and a media frenzy to cover the case.

As a result, the largely hidden and secret local economies related to Class A drugs and street prostitution became a matter of public debate. In an age of twenty-four-hour news the day-to-day investigation by the county police force into these murders was soon leading every hourly bulletin, with a range of experts lining up to explain what was going on, or at least what they thought was going on.

All this attention was more than justified, for the five murders that had taken place were a stark reminder that, whatever the changing nature of Britain within a global economy, some issues – such as illicit street sex and poverty – are stubbornly immune to new Government initiatives, local policing tactics or the civic boosterism that seemed to characterise the Borough Council's motto.

And in the same way that Orwell bemoaned the fact that the type of murder that was taking place in England in the 1940s was changing as a result of the Second World War, so too the murders that took place in Ipswich in 2006 seemed both to reflect something of the changes that Britain had been experiencing economically while at the same time – at least on the surface – harking back to the days of Jack the Ripper. Orwell, writing specifically about the so-called 'Cleft Chin Murder' in 1944 by an American army deserter called Karl Hulten and an English waitress called Elizabeth Jones, was complaining somewhat ironically that the background to murder at that time had become tainted by the empty values of dance halls and American films, and that this stood in contrast to the murders committed in pre-war Britain.

In Ipswich in 2006 the background to murder was changing too, if only because these murders weren't committed by some jilted lover, or an angry husband in a domestic dispute, but instead by that most post-modern of 'inventions' – the serial killer. And just as in Orwell's day the newspaper-reading public got their 'greatest amount of pleasure' from a good old-fashioned murder, so too the public can now think of no better way to be entertained, fascinated and appalled than hearing about the exploits of those who kill and kill again. Whether in the form of films or books such as *The Silence of the Lambs*, *Manhunter* or *Hannibal*, or in TV programmes like *Cracker* or *Wire in the Blood*, the serial killer and those who try to stop him (of late usually psychologists of various kinds) have become staples of the entertainment media. And yet the Ipswich murders weren't entertainment, even if they were 'news' – they were all too depressingly real, and this book takes you straight to that awful, sad and frightening reality.

We break new territory too, by being among the first people 'on the ground' in Suffolk, with access to the sites where the bodies of the five young women were dumped; and using contacts within the police, other criminal justice agencies, the media and also the family, friends and acquaintances of the convicted killer Steve Wright, we argue that he was responsible for other unsolved murders dating back to the early 1990s. And, based on what we learned in Ipswich, we suggest how public policy should respond to the supply and demand of street prostitution in this country, and urge the Government to use this case to take more decisive action than they have hitherto done.

In this book we try to tell the story of what actually happened, and build up a picture of the people and places at the heart of that story. We offer pen portraits of the victims which we have constructed through talking to their family and friends, and using other records – where they exist – we try to describe their lives. We also present the stories of other young women still working in the red-light area of Ipswich, and who sadly also help to reveal how persistent the demand for street prostitution continues to be even in the wake of serial killings. And we build up a profile of Steve Wright, although we have not interviewed him directly, despite several requests that we be allowed to do so. Even so, we have been able to piece together his life from details that emerged from interviewing people who knew him and from information revealed at his trial. After Steve Wright's conviction, his partner, Pam, would give us a personal insight into her life with a killer. Using this background and our knowledge of other serial killers we suggest something about what motivated him to kill.

However, where we are able, we also try to move beyond the confines of the true crime genre, broadening the specifics of the Ipswich story and putting it in a more general context of serial killing in Britain. We explore 'cop culture', public policy and offender profiling, subjects that take the reader to the middle of the events that were to unfold in Ipswich, and which throw light not only on how the murders were investigated but also on what we should do to prevent further cases of this kind.

Our narrative is dominated by a serial killer, and here we should reflect that two traditions are employed when writing about serial killers. Broadly, these can be characterised as 'sociological' and 'medico-psychological'. The latter has tended to dominate both academic writing about serial killers and the true crime genre. To elaborate, medico-psychology tries to 'explain' serial killing by looking at the serial killer's individual psychology, with the implication that if we were but to look closely at the killer's genetic make-up, his sexuality, his childhood relationships and so forth, then we would eventually discover the reason why he repeatedly killed. On the other hand, a sociological approach seeks to understand the individual serial killer as an aberrant product of the social structure he inhabited. This tradition tries to understand why some societies produce more serial killers than others, and why some periods produce more serial killers within the same society. Finally, a sociological perspective would seek to understand serial killing from the angle of who it is that is victimised.

We have tried to blend these two traditions. We seek both to understand the psychological motivation of Wright – and build up a profile of him – but at the same time never to lose sight of the fact that he concentrated his murderous efforts on a marginalised group of vulnerable young women. In one sense we are also trying to understand what created their vulnerability, one that Wright was able to exploit over and over. Ultimately, we argue that these young women were made vulnerable by a variety of factors related to, for example, policing, moralising about street prostitutes and drugs policies. Seeing their murders in this multidimensional way inevitably broadens 'responsibility' for what happened in Ipswich from being the individual, personal responsibility of Wright himself, to a responsibility that we might all share. At the heart of the book we therefore question how we can begin to change our society to help prevent other young women working in prostitution from becoming prime targets for serial killers.

We have interviewed almost all of the key figures involved in the case, and have had access to the various records kept by Sky News throughout the murder investigation and during Wright's subsequent trial. Likewise, we visited the various places at the centre of this story – from Ipswich's red-light district to the sites where the bodies of the five young women were discarded – and attended each day of Wright's trial. We have also analysed a variety of Government publications related to prostitution, and looked at how the sex industry is regulated elsewhere. And we have analysed all of the secondary literature relating to the Ipswich case, and used this where it helps to prompt the narrative. We would like to place on record our thanks to those people who agreed to be interviewed by us, although all preferred to remain anonymous, for different reasons. As a result, we have sometimes had to generalise the information that they gave us, for to report it otherwise would also identify our informants.

Orwell concluded his essay on the decline of the English murder by commenting that it was 'significant that the most talked-of English murder of recent years should have been committed by an American and an English girl who had become partly americanised'. He continued:

> But it is difficult to believe that this case will be so long remembered as the old domestic poisoning dramas, product of a stable society where the all-prevailing hypocrisy did at least ensure that crimes as serious as murder should have strong emotions behind them.

We believe that the Ipswich murders stand as a dreadful symbol not just of the social and economic realities faced by some people in Britain, but also as a tragic reminder that those who want to kill and kill again can only achieve that goal when those things that bind us together, and which keep our lives connected to those of our friends and neighbours, are weakened and then, for one reason or another, all but disappear. Societies in which individuals feel cut off from each other, or where they believe that in the struggle to survive they simply have to look out for themselves and no one else, are precisely those societies that see the greatest number of their inhabitants falling victim to serial killers. Sadly, in this way the Ipswich murders also show the type of society that Britain is fast becoming, and what might happen in that society as a consequence. And so we hope that these awful events will be 'long remembered', not just for the strong emotions behind them, but also because they should prompt us to take action.

Chapter One

Ipswich: The Red-light District

Question:
'In the light of the recent disappearance of two women from the town's red light area is Cllr Green prepared to reconsider his negative response to Labour's proposals for tackling prostitution in Ipswich, in particular with respect to the deployment of mobile CCTV cameras in this area?'

Answer:
'Thank you Mr Mayor. Thank you, Cllr Ellesmere. At the present time there is no evidence of where the two women concerned disappeared from. I would refute that there has been a negative response to the issue in question ... The use of mobile CCTV is a tactical option but must be considered alongside other priorities as well.'

Question:
'Given that no mobile CCTV cameras have been deployed in the area, ... given that there is no improvement in reporting procedures for prostitution and kerb crawling ... and given that there has been no extra help to get women out of prostitution or increased drug treatment, does Cllr Green really believe that this Council is doing all it can to tackle street prostitution in Ipswich?'

Answer:
'Thank you, Mr Mayor. Thank you, Cllr Ellesmere. The
short answer to that is yes.'

(Source – Ipswich Council Meeting minutes, 29 November 2006)

The Council meeting had been a tense one, but not because
two prostitutes had been reported missing. That issue had
been somewhat overshadowed by a debate about the failure, or otherwise, of a Council street project. That was
over a week ago, and tonight darkness had begun to
envelop Endeavour House, the smart new five-storey glass-
fronted Suffolk County Council headquarters in Russell
Road. As the last few councillors filed on to the street, or
emerged from the car park to head home, the dull orange
fluorescent street lamps were already doing their best
to tarnish the magnificence of the multimillion-pound
building and turn the area into a place few would wish to
loiter in for too long beyond normal working hours –
unless of course these are the streets on which you ply your
trade.

On the other side of the road a girl in her twenties
barely noticed the activity outside the Council building.
Sheltering from the cold and rain beneath the fake fur-
lined hood of her oversized black Puffa jacket, she wasn't
interested in anyone getting into cars, unless, of course, it
was her. Shuffling along, barely at walking pace with hands
in pockets, her handbag trailed just inches from the ground.
She only peered out from behind her hood when she heard
a car turn into Russell Road. Forlorn, she watched as the
car passed.

Julie – not her real name – didn't seem surprised. This was
not where she normally worked and in another two minutes

she'd be on Sir Alf Ramsey Way, which was more familiar territory for her, and for her regular clients. But that night she'd take whatever business she could. So, she agreed to become our guide to the red-light area of the town and to tell us a little about her life and circumstances.

Julie knew both the missing girls, but not to talk to. There was some camaraderie between the young women who earned their living on the streets (with one or two especially keen to look out for each other), but that shouldn't be taken too far. After all, the success of one meant that another went hungry, but that night there wasn't that much success for anybody – there simply weren't that many punters to go round. Some clients, hers included, fearful of an increased police presence across the red-light district, were staying away, choosing instead to contact their regular girls by mobile phone.

Julie told us a little about her life. She had gone on the game when she was fifteen. She'd done so because she was short of money, and her then boyfriend had said it was an easy way to make some cash to buy the drugs on which they were both increasingly dependent. They'd met while they were both in care, and they seemed to gravitate towards each other naturally. They shared so much – both hated school and so hardly ever attended, and both shared the guilty secrets of abuse by foster parents, brothers and sisters, uncles, fathers and granddads. Julie lost touch with her boyfriend after he'd been sent inside for the second time, but he was quickly replaced by a succession of others who were only too happy to pimp her around the town. It wasn't long before Julie thought that this was all the life she deserved or was entitled to, and she found it increasingly hard to see a way ever to make something of herself, and escape selling sex.

As we talked, the waif-like figure continued on the short journey that she had travelled many times before, and passed another equally impressive new building on Russell Road – the state-of-the-art Ipswich Crown Court.

The two buildings seemed to reflect not only each other in their glass façades, but an English provincial town ploughing money into its infrastructure, modernising and redefining its position in a new world of outsourcing and globalisation. Desperate not to be left behind, Ipswich wanted to present itself not only as a player in the regional economy of Britain but also as a place that could punch above its weight and compete against the best that Europe and Asia could offer. There was no room for the 'oldest profession' in this shiny new vision of civic pride.

But no amount of CCTV cameras, or new initiatives, or fancy talk about globalisation was going to make prostitution disappear. Prostitution simply adapted and found new recruits like Julie to swell its ranks, and nor did the demand from their punters magically disappear. And, ironically, it would be this oldest of professions that would become the focus of national and international media attention for the town – wanted or otherwise – and the backdrop for a string of murders that would leave Ipswich gripped by fear

Sex and the City

Mention Portman Road and most people would probably point to the football stadium of that name – the home of Ipswich Town FC and the Tractor Boys since the late 1880s. But few outside the area would realise that Portman Road, one of a handful of wide, nondescript roads in the shadow of the 30,000-plus all-seater stadium, is now almost as well known in Ipswich for being the centre of the town's red-light district. The surrounding industrial area, along with a handful of residential roads nearby, mark out the accepted perimeter of the red-light area: London Road to the north, Russell Road and Sir Alf Ramsey Way to the south, Portman Road to the east and West End Road to the west. Running through the middle is Handford Road.

Across the entire town sixty CCTV cameras observe its 140,000 citizens twenty-four hours a day, and sixteen cameras are specifically dedicated to the red-light district. Carefully positioned so as to maximise the police's surveillance, they monitor the many desperate transactions that take place against what had become a rather depressing backdrop. But don't imagine a 'take-your-pick' scene with streets lined with women hanging off the kerb edge touting for business, for the fifty or so regular women working here were often difficult to find. Doorways to businesses, dead-end service roads and parkland would be used as cover as the young women waited for clients. Only a slow-moving car, often at a pre-arranged time, would bring the girls out into full view. But depending on the weather – or, more likely, the immediate need to make a living – some stood openly advertising themselves, pacing up and down to show what was on offer, or rather as a simple means to keep warm.

Not all the residents within this small area welcomed Ipswich's burgeoning trade to their neighbourhood. Local women spoke angrily of being accosted or propositioned, and some of the men would describe their embarrassment at being mistaken for punters. Others described finding used condoms or dirty needles in their gardens. One elderly resident remembered how she used to visit the local park in the centre of the red-light area: 'I don't go there any more. My grandson loved to go to the playground in the park, but you always see condoms on the floor. It's awful.'

Whatever the rights or wrongs of the sex industry, some might have thought that the arrival of the electronic prying eyes of the police would have offered the young girls selling sex on the street the security they need. After all prostitution is a dangerous profession. But most of the girls we spoke to complained that the cameras were at best a double-edged sword. They might prevent attacks within the red-light district itself, but the girls claimed that as a result of the cameras' presence they are now forced to make snap judgements about a prospective client.

'You have to be really quick now, even with the punters you don't know,' Julie explained to us. 'By coming here they know their cars and faces might get caught on the cameras, so they tell me what they want, we have to agree a price and I have to decide if he's dodgy or not. And sometimes they are.'

By now Julie was on her usual patch, Sir Alf Ramsey Way, named after the former manager of Ipswich Town who, as manager of his country, led England to victory in the 1966 World Cup.

'You've gotta be prepared to look after yourself, and get tough if you have to,' explained Julie. 'I've been fucked up a few times, raped and that – but those are the risks you take. And there's no point carrying weapons and stuff – because they can use 'em on you if they find 'em.'

Fifteen minutes later Julie had accepted a lift in a nondescript saloon car. Her pocket would soon be lined – albeit thinly – with money, depending on the service she was asked to perform. In Ipswich, in December 2006, £40 would buy you straight sex; £20 would get you a blow job (although slightly more if you didn't want to wear a condom) and £15

a hand job. Even so, if you shopped around and found someone really desperate it would be cheaper.

Many of the prostitutes we spoke to echoed Julie's feelings
about the CCTV cameras. They agreed with her that, along
with an increased police presence and the threat of Anti-
Social Behaviour Orders (ASBOs), they had been forced into
unfamiliar and badly lit areas in order to carry on working.
They knew they were putting their safety at risk, but, after
all, it's not a job governed by health and safety regulations.
Accepted conventions are as good as it gets, and the informal
protection that can come from friendships made on the
street – you look out for me, and I'll look out for you. Some
of the women thought that with the influx of Eastern
Europeans they had started to experience greater levels of
threats of violence, which in turn had led to various support
groups expressing concerns about their safety. According to
a report for the Ipswich Crime and Disorder Reduction
Partnership published in 2004, prostitutes told Council
researchers that they felt, more than ever, under threat of
attack. As Lyn Jones, who compiled the report, concluded:
'The main concern was [the prostitutes'] safety. Over 60 per
cent of the women said that the fear of attack from "punters" or clients was their biggest problem. This is a very real
fear.'

Typical comments from young women working in Ipswich's
sex industry included:

- 'Foreign blokes walking around don't take no for an
  answer'.
- 'Kosovans are threatening'.
- 'Asylum seekers never pay'.
- 'They [asylum seekers] think they can get it free and
  want sex without condoms; [it's like] gang rape'.

   The report also highlighted the working girls' opinions of the police. Less than flattering, they revealed that the tension between the two groups was real and deep-seated. Typical comments would be: 'They [the police] don't give a stuff, not helpful'; '[they] look at you like you are dirt'. Such an uneasy relationship meant that younger sex workers would be very unlikely to report incidents of violence to the police, as they did not expect to be treated with respect.

   The law of averages suggests it is highly likely that some of the murdered women themselves contributed to the survey. What's more, by late 2006, two years after the survey's publication, officials were admitting that many of the safety recommendations made in the report had not been implemented. Indeed, even with two girls reported missing, little seemed to have improved. As one Labour councillor, Martin Cook, explained: 'We don't think the Council has been doing enough.' Cook should know: his ward encompasses part of the red-light area and he knew that the static cameras were not delivering the hoped-for results. 'We were asking for mobile CCTV cameras to be deployed because there was very poor coverage, but that wasn't acted on until this week. That's too late.'

   By then two young women had already gone missing and it was indeed too late.

Slags, Hookers, Toms, Brasses, Whores, Prostitutes, Vice Girls, Sex Workers, Women, Mothers, Aunts, Sisters and Daughters

Julie returned to Sir Alf Ramsey Way. 'He was one of my married ones,' she told us, explaining her brief absence. And he was a regular. 'All he wanted was a blow job, and he comes so quickly, it's all over in seconds, really.' That would be £20 then.

Like so many towns and cities across Britain, Ipswich's red-light district sits right at the heart of the town. And yet the lives of young prostitutes who work there are far removed from those who consider their lives to be, by and large, normal and respectable. Theirs is an existence within a culture that might as well be from another world. They might be out on the town but they are not hoping to have a good time, like so many other young men and women crowding the pubs and clubs at Happy Hour and beyond. Instead, they walk the streets with colleagues. Their worn stiletto heels scrape the cold, damp, seedy pavements as they search for money, because in nearly every case they are desperate for drugs. Their hopeless alienation is alleviated only by the Class A substances of choice, usually heroin or crack cocaine.

Most of the young women we met had left home as vulnerable young girls, and most are now struggling with problematic drug use.

'I started on spliffs and that, but my boyfriend started giving me heroin because he reckoned it'd give me a real kick. He weren't wrong.' Julie explained that she had left home three years ago when she was eighteen, by which time she had also been on the game for three years. Her home life hadn't been great – her parents would regularly have screaming matches after her dad had been caught sleeping with other women, and Julie had had to spend some time in care.

'They didn't really give a shit about me anyway,' she sighed. Even so her upbringing was better than that of many of the other women who were working Ipswich's streets. Julie knew of a couple of girls who'd been regularly abused by members of their families, and, while she said that hadn't happened to her, at other times when her guard was down she seemed to hint at having been abused, but she wasn't prepared to say by whom. In many cases girls with unhappy home lives are prime targets for men wanting to groom them for sex work, and before long they are too far gone to be retrieved – even if they wanted to be.

Drugs are the context in which prostitution takes place in this country, whether we are describing Ipswich, Glasgow, Belfast, London or any other town or city in Britain. So, too, Julie's first involvement with prostitution at the age of fifteen confirms one recent study which suggested that this was the average age of 'looked-after' prostitutes. Fifteen. It should be the age when you start your GCSEs, but school and these young women don't go together. Most quite quickly sink into a world where education is a distant and often unpleasant memory, and where even life and death are no longer their main concerns. Heroin and crack become their only imperatives – £100-a-day habits which have to be paid for somehow.

'You do what you do to get enough cash to get the next heroin hit. I've got three dealers' numbers in my mobile,' boasts Julie, almost as if she was describing having financial advisers. 'I'm one of their best customers, so they always sort me out. If I can't get through to one, one of the others will supply me. No worries!' Even so, we can detect the sarcasm in her voice – she's clearly had more than one run-in with local dealers.

This is how it works. A pimp or dealer might tell a woman that her next fix will cost £60. From then on the clock is ticking. One job might be enough to fund the next score of heroin, but it's unlikely. Full sex in Ipswich could earn you just £40, but add another girl into the mix and

lesbian sex could net just enough to pay for the next injection. Alternatively – and more quickly – three blow jobs at
£20 each would be enough. It's not uncommon for a string
of sexual favours to mount up to a single fix if a girl has a
serious cash-flow problem. Even so, there is money to be
made and it's not uncommon for some women to pocket
well over £1000 a week – but once their pimp has taken his
cut, whatever's left goes towards paying the bills. As for the
many mothers on the game, a few quid might just make it to
the kids' Christmas present fund.

Life like this becomes a vicious spiral with little chance of
escape. At the most basic level, the horrific withdrawal
effects from a drug like heroin are but one of the many reasons why women continue to sell their bodies. Then there's
the question of esteem – how do you put this life behind
you? How do you 'start again'? It's a constant battle and one
that is seldom won. So the girls quickly learn to develop a
good memory for faces. Well-paying customers register as
vividly as the punter who likes rough sex or the ones who
turn violent. Memory becomes part of their survival strategy.
'One bloke I see sometimes is lovely,' admits Julie. Then she
explains: 'His missus left him so I go to his place. We just
chill out, he cooks and later we have sex and he even asks
me to stay the night. It's like I'm his girlfriend. He pays for
it mind!'

That final 'He pays for it mind!' immediately removes
any lingering notion of domesticity.

In Ipswich, as with every other red-light district in
Britain, the punters come from all walks of life, and just as
many countries. They include the unemployed as well as
professionals. These men use young women in the sex
industry for all sorts of reasons – loneliness, a marriage or
relationship break-up, or simply because they have an

unquenchable thirst for sex, especially kinky sex, which seems to drive them on to the streets to satisfy their needs. But they don't have to be there for long. Picking up a woman isn't complicated. Sometimes girls will jump into the passenger seat without even a 'hello'. A quick exchange takes place about the kind of sex the punter has in mind, then it's off to a more discreet location – perhaps a 'dogging' site, or one of the young woman's own suggestions. Once there, sex can happen in lots of ways. If it is a well-known dogging site, for example, inside the car with the lights on is the done thing. Elsewhere, masturbation or a blow job – with or without a condom – can quickly be provided in the car. It's not uncommon, however, for some men to ask for sex on the bonnet.

But the punter may suggest a more private location of his choice, and if he lives alone the prostitute is sometimes invited back to his house. But there he is in control and on his own territory, and this is when the women face the greatest risks – even death.

Disappearances and Discoveries

Christmas is fast approaching. Just twenty-three days to go. Ipswich town centre is busier than usual, full of shoppers who prefer to avoid the last-minute rush. There is a flood of blue shirts in the centre, too. Ipswich Town have been hosting Burnley at Portman Road. The Tractor Boys were at one stage facing a gloomy night ahead – they were 1–0 down in the ninetieth minute, but striker Alan Lee's stoppage-time penalty had put a smile back on the Ipswich manager's face, not to mention those of most of the 20,000 fans packed into Portman Road, who were now spilling into the town. Their smiles were matched by those of the kids arriving for that night's pantomime performance of *Dick Whittington* at the New Wolsey Theatre, just a few hundred metres away from the stadium.

To most people the seedy, dark, murky life of the red-light district couldn't have been further away, even though it was on their very doorstep. But soon it would be much closer than it had ever been before, filling local, regional and national newspapers, with scores of broadcast journalists representing every major radio station and TV channel in this country and many abroad, too. The police had already discovered the naked body of a woman on the outskirts of Ipswich, but the news had yet to filter through and disrupt the festive mood of the town centre.

Tania Nicol

Several weeks earlier, on 30 October 2006, Tania Nicol slipped a tiny foot under the thin strap of her new, sparkling, pink stilettos. She left the silver buckle loosely fastened against her olive skin as she might have to walk a fair distance. She loved her new shoes and her cut-off jeans would show them off to perfection. She took a last-minute look in the mirror. She had lost about a stone over the past year – her friends had noticed, and so had her parents. A final check that her long, dark hair was in place, and then her tall slender figure was out of the door. It hadn't been a lingering look – she knew why her complexion was spotty, but she couldn't do anything about it. Not at the moment anyway. As if in a hurry, she slammed shut the door of the house she shared with her mother, Kerry, and her fifteen-year-old brother. She headed along Woolverstone Close in the direction of Ipswich town centre, the night just warm enough for her to wear a small white top. It was a walk she had done since she was a schoolgirl. Indeed, a ten-minute meander through the streets of the Chantry area of Ipswich and she would have come to her old school – Chantry High.

Unlike most of the young women who worked the streets, for Tania schooldays had by and large been good. One of the more fun-loving of the school's 1200 pupils, she could sometimes be found at the back of the class giggling with her friends, and it wouldn't have been uncommon for her to be told off by her teachers when the noise got a bit too much. Friends would remember that she had her quieter moments, though that didn't stop her from standing out from the rest. She was always well turned out, and she harboured the hope that her pretty looks and big brown eyes would one day help to make her a pop star. Maybe she had the *X Factor*? But the good times came to an end after she fell in with the wrong crowd. She knew her dad hadn't approved of her new boyfriend and at more or less the same time she began skipping school and stopped going to Sea Cadets. Her parents had been so proud when she and her Sea Cadet group met Prince Andrew at the docks in Felixstowe; now her uniform had been consigned to the back of the cupboard. She wondered whether her parents had known then that she had also started smoking cannabis.

Chantry High's motto is 'Dare To Do Right', but on the night of 30 October Tania was no longer in school uniform. The clothes she was wearing could not have been further removed from her blazer. As she headed into town she must have wondered, as she had done so many times before, if she was about to go against those four words inscribed on the school's coat of arms.

Like many of her friends who'd just left school, Tania

moved from one low-paid job to another, at one stage working in an Ipswich hotel. That job was short-lived, and she soon had designs on catering for a very different type of clientele. She had also become addicted to drugs, and she needed better-paying work to feed her addiction.

That's when Cleopatra's in Ipswich entered her life. The world of massage parlours was just as murky as that of street prostitution. She was the perfect candidate to work in a parlour: pretty, friendly, caring, reliable and, most importantly, honest. It was far from pop stardom but it paid reasonably well, and hard currency was what she needed. Anyway, the customers were generally regulars and she got on with the other girls there – some of whom had been provided with accommodation. She became known as 'Chantelle' by the punters – she liked the name and it meant the work she was doing was kept separate from her real life. She could then escape back to her own bed in Woolverstone Close and be Tania again. But that secret life had begun to encroach upon her home life. Punters or managers from the massage parlour – she didn't know which – had begun calling her home asking for 'Chantelle', which had confused and worried her mother.

She also knew that she was a lot safer working at a parlour rather than working the streets. But the trade-off for the bitterly cold weather, dodgy punters, CCTV and ASBOs was that those girls didn't have to pay commission. If they made £30, they'd get to keep all of it. The massage parlour, on the other hand, came with overheads – electricity, hot water and her room with the low ambient lighting had to be paid for, and so the £30 she earned had to be shared.

Like Tania's previous jobs, this too was to be short-lived. As shady as the massage parlour industry is, it is a business nonetheless, with standards like any other business. Owners would not stand for their girls being addicted to drugs, especially as this often meant that they were looking after their partner's drug needs as well. There were concerns that Tania's drug dependency had gone too far and she was asked to leave. She did so with little fuss, but with the next fix to find, the once upbeat, smiling teenager took to selling sex on the streets.

At one stage Tania did manage to get her own flat, on the same road as her father. He and her mum had split up when she was twelve, but her dad only moved half a mile away so she'd still see him at least twice a week, apart from when he was away working as a lorry driver. But as the drugs took hold she stopped paying the rent and bills. She would spend all day sleeping off the previous night – her haphazard lifestyle meant that everything else went by the wayside, and once again she was forced to move, this time back to her old room at her mum's house. It was then that her parents discovered she was taking heroin.

'There were no arguments and everything seemed to be OK, until one day Kerry and I walked into her room and found a syringe on the windowsill,' explained Tania's father, Jim Duell. 'We thought: we've got to do something. We all sat around the table to talk about this, to confront this. Tania told us she had been to get prescriptions for methadone, so clearly she was trying to get off heroin. She said she hadn't taken drugs for three weeks, but I just think we didn't realise the seriousness of her addiction. Every time we confronted her about it afterwards, she would get agitated. When she came around to visit me, I would gently try and broach the subject, but there was a danger that she would react badly and then I wouldn't see her for several weeks. I believe she was living in hell, quite honestly.'

What Tania's parents didn't know was that she had been

arrested by police when she was eighteen for working as a prostitute. Because she was an 'adult' her family was not informed.

'As far as I'm concerned, she was just a girl. Regardless of anyone's age, her kin should be told – and we were not told. If we had been told I'd have been going down there to find her. Of course we would, wouldn't we?'

So Tania's life as a prostitute remained a secret from her family and the drill was the same that night in October as it had been over recent months. Sometimes she would get a lift into town from a man called Tom Stephens. When they got there, he would park in the red-light area, and while she worked he'd sit in his car by himself and talk to the other girls. If any of them needed a lift to score drugs or be picked up from where a punter had dropped them off, he would oblige. Sometimes they paid him for a lift, other times he would get paid with sexual favours.

But tonight Tom wasn't around, so she would get the bus instead. And if a regular punter called, she would divert. She would also call her mother. She always did, if only to stop her worrying about where she was and who she was with. In fact her mother beat her to it. Shortly after leaving the house at 10.45, while she was on the bus, her mum phoned. It was a quick call, but it put her mother more at ease, and Tania could concentrate on her work. Little did she know this would be the last conversation they would ever have.

By 11 p.m. she was on foot again, striding purposefully towards the red-light district. As she passed the Sainsbury's garage on London Road she was caught on CCTV. And then . . . nothing. It was as if she had vanished into thin air.

Steve Wright's partner had gone to work at 11 p.m. – Pam worked the night shift at a call centre on an industrial park near Nacton, south-east of Ipswich. She wouldn't be home until after 8 a.m., so he had the whole night to himself. In his dark blue Ford Mondeo, he pulled away from his house in London Road and made for the red-light area. It wasn't the first time he'd sought the services of prostitutes – ever since he first travelled to Thailand in his twenties, he'd got a taste for paying for sex. And now, more than twenty years later, he was still looking for sex, this time cruising around the Portman Road area. Sometimes he would go out smartly dressed. It made the girls feel safe. His car was clean too. He tried to keep it spotless because he'd only recently bought it second hand. After a six-month driving ban for speeding offences in May 2005 had come to an end, he'd decided to treat himself to a new car. Money was tight so he bought it on hire purchase. It would get a good wash from time to time, he made sure of that. But it was a ritual he would repeat increasingly over the coming weeks, with even more vigour.

At around midnight that night, in the distance, though partly obscured by the Christmas tree air-freshener swinging on his rear-view mirror, he saw the dark-haired girl touting for business, so he pulled over. She seemed quite young to him and he thought her skin was a little spotty. But other than that, she was just what he was looking for. In an instant he knew that his car would need another clean – a meticulous one; this time he might even do it that night under the cover of darkness so no one would see.

The following morning her mother woke to find that Tania's bed hadn't been slept in. Worried, Kerry Nicol dialled a list of numbers Tania had called the previous evening to find out where she might be. One of the calls took her to a man called Tom Stephens.

Stephens would phone the Nicols' house later that evening

to speak to Tania. Rather than tell him she hadn't come home the previous night, Kerry explained she was still asleep in bed. He called back the following day, again looking for Tania, and this time Kerry explained there was still no sign of her daughter and she was thinking of calling the police. Stephens replied that if he were her, he'd definitely call the police. So she did.

Officers decided to wait and see if she'd make contact over the busy weekend of 4 and 5 November – perhaps because they realised how Tania earned her living and knew that it wasn't uncommon for girls in the red-light district to go missing for days on end. Getting used to the knowledge that her daughter was a prostitute with a serious drug problem was bad enough, but what was just as worrying for Kerry was that despite the vast number of calls to Tania's mobile phone, each time it diverted to voicemail. The handset eventually lost contact with the phone network.

The few inquiries the police had made while hoping she would reappear had thrown up little, so by the following Tuesday they decided it was time to take more action – a public appeal. 'We're extremely concerned for Tania's welfare because of her lifestyle and the fact that she is known to work as a prostitute,' announced Suffolk Constabulary's Detective Chief Inspector John Quinton. 'We are also interested in any previous or current associates with whom she had regular contact and who may have an idea of where she might be,' he added. 'We need to find her to be sure that she is safe and well.'

The words resonated in Kerry Nicol's ears. Publicly she simply would not accept that anything bad had happened to her daughter, yet she knew that this behaviour was out of character: 'This is unusual. Tania usually makes contact with me to let me know she is with friends and OK.' Little did she know what lay ahead, although secretly she feared the worst.

Tania's father felt the same. 'Initially we were told she may have taken an overdose and could be at an address somewhere. I thought maybe Tania hadn't been able to pay her dealer and they'd taken her somewhere and finished her off. I'm not someone who walks around in a daydream, I had pretty much realised that going missing for three weeks means something pretty serious has happened. It could be obvious, but Tania would have come home to get a change of clothes. I went to bed one night and had a vision of a piece of rope being broken in half. I said to myself: that's Tania's lifeline snapped.'

All Tania's family could do was wait and hope.

By 2 December Trevor Saunders hadn't ventured down to the brook for well over a week, having been kept indoors by unusually prolonged heavy rainfall. Flooding was a real possibility, and while he knew the local waterways like the back of his hand he'd have to wait until the rain stopped and the levels dropped before he could stroll down again to Belstead Brook to check on any blockages. When the rain stopped that morning, Trevor was at last able to venture outside.

The owners of Hintlesham Fisheries, the Dowding-Youngs, had moved in four years earlier, but Trevor, a water bailiff, had been a fixture there for many years. Whenever anglers telephoned the main house to find out about carp and coarse fishing in their two lakes to the rear, more often than not they would be referred to Trevor. It was a quiet location for anglers, and you could drive the couple of miles along the A1071 from Ipswich without even noticing the village of Hintlesham. A week might go by with no visitors; the following week four or more might arrive to spend £10 for an entire day's fishing. With carp weighing up to thirty pounds swimming in the lakes, it would often attract people from out of town.

Belstead Brook was only a two-hundred-metre amble down Thorpe's Hill from Hintlesham Fisheries, so it didn't take Trevor long to get there. The brook was still somewhat swollen from the rain, and the water was running at quite a speed in the direction of Copdock, about a mile and a half downstream. Checking blockages was a regular chore for Trevor, and, just as he'd thought, the high water had dragged a lot of loose twigs and branches into the by now narrow channel. The brook was particularly sinuous, and one bend seemed more clogged up than the others. Whatever was causing the blockage would have to be cleared.

Trevor brushed away some twigs and leaves, and then he saw a smooth, round surface sticking out of the water. He couldn't quite make out what it was, and knew he'd have to wade into the brook to fish it out. Knee-deep in the water, he could now see what looked like buttocks, then two legs. The mannequin must have been here a while because it was covered in a shiny slime. But how on earth could a dummy end up here? It looked as if someone had tried to hide it. Then he froze. In a split second he realised he had found the body of a woman, wedged face-down into the bend, her back visible above the waterline. A hesitant step closer and he could see that she was naked but for a pair of earrings. Trevor rang the main house on his mobile as fast as he could. 'I think I've found a body.'

The police had devoted most of their manpower that day to an Ipswich Town home game, but now, with this more pressing matter to attend to, they'd have to free some officers to attend the scene. Even so, access to the woman's body wasn't going to be easy. Not only was it nearly fifty metres from the A1071, but the naked corpse was also wedged hard into the bend in the brook. The fire brigade had been called to clear the immediate area, making the body's recovery simpler and also protecting any forensic evidence. As the hours passed, police cars started to gather on the nearby main road. By day the A1071 is one of the busier single-lane country roads leading into Ipswich, but at night the volume of traffic normally subsides, leaving the road in darkness. There is no street lighting on the A1071 and that night there were no cars either – the police had closed the roads for three miles around Hintlesham.

The absence of street lighting had made setting up a police inner cordon just that little bit trickier: there was nothing to attach the police tape to. The blue and white tape bearing the words 'Police Line Do Not Cross' was instead tied to the gate post of a field which ran down to Belstead Brook, close to the small bridge over which the main road passes.

As darkness fell over the isolated location the police had already begun to suspect that the woman had been murdered, although the press were told only that investigators were looking at 'suspicious circumstances' surrounding the discovery. They had also begun theorising about where her body had originally entered the brook. Different hypotheses were offered up, but even at this early stage the front runner seemed to be that she'd been jettisoned from the small bridge under the cover of darkness – darkness similar to that which was now enveloping Hintlesham – but that wouldn't explain why she had remained undetected for so long.

A post-mortem examination and additional tests due to be carried out at Ipswich Hospital the following day by a Home Office pathologist would help establish a cause of death, but Suffolk Police's most immediate concern was to identify the victim. Perhaps they had found Tania?

Gemma Adams

She always had her mobile phone with her. It was a vital tool in her business. As well as helping her keep in touch with her boyfriend, it was also a connection to a life she had largely left behind. Her parents would often call her but when their number came up on the screen, she invariably let it ring out. She knew they just wanted to make sure she was all right. Sometimes she would answer but would quickly curtail the conversation, afraid that talking too long might give them clues as to her desperate situation. She didn't want that. Texting was slightly different – emotion was harder to detect in a text. Every day, either while she was at her flat in Blenheim Road just outside the town centre or out working in Ipswich, her mobile would sound its message alert. Another text from Mum and Dad. Her replies were becoming less frequent; she'd manage a quick message of reassurance every couple of weeks or so, but that was it.

Twenty-five-year-old Gemma Adams placed her mobile in her black handbag. Over the past two weeks she'd checked it on a number of occasions to see whether her friend Tania had made contact to say she was OK. She'd seen her picture on the television a few times since she had gone missing at the end of October. Gemma was worried for her, but it didn't make her think twice about heading into Ipswich that night of 14 November.

Tuesday was invariably a quiet night, but her regular clients would be around and she might even pick up other business if she was lucky. She'd been working as a prostitute for a few years now, and she knew the risks.

Over the summer she had spent some time working at Cleopatra's massage parlour. It was certainly safer there than on the streets – CCTV cameras had been installed in each parlour for the safety of the staff. But she wasn't happy that the business took too big a cut of the money she made. So she began to make arrangements to meet a few of the clients privately. Some came to the parlour especially to see her and not the other girls, so she felt it made sense to arrange to meet them elsewhere. That way she got to keep all the cash. Compared with other girls working on the street, Gemma's clients felt she was different. It was a market she was determined to exploit.

She knew she could handle herself, and anyway her long-term boyfriend, Jon Simpson, was with her. The contrast of her long, straight, blonde hair and pale skin against the hood of her short black waterproof jacket was striking. She'd also decided to wear light blue jeans with studded pockets, a red top and white and chrome Nike trainers, and the obligatory jewellery – rings and earrings. Together she and Jon set off in the direction of Handford Road; it would take them only a few minutes to reach it.

Gemma often wondered if she would bump into her parents in Ipswich. After all they, along with her brother and sister, only lived on the outskirts of the town in Kesgrave. But the streets she walked at night were not the ones frequented by Brian, her father, or by her mother, Gail. Their lives, though close at hand, couldn't have been further removed from hers, but it hadn't always been so.

Gemma had grown up in the well-to-do area of Kesgrave in a happy, loving home. Her life was full. If she wasn't at Brownies, she was taking piano lessons and if she was doing neither of those she was having riding lessons. But the animal to which she was really devoted was her dog, Holly. She had been rescued after being found abandoned in a shed.

School didn't excite Gemma even though she was intelligent and popular. She was down-to-earth and modest, and, despite a striking smile, she seemed unaware just how pretty she was.

Gemma had left school at sixteen to take a GNVQ in health and social care at Suffolk College. Her parents had had high hopes and thought she might even end up joining the police force, but by then she had met her boyfriend and they soon moved in together. From that moment on her life would change direction. It was the beginning of the end. For Gemma it had started with the occasional experiment with cannabis at parties. Her job with an insurance company in Ipswich had begun to nose-dive, too. She had failed to turn up to work once too often and after she started arriving in an unfit state she was sacked. Heroin had begun to take control of her life. Unemployment and a daily obsession with landing her next fix forced Gemma out into the world of prostitution.

Her parents had tried to intervene, and in the early stages there had been some hope that Gemma might beat her addiction. She allowed her parents to take her to see their doctor, and then the community drugs team. 'She wanted to sort herself out,' said Brian Adams. 'For a time she was on a course of methadone but soon went back on the heroin.

'We never knew she was working as a prostitute until she went missing. If we had known, we would have done everything in our power to stop her, just like we tried to get her off drugs.'

But Gemma's addiction to drugs proved stronger than her family ties, and so she began distancing herself. Birthdays and Christmases passed without her going home to see her family. And now Christmas was coming round again. She knew she would be asked to go home – she would decline, just as she had for the past two years.

Gemma and her boyfriend soon reached Handford Road. Within minutes she was on her own. In a strange way, although she knew that her exile from her family was self-imposed, just as she had rescued Holly she dearly hoped that someone would rescue her before it was too late. When Jon had left her a few minutes earlier he'd made her promise to call him later. It was early – just 10 p.m. – but it wouldn't be long before she had her first customer.

He pulled up in a dark car on London Road at 10.30 p.m. After agreeing a price for what he wanted, Gemma got in. He didn't want full sex, so it wasn't long before she was back on the street and only £15 the richer. It was now about 11.20 p.m. Lucky for her, she thought, her second punter pulled up shortly after midnight. He did want full sex, so together they went to a nearby car park. He paid £30 – a quid a minute. Half an hour later – just before 1 a.m. – the five-foot-two-inch, slim girl was back in the red-light district again.

Business was good tonight. It wasn't long before she was negotiating her next fee. The man wanted oral sex and they both settled on £20. He drove her to a secluded spot in Copdock where the old A12 reaches a dead end. There, he offered her another £10 for full sex. She agreed. By 12.45 a.m. she was back on the street.

One of her haunts was outside the BMW garage on West End Road. She would soon be picked up by her final client of the night, who wanted much more than just quick hand relief. He wanted an adrenalin rush of a very different kind.

Since 4 November Steve Wright's partner, Pam, had been off work. She'd been ill for a few days and then she'd taken a few days' holiday. Her nightshifts had allowed him to do as he pleased late into the evening, but because she'd been off he'd been forced to stay away from the red-light district. This evening she'd gone back to work, so the coast would be clear. As usual, she left home shortly after 11 p.m. It was cold, so he'd put on a thick lumberjack-style shirt. Getting into his car, which he always parked on the driveway in front of the house, he made sure he had at least one pair of hard-wearing gloves stuffed in the driver's door pocket. He might need them later. He didn't have to travel far beyond London Road before spotting her. Immediately he knew his car was about to get another thorough clean, inside and out.

A couple of hours later, at 2.55 a.m., Suffolk Police took a phone call from a worried man to say his girlfriend hadn't contacted him. Jon explained to the officer in the control room that the last time he had seen Gemma was at 10 p.m. in Handford Road; that she'd promised to call him later, as usual. Furthermore, he explained, she hadn't come home either.

Most calls of this nature would not normally be given priority. After all, Gemma had only been out of touch for a matter of a few hours. But when Jon explained that she had been working on the streets, alarm bells began to ring. Tania Nicol had disappeared from the red-light district more than two weeks earlier, and still hadn't been found. It now seemed a second young woman was missing.

Earlier that evening Gemma's phone message alert sounded twice in quick succession. She would normally be quick to reply to her boyfriend's texts, but this time she couldn't get to the phone. She was in trouble.

It was entirely possible that Gemma had gone back to her family, and the police wanted to make a few obvious yet necessary inquiries. Jon agreed, but at the same time he knew it was highly unlikely, especially as by now she would be thinking more about where she could get her next heroin fix. Home, he felt, would have been the last place she would have wanted to go. It was excruciating as the police relayed their concern to Gemma's parents. 'The police informed us that she was missing and that she had been working as a prostitute,' said Brian Adams. 'Our world just crumbled, really, when we heard that.' Since 15 November Gemma's family had been waiting for news, both dreading and needing to know what had happened.

But it had been a longer wait for Tania's family. And now with the discovery of a woman's body in a brook in Hintlesham, for both families the already unbearable anxiety of not knowing where their daughters were was being compounded by the knowledge that the dead woman could be their loved one. And while neither family wished the devastating news on the other, each silently prayed that the victim was not their own daughter.

With two women missing and a body yet to be identified, the media had begun to show a greater interest in the story. They knew from the pictures of Tania Nicol and Gemma Adams that, despite having so much in common, their appearances were very different. Their hair and skin colour, for example, were poles apart. It wouldn't be difficult to rule out one of the girls, but depending on how long the body had been in the water at the bottom of Thorpe's Hill, it could take a little longer to establish who the girl was and how she had been killed. Of course it was possible that it was neither girl, but that seemed unlikely.

The police arrived at Gemma's parents' house in Kesgrave and asked them to accompany them to Ipswich Hospital. As they did so, across town the Nicol household breathed a guarded sigh of relief. Brian Adams later explained what had happened and what the rest of the family had been going through:

> The police came round and asked if one of us could identify the body. I couldn't do it. Gemma's mother and sister identified her. My wife was utterly devastated, we all were, and still are. Gemma's brother and sister are suffering terribly. Normally, if you have a nightmare, you wake up and the pain is gone, but this is with us day and night. We are going through Hell. We have lost a wonderful, beautiful daughter in the most dreadful way. Heroin was her undoing. It is just the most awful waste of a young woman's life and it has destroyed our family. We are praying that the madman who did this is caught soon.

Gemma's younger brother, Jack, felt compelled to let his sister know how much she had meant to him. On the website of the local paper, he wrote: 'Gem, you will never be forgotten. I know you're in a better place now and I will always love you.'

As if to make matters worse for the family, however, the post-mortem on Gemma's body had proved inconclusive. With no obvious cause of death, more tests would be needed before her family would be allowed to bury her. In the event, Gemma's funeral and thanksgiving service wouldn't take place until 15 February 2007, three months to the day that she had gone missing.

Shortly after the family's grim experience at Ipswich Hospital, Suffolk Constabulary confirmed in a press statement that the body was that of one of the missing girls: 'Following the discovery of a woman's body in a brook at Thorpe's Hill in Hintlesham at approximately 11.50am yesterday, Saturday 2nd December, police can confirm that formal identification has taken place this afternoon [Sunday 3 December] and the body is that of missing twenty-five-year-old Ipswich woman Gemma Adams.

'A post-mortem examination has been carried out today at Ipswich Hospital by a Home Office pathologist and further tests will now have to be carried out to help ascertain the cause of death.

'Police are treating the death as suspicious.'

It would be another twenty-four hours before the police confirmed that Gemma had been murdered.

'The main focus of our investigations over the next few days will be in the area Gemma's body was discovered,' said Detective Chief Inspector David Skevington on Monday 4 December. DCI Skevington had been placed in charge of the murder inquiry. 'It's a remote area, often used by anglers, dog walkers and ramblers; it is not an area that is easily accessible by car,' he said. 'Specialist search teams are currently conducting searches in the area the body was discovered.' He also confirmed: 'When Gemma was found, her body was naked and we therefore need to try to find her clothing as a matter of urgency.'

By 'specialist search teams' DCI Skevington had meant 'scenes of crime officers' (SOCO) and 'dive teams'. Even though Gemma had been found naked it didn't rule out the possibility that whoever dumped her body had left footprints, clothing fibres or DNA at the scene, nor did it necessarily mean that she had been completely unclothed when she had been discarded.

Teams of between four and six divers wearing wetsuits began searching Belstead Brook. The water was only about one metre deep, but it was moving at a pace and it was freezing. Parts of the brook were also overgrown, but where possible, side by side and with the flow of the water, the officers began a fingertip search of the banks and bed of the winding tributary. They were heading in the direction of Copdock.

As police issued further public appeals, it became clear they had made no major breakthrough in the investigation for days. Tania Nicol was still missing and, despite a good response for information from Gemma's friends, the police had few solid leads. They thought their luck was about to change on Friday 8 December, six days after Gemma's body was found.

A car exhaust centre on Norwich Road in Ipswich had suddenly been shut by the police after a phone call from a member of the public who had found a pair of discarded Nike trainers similar to those worn by Gemma the night she disappeared. The premises were cordoned off and officers searched for the rest of the day. 'We will now be sending the shoes off for a detailed forensic examination to establish whether they are relevant to our inquiry,' explained DCI Skevington the following day, but they were later ruled out of the investigation.

The discovery of the trainers had for the time being shifted the media's attention away from the police divers in Belstead Brook. It was an untimely distraction for the divers were about to make a much more macabre discovery.

It had taken them a number of days to search the narrow waterway, but by Friday 8 December the team had arrived just over a mile downstream from Hintlesham in the village of Copdock. The brook at Copdock becomes somewhat shallower, but it widens almost threefold. It flows beneath a twenty-metre-long concrete archway supporting a dual carriageway – otherwise known as the old A12. The new faster-moving road now runs parallel and can be seen in the near distance. Beyond the bridge, the brook returns to its usual form, just a couple of metres wide and one metre deep.

The dive team hadn't been at work for long. It was just before 11.30 a.m. when the officers reached that section of the brook running parallel to Mill Lane leading up to Copdock Mill. There, again wedged against one of the banks, covered with twigs and branches and coated with a slimy film, was the naked body of another young woman.

Despite no formal identification having taken place, the initial striking similarities were not lost on the police. The victims were both women; they had been dumped in the same brook less than two miles apart; and both had been stripped completely of their clothing. It seemed likely that the second woman also worked in the red-light district.

The forensic team had to move fast to secure evidence. Not only had this body been dumped in water, but it was also raining again. The body was removed quickly, long before most journalists arrived at the scene. And as had been the case with Gemma Adams six days earlier, this latest victim was transported by a black coroner's ambulance to Ipswich Hospital for a post-mortem examination.

'I was with two family liaison officers as we knocked on Kerry's door,' explained Tania's father, Jim. 'As we went into the living room, one of the liaison officers' mobile rang. It was a brief call. I said to them, "Please take a seat", and the officer who'd taken the call suggested maybe I should instead take a seat. He told us that a body had been found, but at that stage, they weren't sure it was Tania. It was the news I was expecting. Strangely, there was no sobbing and no tears. I went out for a walk, and I felt I was walking on air. For me that was my assurance the Lord had taken her and was looking after her.'

To be sure the second body was Tania's, she had to be formally identified.

'I said I would go and identify her,' said Jim. 'Then her aunt kindly said she would drive up to Ipswich and do it. In the end, the police said no one should come and see her, and instead they would use fingerprints as the form of identification.'

At Suffolk Constabulary's Martlesham Heath headquarters the following morning the press, who on the discovery of a second body were now gathering in greater numbers, waited for news of the woman's identity. As the press officer emerged from a meeting room with Detective Superintendent Andy Henwood in tow, and before either had the chance to enter the press conference room, a whispered 'Is it Tania?' was met with a nod, followed by a 'Yes'. Within seconds, and before DS Henwood had even sat down, Sky News had flashed the news live on air. Moments later, we broadcast the statement live: 'Formal identification has taken place today and police can confirm that the body is that of missing nineteen-year-old woman Tania Nicol.'

The police continued:

Following the discovery of Tania's body in the brook at Copdock we are now beginning a linked murder investigation. There are obvious similarities between Tania and Gemma's disappearances and subsequent deaths . . . however we will be seeking further opinion from specialist advisors to confirm this view. A team of specialist search officers remain in the area around where Tania's body was found in Copdock today and cordons will remain in place until the searches are complete. Our inquiries are continuing to try to ascertain where and when Tania and Gemma's bodies were placed in the water and the circumstances of their deaths.

Reality had set in. The police knew it. The press knew it. And not only had Ipswich begun to wake up to it, but the whole country was starting to realise that Britain's latest serial killer-in-the-making was at large, and his hunting ground was the red-light district of Ipswich. Would he strike again, and if so when and where? Would it be close to his first two victims, and would his target again be a prostitute? Would she too be stripped of all her clothing and then dumped in water?

Unbeknown to everyone, the answers to these questions were already lying in woodland some six miles away in the Ipswich suburb of Nacton.

Chapter Two

Killing for Kicks

Anneli Alderton

She scraped her long blonde hair back into a high ponytail, and posed briefly in front of the mirror. The time the twenty-four-year-old had spent working out at the YMCA gym had served her well. Anneli looked good and, considering the night she had ahead of her, she felt OK too. Dressed in a black jacket with a fur-trimmed hood, grey top, blue jeans and white trainers, she packed her nylon shoulder bag with all the things she might need. Drawing the cord tight, she slung the bag over her shoulder and headed for the door, leaving the bathroom in a terrible mess.

'Goodbye, mum. I love you,' she shouted on her way out.

As she left the pebble-dash terraced house decorated with Christmas banners reading 'Welcome' and made her way to the railway station, she wondered whether she had made a mistake in not telling her family. She had already told one or two of her friends, but had decided, on this visit at least, against telling her mum.

Her mother Maire had lived with her partner Tim Smith for a little while now and even though her visits to them both at the house in Harwich had been less frequent of late, she had worried whether a mother's intuition might have divined the big news she was hiding. It hadn't, so she would keep quiet. She would tell them soon, though, she promised herself that much, and pressed her stomach, as if to protect the unborn child inside her. She was happy she was three months pregnant and didn't mind if it was a boy or a girl, so long as it was healthy.

It was twenty-two days till Christmas and Anneli reasoned that the announcement of her pregnancy would be the best present she could give her family. Ever since she had lost her father, Roy, to lung cancer in 1998 – when she was sixteen – family had been even more important to her and was the one constant in her turbulent life. This Christmas she'd spend time in Ipswich, surrounded by the people she loved.

Anni, as she was called by her mother, was ten years old in 1992 when she followed her mother to Cyprus to live. A bright student, she mastered the Greek Cypriot language quickly. But her father, who separated from her mother when Anni was four, still lived in Ipswich, and from the age of fourteen Anni began taking trips back to Suffolk to stay with him during school holidays. It soon became a permanent fixture and it would prove to be a turning point in her life.

Enrolling at Copleston High School in Ipswich, Anni achieved good grades in her exams and had ambitions of being a model. She had the confidence for it, but she was nonetheless vulnerable. Having been close to her father, after his death her behaviour at school and at home had become more and more rebellious and, when she fell in with the wrong crowd, drugs began to play a role in her life.

Anni's downward spiral didn't go unnoticed by her mother, who by now had returned to the UK. She tried in vain, time and again, to help Anni kick her drug addiction. What did go unnoticed at the time, but which Maire Alderton would find out about soon enough, was that Anni had turned to prostitution to fund her addiction, and what seemed to go hand in hand with the path Anni was taking – time in prison. Four times, in fact, between 2000 and 2006. After being released first time around, Anni moved back in with her mother and seemed more relaxed at the prospect of a brighter future. That future couldn't have seemed more distant when, upon release from her fourth sentence in September 2006, she soon returned to the streets of Ipswich's red-light area.

Since Anneli had been working as a prostitute, she had earned her new nickname: 'Crackhead Annie'. It was a nickname that would also explain this evening's trip to Ipswich's red-light district. Her drugs habit wasn't cheap and – as her nickname suggested – neither was it modest. With Christmas around the corner presents needed buying too, and there'd soon be another mouth to feed. She would work hard tonight for those few vital pounds.

Walking along George Street, Anneli arrived at Harwich Town railway station shortly after 5.30 p.m. It was already dark and cold, but the warmth of the 17.53 to Colchester would keep the chill out for a few minutes. It being a Sunday night the train would be quiet. In fact, as Anneli boarded the train she noticed she was practically the only passenger.

Dover Court. Harwich International. Wrabness. A cold wind penetrated the coach at each stop. It was barely a twenty-minute journey, yet she was restless and eager to get to her destination, standing for most of the way as if to make the train go quicker. On edge and endlessly preening herself in her reflection in the window, Anneli's discomfort was soon at an end.

Mistley. Manningtree. Change. Arriving on platform one of quiet Manningtree station meant she'd have to take the underpass to the other side of the track. It was only a short walk, yet still a concern for a girl on her own. There were CCTV cameras in the underground walkway, but Anneli could look after herself. She'd had tough moments with some of her clients and anyone following her here under the gaze of the cameras didn't bother her in the slightest.

What did bother her a little was the fact that the body of a girl had been found the previous day in Hintlesham and that the police had said they still had no explanation for the death. She was worried the body was that of either Gemma Adams or Tania Nicol, both of whom she knew. There'd been a lot of talk in the red-light area about them going missing, and now that a body had been found people would begin to fear the worst. This in itself made her jumpy, as did needing her next fix. It made her feisty, too. She would try to be calm, mindful that her temper had got the better of her back in August when she was arrested for being drunk and disorderly in Colchester after attacking a police officer.

Little did Anneli know that the body the police were trying to identify was indeed that of Gemma Adams, and that Tania Nicol was lying still undiscovered in a brook in Copdock, less than a couple of miles from where Gemma had been found. Nor did she know as she confidently boarded the 18.34 from Manningtree to Ipswich that this would be her last trip. She was about to become the killer's third victim.

Steve Wright's day had started early. His work at Felixstowe docks, loading and unloading freight, had dried up a little of late, so he'd be working the early shift as a fork-lift truck driver. He'd told his recruitment consultancy he wanted to leave his previous job at Celotex because he wanted more money – by 30 November he was in a better-paid job at a company closer to home, although he still worked at the docks when his shift patterns allowed. To get to Celotex he used to drive along the A1071 to Hadleigh, which took him through a village called Hintlesham and over a small brook he'd always thought picturesque. But now he could walk to work. The Hadleigh industrial estate was just a five-minute stroll from his London Road home, so he didn't mind starting work at 6 a.m. and finishing at 2 p.m. At least he could see more of Pam.

She was back at work again, so the urge that evening to take a drive into the red-light district was overwhelming, even though the police presence in the town was greater than ever since the discovery of the body of his first victim in Hintlesham. If he was going do what he wanted to do that night, he'd have to steer clear of the A1071. Giving it a moment's thought, Wright remembered where his previous recruitment consultant had been based – Nacton village, near where Pam worked. It was quiet there; and private. He would break from his usual routine and give the police pause for thought.

The car negotiated the narrow lane that ran between the old Felixstowe road and the village of Nacton, south-east of Ipswich. It was 10.30 on the morning of Thursday 7 December. The driver, thinking only of the day ahead, suddenly caught sight of something out of the corner of his eye, something that looked out of place in this wooded area where even the local Amberfield School was barely visible through the trees. He didn't stop to take a closer look. The discarded mannequin was someone else's business, he thought, and continued on his way.

Anneli Alderton's body would remain undiscovered until 10 December. Travelling along the same stretch of road through Nacton one driver did decide to take a closer look at what had to another seemed like a tailor's dummy. A week to the day since arriving in Ipswich from her mother's house in Harwich, the naked body of Anneli – victim number three – was discovered barely ten metres from the side of the road, and just thirty from the main entrance of Amberfield School.

At a police press conference two days later, Detective Chief Superintendent Stewart Gull, who was now in charge of the investigation, confirmed not only the identity of the woman, but that for the first time pathologists were able to establish the cause of death.

'Detectives have confirmed that the murdered woman is twenty-four-year-old Anneli Alderton from Colchester and appeal for anyone who may have seen her shortly before her death, to come forward,' announced DCS Gull. He continued: 'The body was removed from the site yesterday afternoon – Monday 11 December – and taken to Ipswich Hospital. A post-mortem examination, carried out by Home Office pathologist Dr Nat Cary, last night, revealed the cause of death was asphyxiation.'

Not only that, but the killer had put Anneli's body in a particular position that puzzled the police. Her naked body was placed in the shape of a crucifix, arms outstretched, left knee raised and her long blonde hair pulled out straight behind her.

It was the first time they would encounter such a sight – but not the last.

Reporters had been waiting in Harwich for Anneli's mother to return home from the hospital. Dressed in black, Maire Alderton fought back tears and told journalists: 'I have just come back from identifying her body and am just trying to hold things together. Anni was a lovely, bright girl and I just loved her so much.'

Anneli's sister-in-law, Jane Lowe, told reporters that, while Anneli had acted tough, underneath she was a 'lovely person, really warm and generous'.

But it was her eighty-one-year-old grandmother, Joan Molloy, who summed up for the press the tragedy that was the life of Anneli. She said that she had seen her granddaughter the previous Christmas, but had been upset by the transformation in Anneli. And now she was dead. Joan continued:

> She upset everybody at Christmas, because she was a totally changed character with a terrible vocabulary. There was swearing and arguing, Anni was not the little girl I knew. She was a perfectly nice little girl and had a happy upbringing. I was gobsmacked to hear my granddaughter was dead, but the Anni I knew as a little girl had died years before. I remember her as a normal, artistic, bright little girl – happy and alive. She has been a girl more sinned against than sinning, but became addicted to heroin.

Anneli's family had been distraught after being told she'd been murdered. But then came the second shock – she had been pregnant. So they had lost two of their family in one single, evil act.

Police now had their first cause of death – strangulation. It had been impossible to establish the causes of death for Gemma and Tania as they had been killed some time before they were discovered. So the police had something to work with, but were they chasing their tails? How many others had fallen victim to the killer? The mood among the women in Ipswich's red-light district was reflected in their actions. They were keeping an eye out for each other, and, more importantly, keeping an eye out for those who hadn't been seen for a while. It wasn't uncommon for some of the girls not to be seen for days, but two names were quickly brought to the attention of the police – Annette Nicholls and Paula Clennell.

Steve Wright read the newspaper like anyone else. He watched the news like everyone else, too. He could see the police chasing from one murder scene to the next. He knew he was always one step ahead of them and with his first two victims he had made sure that they couldn't catch up with him easily. He'd stripped Gemma and Tania and dumped them in a brook he knew, so careful was he to avoid leaving any clues behind. Anyway, they had been so well concealed, he knew that by the time the police found them, if he had left anything behind the winter elements would soon put that right.

When the police announced they had found their first body, Wright had been intrigued to learn it was in fact that of his second victim. When it appeared the police had very little to go on following the discovery of Gemma's body, he felt confident that if they found Tania – his first victim – whom he had dumped close by and in the same stretch of water, then there would be even less evidence to go on with her body. He'd killed Tania two weeks before he'd murdered Gemma.

Having not yet found Tania, all police activity for the moment was concentrated in and around Hintlesham, close to the scene of Gemma Adams' discovery. The police, he mused, had no idea that, while they flooded Hintlesham with officers, he had already left two more bodies for them to find – Tania and Anneli. He had been a little wary with his third victim – Anneli, the blonde with the crack habit. He'd found the perfect place to get rid of the first two victims, but that area had become off-limits because it was crawling with police. So he'd decided to dispose of his third victim just far enough away, and in a similarly poorly lit location. Nacton was remote enough, yet close enough, and it was a place he knew because his previous employer's head office was based there and he'd visited the area more than once. It was dark when he pulled over. Headlights off. Wright carried his naked victim into the thick undergrowth. She wasn't heavy, but he knew local people were beginning to become vigilant and so he had to be quick. Had he walked a few metres further, he could have placed his third victim in water, too, but there wasn't much moonlight that evening and instead he dropped her to the ground, far enough from the road, he felt, so as to be concealed from passing traffic. He would later discover that was not the case.

But could he kill a fourth time, even before the police discovered his second victim and realised they were dealing with someone who had now developed a taste for his victims? At that point to kill again would be tricky, to say the least.

It was the early hours of the morning, early in the week, and he was on his guard because of the increased presence of police in the red-light district itself. Then he saw her. Annette Nicholls wasn't standing in what he considered the heart of the red-light area, but, rather, on the outskirts. She was about the same size as his third victim, though this one was brunette rather than blonde, not that it bothered him. His first had been brunette, his second blonde, his third blonde again and now his fourth would be brunette. He pulled up and she leaned in through the window. She was perfect. She was the one.

'Netty': Annette Nicholls

It was on nights like this one that Annette hated her job most of all. She didn't like working on the streets at the best of times, and now there was a killer out there. There had been a lot of talk among the girls she worked with that the killer might be someone they all knew. She had met a few dodgy clients during her time, and not long ago she'd had one of the most frightening experiences of her life. In the summer she had been attacked in the street and then dragged into an alleyway. She'd finally gone to the police in October and a man was later arrested on suspicion of rape.

She had known Gemma Adams whose body had been found a few days before, which brought things just that little bit closer to home. But what made her conscious about being out on the streets on this night was more a fear of being seen by someone she knew. Truth be told, she was a little embarrassed to be working as a prostitute.

This wasn't how her life was supposed to be, and she would try her hardest to make sure it didn't stay that way either, if only for her eight-year-old son who she cared about more than anyone.

Her existence was a far cry from nights out clubbing in town with friends. A far cry, too, from the fun she used to have with her son having water fights with the neighbours as he was growing up at the family home on the Greenwich Estate. And four years ago her life had been on the verge of taking off in a very different direction from the one it was now taking with her friends and clients in the red-light district of Ipswich.

Unlike some of her friends from school, a life on state benefits was not for her. She had been encouraged by her close-knit family to take up an NVQ beautician's course at Suffolk College in Ipswich. She was soon a qualified beauty therapist and had plans to open her own business. Her family was proud of their 'Netty', as were her friends, many of whom benefited from her expertise as they prepared for a night out on the town. But, more than that, Netty was proud of herself, too. For a twenty-five-year-old bringing up a young son, completing her course was some achievement and she felt she had done well.

But almost overnight her bright future was transformed into a dull, distant dream. She started visiting her family less and her get-up-and-go had instead been replaced by drug addiction. Class A substances had begun to take control of her life – heroin her substance of choice, or, rather, her need. She had always been quite easily led and now with money – and lots of it – needed to fund her habit, within a matter of months she was reduced to climbing into cars with complete strangers for sex. Sometimes she would steal money when the client wasn't looking, and that had got her into tricky situations more than once. But it was a means to an end – she could get her fix while knowing her son was in good hands. Her mother was taking care of him.

It was a while since she last scored some drugs, and she needed cash quickly. Perhaps her taxi driver friend would lend her enough for a quick hit? But she thought better of calling him. He'd given her lifts over recent weeks and most of the time she was forced to apologise for not having the cab fare on her. He'd let her off, but she could tell he was getting a bit annoyed by her lack of cash. They'd exchanged numbers – Netty had given him one of her many mobile numbers – and they'd even begun to stay at each other's homes. Soon he started lending her money to buy drugs. But she hadn't seen him for about four days now – not since the last time she phoned him asking for £15. On that occasion, he said if she wanted the money she'd have to come and get it. So a friend had given her a lift in his white Ford Escort. She felt she couldn't call him tonight and again ask for money. Instead, she called a supplier she knew. When they met up, he wasn't pleased she'd come without cash, though it wasn't the first time he'd been asked for drugs up-front. No deal. He wasn't going to extend her drugs tab. He headed off on foot, and she followed behind, struggling to keep up with his big strides. But he wasn't able to shake her off, so he relented.

At twenty-nine, Netty's dreams had evaporated. Still, at least she looked immaculate tonight, she thought. She'd dressed herself from head to toe in black – boots, leggings and decorative top. Hair, nails, lips. All had been done to perfection. Well, after four years training as a beautician, she certainly hoped so.

She had lost quite a lot of weight over recent months since she moved in with her boyfriend on the Ravenswood Estate and so the cold of the December night was getting to her more than ever. That was another reason why she particularly loathed standing on the street waiting for a client to pull up to the kerb or for her mobile to ring.

She hoped that no one outside her world in the sex trade knew what she did to make money and she wanted to keep it that way. Netty wasn't just embarrassed, she was ashamed of the direction that her life had taken. What was worse, she had been born and bred in Ipswich and so the chances of keeping her work in the sex industry a secret from her parents were slim. Only a few weeks earlier she had seen her cousin Tanya cycling past while she had been touting for business close to the BMW garage on West End Road.

Tanya had pedalled over to say 'hi', and had told her that she was really worried about her being on the streets when two girls – Gemma Adams and Tania Nicol – had been reported missing. Netty told her cousin not to worry and that she was OK, but she knew that wouldn't allay her fears, and so made her promise not to tell anyone else she'd seen her there. She knew just how upset her parents would be if they found out. She didn't look like an addict, so they would never have known – the make-up helped, too, another skill from her former life that was now coming in handy. The punters liked a bit of slap as well.

The flashing of the car's headlights disturbed her daydreams and her fears about her parents finding out were now pushed to the back of her mind. Back to business. She watched the car slow down as it approached. This wouldn't be her first job of the night, but it might be the one to secure the money she needed for her next score. The window was rolled down; she peered inside. Within seconds the car had pulled away with Netty in the passenger seat, chatting with her killer.

Steve Wright knew he'd taken a risk with his fourth victim. She was also his second in almost as many days since the discovery of Gemma Adams over the weekend. He was playing with fire, but he liked that. Not only was he now killing for kicks, but he needed his kicks at a faster rate. But as he killed, he knew he was being less meticulous about where he was discarding his victims. He'd not placed Anneli in water and he'd decided to follow suit with his fourth – the brunette. There were more police around now so he'd have to be quick getting rid of her. Nacton had been quiet and dark – just as he liked it – but what it didn't provide was early warning of approaching vehicles. The narrow, twisting road meant that car headlights would only be seen at the last minute, and the last thing he wanted was to be caught in the full beam of a car's headlamps dragging his latest naked victim from the boot or back seat. He had no idea whether the blonde's body had been discovered by police yet. He'd neither seen nor heard any reports in the past couple of days, but it was just too risky to go there on the off chance he could dump another victim in the wasteland.

What he needed, rather, was a straight road where cars could be seen coming from hundreds of metres away. The old A12 where he'd dumped his first and still undiscovered victim, Tania Nicol, would have been ideal. It was dimly lit and, compared to the new A12 that now ran parallel to it yet out of sight, was much less used, too. But it was too close to Hintlesham where Gemma Adams had been found. Still, too many cops for his liking.

The old Felixstowe road it would be, then. Ideal. Close to the small, quiet village of Levington and, as with the old A12, it offered long, straight approaches where cars could be spotted four to five hundred metres away. No street lights either. Dual carriageway bordered by knee-deep undergrowth. A swift getaway, and, should he decide to kill again soon, an ideal place to deposit future victims.

The naked body of Annette Nicholls lay barely five metres back into the undergrowth on land between the old Felixstowe road and the railway line that ran between Felixstowe and Ipswich. It would not be long before Wright, true to his habits, would return to the scene. He would not return alone, but he had yet to select the next prostitute he would bring there, a task that would only take him a matter of days.

With the discovery of Tania Nicol's body on Friday 8 December, the police were now two, rather than three, bodies behind the killer. In Nacton, Anneli Alderton's body lay still undiscovered. Less than a mile away, close to Levington, was the body of Annette Nicholls. For now, however, the police had only two bodies. As far as they were concerned, both women had been killed in strikingly similar circumstances, although at that stage they were not linking them officially. But the ante had been upped and the media were cottoning on to the fact this was probably the work of one person and so had already begun to flock to the town. Suffolk Constabulary increased the number of staff that they were dedicating to the case.

All this attention would make things a little trickier for the killer. By now he would know from press reports that they'd only found the first body because someone had gone to check for blockages in the brook after days of heavy rains. If that hadn't happened, the police would never have found the second – Tania. Still, he must have thought that they had nothing to go on, and with the weekend fast approaching there'd be a few girls out on the streets. Perhaps he thought he might just cruise around to see who was available to satisfy his needs. His needs? They were sexual, all right, but not in the usual way. Strangulation was as intimate as it got.

Paula Clennell, 'Mystery Angel'

Paula woke up after crashing out on pensioner John Davies's bedroom floor all day, walked into his living room and opened the card she'd bought for her three children. She had met John outside his local pub close to the red-light area one night. She had asked him for a cigarette and John had obliged.

'You're Taffy aren't you?' Paula had asked.

John had nodded and they chatted for a while before going their separate ways. Knowing where he drank, Paula made sure of an impromptu meeting the following evening. This time she invited herself back to his for coffee. John's sheltered accommodation was modest, yet warm and comfortable – and for Paula it offered her temporary sanctuary from the harshness of Ipswich's red-light area. John knew what Paula did for a living, but, being a fair man, he told her she could visit whenever she wanted on the understanding that she didn't use drugs in the house. Paula respected that.

'She was out of this world,' said John. 'She would come in after being out all night, sleep all day, waking up around tea time. She was always exhausted from the drugs and walking around all night – that was her life. Still, she'd wash up, make the bed and sometimes offer to do the ironing. I never asked her to, she would just want to do it. Then she'd make herself her favourite sandwich – ham, cheese and beetroot. She was really fun to be around. She was more like a daughter than a friend.'

Now, with her sandwich in her lap, Paula grabbed a pen and began writing to her three daughters who had been taken into care when social services found out she was taking heroine:

To my 3 little angels,

If you only knew how much I really miss you all, more than anyone can ever imajin. The past couple of years have been so hard for me to deal with, but the only thing that has helped me cope is that you're all together, as you should be.

I never have stopped and never will stop thinking of you all. I hope you will find it in your hearts to forgive me, my girls, but one day I will get the chance to explain the whole situation to yous, and I know yous will understand.

Obviously I know you're all too young to take it all in, but you will get to read all your letters I send to all three of yous and you'll see that I always have and will love you all.

Oh my little angels, you're always in my thoughts. Not

one day goes by that I'm not thinking of you all. I am always talking about yous, telling how my 3 beautiful little girls are my whole life. The best thing I done for yous was what I done to give you all the life yous deserved. I just hope it was the right thing, and that's why I need a photo of yous so I can see yous all grow up. At least if I can have that it wont feel like you're gone, as in my heart yous are always there with me.

I love you with every beat of my heart and always will. Love you lots and lots.
From Mummy
Paula
xxx xxx xxx

It was getting late and Paula didn't have a photo of herself, but she would get one done, slip it into the card and send it off as soon as possible. John was asleep, and she pinched the packet of cigarettes he kept down the side of the sofa. She'd own up later. Then she headed out of the front door.

It was 5 December and Paula was on the streets again tonight. She and the other girls had been extra cautious since Gemma and Tania had gone missing and, now that Gemma had been found murdered, everyone was on edge. The funny thing was, the red-light district felt like the safest place in Ipswich – police were everywhere and so were the media. Surely the killer wouldn't be so foolish as to show himself now? She'd seen television crews driving around and heard that some of the other girls had done interviews for cash, too. Nice work if you can get it, she thought. And, sure enough, it was soon her turn.

She'd been hanging around for a while in between

clients so the TV crew didn't take long to descend on her. She didn't take much persuasion – it wasn't every day you appeared on television and, anyway, it broke up the monotony of the evening, and there might be some cash in it for her, too. But she decided she wouldn't give them her real name. Instead of Paula, she would call herself Kelly and the hood of her coat would hide her face during the interview that would be shown that night, just to protect her identity.

Paula – or Kelly – told the reporter from Anglia TV that she was prepared to be out on the streets because she needed the money, but admitted that the murder of Gemma Adams and the disappearance of Tania Nicol had made her 'a bit wary about getting into cars'. The streets of the red-light district were quiet because, she said, 'the girls are probably wary about coming out now'. Not that it would stop her from getting into the next car that came along. She also said that Gemma's murder had made her feel 'sick'. 'Gemma was a nice girl, always smiling.'

She was also keen to stress that the streets weren't safe. 'I've had a couple of nasty experiences but nothing like this with the foreigners. They're the only ones who have ever been out of order,' she said. 'I haven't been properly attacked but I have had a few pretty bad experiences, like I said, with foreigners. They think they can do anything to a woman and get away with it. It makes me feel sick to the stomach but if you need the money badly it's better than going out thieving. It would be safer to get a flat and work from there, but it's getting a flat that's the problem.

She told the TV crew she even feared she might be the next victim, but what she didn't tell them was the extent to which she had been in trouble with the police. She'd lost count of the number of appearances she'd made in court for offences related to her job. It was just an occupational hazard – almost like paying taxes, but not quite. And that was only the half of it. What she couldn't beg, steal or borrow she'd earn doing a job she needed to feed her heroin and crack habit – after all, there were dealers and fines to pay and debts to settle.

As quickly as they had arrived the TV crew were gone – off, Paula suspected, to find their next 'hooker', as she'd seen the girls described in the papers. It reminded her of the last time she had been in the papers herself. A long time ago now – eight years, in fact, when she was only sixteen. She had gone to help a pensioner who'd fallen and badly injured herself. She had called for an ambulance and waited with the elderly woman until paramedics arrived. Her picture appeared in the paper soon after the grateful lady had appealed for her 'mystery angel' to come forward so that she could thank her.

But that was in the past. Paula was hardly a model citizen now, though she could still be angelic when she needed to be – and that was quite often these days. She had left home soon after helping the old lady and at first led a nomadic existence, living where she could. Drugs had created chaos in her life but also, paradoxically, a certainty – everything now became focused on finding the money for the next fix. She often said she didn't expect to live longer than twenty-five years.

If her predictions were right, she would be dead in a year's time. It was a bold statement and had made her think hard about her family. With Christmas around the corner, she was looking forward to buying presents for her 'three little angels'. She would spoil them if she could. Her parents had split up years earlier and her father – like Gemma's also called Brian – lived far away, in Berwick. She hadn't seen him for some years, though she suspected her sister, who lived nearby, would keep him updated about how she was. It had been a long time since she'd seen her mother, too. She hadn't had her mum Isabella's address until recently but now she had it, she had decided to get in touch with her. She wouldn't go and see her; rather, she would write to her.

Paula's spelling wasn't great but she wrote the letter anyway. She had decided to tell her mum that she wanted to meet up and that they could go Christmas shopping together. They'd buy presents for her own kids and she'd buy her sister's children glow-in-the-dark Care Bears. Paula also wanted her mum to know that this time it wasn't just about Christmas but that she would really keep in touch with her. So, she had given her mum her new phone number. She had also told her that she was terrified of being on the streets, but that she needed the money to buy a house – then she could fight for the return of her three children.

Paula was at her boyfriend's house on the afternoon of Saturday 9 December, when she was suddenly woken up by her friend. It was the same friend she had bumped into the previous day on the Nacton Estate when she was scoring drugs. It had been a good week's work, so Paula was flush with money. She had enough for five deals – three crack cocaine and two heroin. She handed over her £75 and headed back into Ipswich on her mountain bike.

But that was yesterday – her friend had already run out of drugs and withdrawal had begun to set in, so she had come to find Paula to borrow some money. Paula's boyfriend had agreed to fund them enough money to score more crack and heroin – they would both return his favour in kind. Together, Paula and her friend fed their habits, taking cocaine in the living room, then heroin in the bathroom. They both took a bath and washed each other's hair before getting dressed. By now they needed more drugs, but Paula's boyfriend's pockets weren't deep enough to oblige them a second time, and that annoyed the twenty-four-year-old. She decided to teach him a lesson, and took herself out on to the streets for a night's work. Her friend followed her out the door and together they headed for London Road. There, on the borders of the red-light district, they parted company.

Paula wasn't one of life's complainers – she just got on with things as she had done now for years. Hanging off the edge of the kerb in her expensive new Reebok trainers, which John had bought her, and navy blue anorak, she pulled the hood of her grey sweatshirt over her head to keep out the winter night. With her hands shoved deep inside the patterned pocket of her jeans, she prepared for a long night ahead.

Over the years Paula had become wily, tough and street-wise, but that didn't mean she didn't get knocked about. She met some weirdos on the street – some of them wanted it rough and others wanted to spank her. She never came back looking as if she'd been really beaten up, but she had her fair share of marks on her backside from the spanking. Anything went, as long as she got paid, but she could hardly have prepared herself for the client that she was about to meet. She hadn't been out long when the car approached.

The punter was one she knew well – she had been with him several times before. Sometimes she would stay at his place for the night on London Road. The thing was, she had only seen him a few hours earlier. He'd taken her to get her fix and now he was back again. It was cold so she got into his car quickly. It was a mistake; the last she would make. Her grim prediction that she would be dead by the time she reached twenty-five was about to become a premature and ghastly reality.

In the same way that Wright had discarded the body of Annette Nicholls the previous week along the old Felixstowe road near Levington, so he had decided that that was to be Paula's fate, too. And just as with all of his victims he ensured that Paula was stripped naked. He'd driven in the dark along the same stretch of road, but, because of the absence of light, it was difficult to know exactly where he had deposited Annette's body. When he thought he was roughly in the same place, and when he felt the coast was clear, he pulled up, headlights off, and dumped his latest prey, just metres from the main road in the deep undergrowth.

Right under the noses of the police he had done it again. He had seen and read about the discovery on Friday of his first victim – Tania; now the police had discovered his third – Anneli – in Nacton. But his fourth and fifth remained undiscovered, although with all the police activity in Nacton he suspected that might not be the case for too long.

For nearly three days the focus of the police investigation had switched to Nacton, where Anneli Alderton's body had been found by a passer-by. A post-mortem quickly established she had been strangled. And, unlike the discovery of the bodies of Gemma and Tania, it had been clear to investigators that the time that had elapsed between Anneli's death and her discovery was much shorter, at most seven days. They would soon discover the CCTV of her on the train from Harwich to Ipswich the previous Sunday. It was the last sighting of her.

Little did the police on the ground or the media helicopters overhead know that, barely a mile from the scene of activity, the bodies of two more women lay waiting to be found. Annette Nicholls and Paula Clennell had already been reported missing. Their photographs were all over the papers and television and Suffolk Police had appealed for the girls to come forward or make contact.

'Annette Nicholls, aged twenty-nine, was last seen by a member of her family either last Saturday 3 December or Sunday 4 December. She is known to work in the area as a prostitute,' said DCS Gull to a packed news conference.

'She was reported missing by her family who became concerned after seeing the publicity surrounding the murders of Gemma Adams and Tania Nicol. She is white, about five foot three inches tall, slim with shoulder-length brown hair.'

DCS Gull explained they were still concerned as to the whereabouts of another girl, also thought to be working as a prostitute.

'Paula Clennell, aged twenty-four, hasn't been seen since Saturday night when she left an address in London Road on a blue bicycle,' he said. 'However, we have now received a report that a friend spoke to Paula on Sunday night at 10.30 p.m. because she was looking for somewhere to stay.'

'She is described as white, five foot seven inches tall, of medium build with shoulder-length mousy hair, blue eyes and a spotty complexion.

'There could be an innocent explanation as to why these girls are missing. We know, for example, that Paula is of no fixed address and moves about regularly. However, in the current climate we are concerned for their welfare and are making urgent inquiries to locate them.'

Mars Bars and Toffee Crisps

Steve Wright left work, went straight home and stepped into
the shower. He loved nothing more than to hurry back, wash
off the day's grime and get into a pair of jogging bottoms, a
polo shirt and his favourite pair of brown fluffy slippers.
His partner Pam hadn't long been up after working nights
but the smell of her home-made lasagne had already begun
to wend its way up the stairs, making his stomach grumble
with hunger. Her lasagne was his favourite.

He liked to have dinner in front of the television, especially if *EastEnders* or *Emmerdale* was on, and there might
be a good action movie on one of the channels, he thought.
But it would have to be finished by about 11.30 p.m.
because he'd promised to drive Pam to work.

They'd never made a point of watching the news together,
but there was a killer on the loose in Ipswich. Three bodies
had been found in the countryside and Pam wanted to see if
the police had caught anyone yet. The bulletin reported that
the naked bodies of two women had been discovered in the
same brook that ran through Hintlesham and Copdock and
another had been discovered in Nacton. 'What sort of monster
could be capable of such crimes?' Pam had remarked partly to
herself but also directing her comments to the man sitting
beside her, who had by now finished devouring his lasagne
and was halfway through his dessert – tonight a Mars Bar,
other nights, a Toffee Crisp. He grunted, barely acknowledg-
ing her concern for the women, as if he didn't really want to
talk about what everyone else in the town could barely ignore.

Like many women in Ipswich, Pam had started to take
notice of what the media was beginning to call a 'hunt for a
serial killer'. When the first of the two women whose bodies

were later found in water had gone missing at the end of October, she remembered the girl's mother had made a TV appeal. She'd thought nothing of it then, but two weeks later, when a second girl had been reported missing, she'd turned to Steve and said, 'That doesn't sound good, there's something wrong there.' Seemingly uninterested, he'd calmly replied that they were probably together somewhere.

And the fact that prostitutes were in the news had brought back a recent memory for Pam. Not long after they'd moved to London Road, Steve had driven her to work late at night in Nacton. As they'd paused at the lights at the end of their road, she'd spotted a prostitute looking in at them, smiling at Steve as if she knew him. She'd wondered what the hell the woman was looking at. Steve said he had no idea. But since then, she had a nagging feeling he was using prostitutes behind her back, but never confronted him about it.

She'd come close to doing so when, one night some months later, she'd rung home within half an hour of Steve dropping her off at work because she'd forgotten her glasses. She'd wanted him to drive them over for her, but he didn't answer the phone. He claimed he'd gone straight to bed when he got back home so hadn't heard the phone ring. She'd given him the benefit of the doubt.

It was nearing 11.30 p.m. and Pam was ready to be driven to work. Steve slipped out of his slippers, straight into his trainers without putting on any socks. He pulled shut and locked the door to number 79 and reversed out of the drive. Since Pam had spotted a prostitute looking in at Steve, he had begun taking an alternative route out of town, avoiding that particular junction. It wasn't lost on Pam, but she was just glad of the lift to work. A kiss goodnight before letting herself into the call centre, and Wright was heading back into town. But he wouldn't be going straight home. Not yet anyway.

The 'Suffolk Strangler'

The following day, Tuesday 12 December, as had been the case with Gemma Adams and Anneli Alderton, it was again a member of the public who would make the gruesome discovery of the next victim of a man who'd become known locally as the 'Suffolk Strangler'. It wasn't an area in which anyone other than locals might go walking. There was a railway to one side of the road and to the other a patch of land two hundred metres wide that separated the road from the A14. But one walker had veered towards the patch of scrubland on the railway track side of the road when he saw it – or, rather, her. The police were called at 3.05 p.m. They arrived within minutes. They closed the road, setting up a cordon and, as was usual practice, a police helicopter was sent up to film what had been discovered. The chopper was soon hovering above, but it wasn't filming the scene where the police had gathered. Rather it was trained on a location less than a hundred metres further up the road. Word came through to the officers from above at 3.40 p.m.: 'We can see a second body.'

Two more naked bodies of prostitutes discovered in a matter of forty minutes. Both were less than a mile from where the killer had dumped Anneli Alderton. That made five murdered so far. The police had a serial killer on their hands, but when would the killing stop? The media that had begun to get word of police activity near Levington had hurried there in numbers and were asking the same question. As television cameras were set up by the side of the road, so too were crews readying themselves for a hastily arranged press conference at police headquarter. DCS Gull announced to the gathered media that they had some 'breaking news' to deliver:

'As you will understand, we don't have a great deal of information . . . but the natural assumption is that these are the bodies of the two missing women, Annette Nicholls and Paula Clennell.'

The two bodies in Levington were indeed those of Annette and Paula. The lives of two families – like those of the three before them – had fallen apart in a single, miserable moment. And not only did each family member have to deal with their own individual loss, they also had to deal with the loss for the children of both victims, children who would not fully understand losing a parent.

Annette's family, though destroyed, had struggled with how to break the news to her eight-year-old son. Annette's uncle, Peter Nicholls, who had been visiting Annette's parents when police announced two further bodies had been discovered, said: 'He has even mistaken the cards of condolence in his family home for Christmas cards. He was just watching television while police came in and out of the house. He sees all the relatives coming around and will think they are there for some sort of party. We're at our wits' end.'

The Nicholls family even took him and eight of his cousins out of school to prevent them being teased in the playground. According to one newspaper Annette's cousin maintained that some of the kids at school had taken to 'playing prostitutes at break-time instead of mummies and daddies'.

But sadness was accompanied by anger, too. For a week Annette's family had feared the worst, yet at the same time had tried to remain strong for each other. Now that they knew Annette had fallen foul of the notorious killer, they had a message for the murderer. Annette's Uncle Peter, whom the twenty-nine-year-old had visited immediately she had heard that he had developed cancer, in a plea to the killer said:

'Why can't you stop? You have done enough damage. Please just leave this town alone.'

A similar message had come from the Clennell family. Paula's father, who had felt the need to come to Ipswich to be close to the hunt for his daughter, told a national newspaper: 'I don't want anybody else to experience this kind of pain. What kind of beast is he? What sort of inhuman monster is walking among us? – that's the scary thing. Until he is caught nobody is safe.' He added:

> I would plead with anybody who knows something to come forward. He must be someone's father, or brother or son, or even husband. Someone must know something – and they've got to turn him in. We must find this bastard – who the hell is he? I'd like to get him for two minutes alone. I know there are some wicked people in the world, some of them genuinely evil. But I can't understand what must possess a man so that he can do this to so many women.

The killer was indeed genuinely evil, and it was that evil that the police would continue to hunt. But not only did the police seem not to have much to go on, despite five bodies lying in a mortuary in Ipswich, but they had also admitted to being 'emotionally overwhelmed' after learning of the discovery of the fourth and fifth victims. A meeting of police commanders had been punctuated by stunned silence when they were given the news. Later, DCS Gull admitted: 'These tragic events have clearly overwhelmed us . . . emotionally', before adding: 'These are tragic circumstances. Whatever people may think of street workers or about prostitutes, these are young girls who come from families. It is tragic, tragic news.'

The pressure was getting to this small police force. Reinforcements were needed if they were to catch a killer who, it felt to some, was laughing at them. But how good are the police at catching the serial killers or prostitutes?

Chapter Three

The Oldest Profession
and the Serial Killer

'They separated about 9 years since in consequence of her drunken habits. For some time he allowed her 5/- per week, but in 1882, it having come to his knowledge that she was living the life of a prostitute he discontinued the allowance . . . a man named Jack Pizer, alias Leather Apron, has, for some considerable period been in the habit of ill-using prostitutes in this, and other parts of the Metropolis, and careful search has been, and is continued to be made in order that his movements may be accounted for on the night in question, although at present there is no evidence whatsoever against him.'

J. H. Helson Inspr. & J. Keating Supt. J Division Metropolitan
Police September 1888, quoted in S. Evans and K. Skinner (2000:
23–25)

There is a sad and recurring relationship between the so-called 'oldest profession' – prostitution – and serial killers. Indeed, the epigraph at the beginning of this chapter describes the murder of Mary Ann Nichols on 31 August 1888 in Whitechapel, in the East End of London, widely believed to be the first victim of Jack the Ripper, the infamous killer who was perhaps the first to take advantage of the vulnerability of women who, for one reason or another, sell sex to survive. In Mary Ann's case it seems that it was the combination of drink and the failure of her former husband to support her financially that led her to live 'the life of a prostitute'. Whatever the cause, the 'ill-using' that Mary Ann was subjected to creates a direct link between her murder and the failure of the police to catch her killer and the murders in Ipswich and elsewhere in Britain nearly 120 years later, when gin may have been replaced by crack and heroin, but when the killers of many of the young women involved in the sex industry remain at large.

Why do prostitutes remain so vulnerable to attack? Again and again they have been the target of violence and murder, whether from Jack the Ripper, Peter Sutcliffe – known as the 'Yorkshire Ripper', although he also killed and attacked other women, too – or from Steve Wright. Between 1888 and 2006 there have been various attempts to change public attitudes towards women involved in prostitution, and of late in our social policy there has been a move to see women – especially young women (and increasingly also young men) – who are involved in prostitution as victims, and to offer them protection, support and a way out of selling sexual services, rather than simply to prosecute them.

Increasingly there has been a recognition of the need to alleviate the circumstances which make young people vulnerable to exploitation and coercion into prostitution, and of the fact that like Julie, our guide to the red-light area in Ipswich, many of those who end up working on the streets suffer from the same catalogue of issues – physical and sexual abuse within their families, homelessness, poor school attendance and problematic drug use.

Nonetheless, despite recent government initiatives nothing

seems to have changed, and for some women prostitution remains a 'survival strategy': the simple economic necessity that led Jack the Ripper's victim Mary Ann Nichols into the life of a prostitute where the seemingly insatiable demand for sexual services guarantees that there is money to be made. However, perhaps the greatest continuity of all between then and now remains our ambivalence towards women involved in prostitution, and a corresponding lack of interest when they are battered, raped or murdered.

Britain's Street-sex Industry

It is estimated that as many as eighty thousand people work as prostitutes – both as street prostitutes and in 'off-street' prostitution in brothels and saunas in the United Kingdom, and that all of them share a number of common characteristics. These would include:

- Abuse in their past – both physical and sexual.
- Difficult lives, with many of those involved being taken into care and failing to attend or being excluded from school, and so having few educational or training qualifications.
- Homelessness – with many running away from home at an early age.
- Problematic drug use – it has been calculated that as many as 95 per cent of those involved in street prostitution are using crack or heroin.

There are well-known and persistent links between prostitution and deprivation, poverty and disadvantage, which in turn can lead to a feeling of hopelessness, vulnerability, a lack of self-esteem and aspiration. As many as half of those who are involved in street prostitution started working on the streets before their eighteenth birthday. All these factors conspire to suggest that, just like Mary Ann Nichols in late Victorian London, selling sexual services remains for some women and men a survival strategy, with around three-quarters of those involved in street prostitution claiming the need to pay household bills and support their children as the motivating factor for their involvement with prostitution. It should therefore come as no surprise that street prostitution in Britain takes place in areas where deprivation is at its highest.

So, too, the link between commercial sexual exploitation and Class A drugs cannot be overemphasised. These are now so closely associated that those who control prostitution in any city or large town are also likely to control the supply of Class A drugs. We know from Government figures that almost all street prostitutes are problematic drug users, and many will sell sexual services not only to support their own drug habit but also those of their boyfriends. It is increasingly common for a boyfriend with a serious drug habit to pimp his girlfriend to support both their habits. In this respect these men are different from the 'classic pimp' so often represented by the media.

Prostitution is not illegal in the United Kingdom, but what is against the law are the activities that surround prostitution, such as soliciting, advertising using cards in telephone boxes and kerb-crawling. Even so, there remains a huge demand for sexual services, one that has stubbornly resisted various legislative initiatives. The Criminal Justice and Police Act of 2001 made it an offence to advertise the services of a prostitute by way of advertising cards in telephone boxes, threatening prison sentences of up to six months, with calls to those numbers being advertised to be barred. However, such legislation merely 'displaced' this activity; and most prostitutes now use mobile phones, especially those with a Pay As You Go tariff, where it is not possible to identify the subscriber, and which can be quickly discarded and replaced relatively cheaply.

Violence and the Sex Industry

More than 65 per cent of the women involved in prostitution in Britain have experienced client violence. Most report being slapped, kicked or punched, although others mention robbery and rape. In response to violence of this kind cities such as Liverpool have set up 'Ugly Mugs' schemes whereby information about 'dodgy punters' is made freely available to sex workers, but overall only about 30 per cent of the crimes committed against prostitutes get reported to the police. This confirms our findings in Ipswich where most of the prostitutes we spoke to claimed that their accounts of the violence committed against them would not be believed. Others refused to go to the police because they were afraid action would be taken against them for warrants still outstanding. The small number who had reported a crime did not feel that they had been treated respectfully either by the police or by court officials, and the lack of prosecutions for crimes committed against prostitutes did little to convince them it was worth bothering.

Recent Government figures reveal that as many as sixty prostitutes were murdered between 1994 and 2004, although there were only convictions in sixteen cases. Put simply, the figures suggest that if you kill a prostitute you are less likely to be caught by the police than if you murder almost anyone else. The average conviction rate for murder in Britain is one of the highest in the world at over 75 per cent, but this drops to around 25 per cent when it comes to the murder of a prostitute. Why should this be so? Leaving to one side for the moment issues surrounding police investigations of the murders of prostitutes, when thinking about murder more generally it is also always best to consider three issues – access, opportunity and motive.

In other words, if you were motivated to kill someone how would you be able to get access to that person, and thereafter the opportunity to kill them? Access would be an issue if our serial killer wanted to kill famous or powerful people, but women who work in the sex industry offer access to strangers in return for money or drugs. Our motivated killer does not have to find ways to create access at all, but rather this is manufactured for him by the economic realities of prostitution. So, too, opportunities to kill abound. After all, the sex that a prostitute sells invariably takes place covertly, out of sight of anyone who might be able to help a woman in trouble with a client. The prostitute gets into a car that does not belong to her, and is driven away from those who might be able to protect her. She is also likely to be using drugs. In doing so she is making herself vulnerable to those who have ulterior motives. Simply considering these first two issues – access and opportunity – goes some way towards explaining the depressing numbers of women involved in the sex industry who end up dead – either at the hands of everyday murderers or serial killers.

Serial Killers in Britain

To be labelled a serial killer a murderer would normally have to have killed three or more victims in a period of more than thirty days. Seeking to identify serial killers with such guidelines allows us to differentiate between those, for example, who murder a large number of people – such as Michael Ryan, who shot and killed sixteen people in Hungerford in August 1987, or Thomas Hamilton, who shot and killed fifteen children and their school teacher in Dunblane in March 1996 – and who thus qualify in terms of the number of victims but not in relation to the period of time. Hamilton or Ryan would be described by criminologists as 'spree' or 'mass' killers.

Nonetheless, defining serial killing is fraught with difficulties. Some criminologists suggest that there should be as many as six points of identification for a murderer to be labelled as a serial killer; others maintain that there need only be two rather than three victims; and some argue that the murders should occur at different locations and that there should be no relation between the victim and the murderer. However, in the British context these stipulations would exclude such individuals such as Dennis Nilsen, Fred and Rosemary West and our most prolific serial killer to date, Harold Shipman, all of whom clearly had a prior relationship with many of their victims, and who murdered them in the same locations.

Perhaps just because defining serial killing is so problematic there have been few attempts to devise a typology of serial murderers. The most comprehensive one is still that devised by two American criminologists, Ronald Holmes and James Deburger, which was based on interviews and analysis of more than four hundred cases of serial murder. They identified four types of male serial killer – visionary, mission, hedonistic and power/control (see Table 1).

Table 1. Types of Serial Killer (Male).

Visionary	Killer is impelled to murder because he has heard voices or seen visions demanding that he kill a particular person, or category of people. The voice or vision may be for some a demon, but for others may be perceived as coming from God
Mission	Killer has a conscious goal in his life to eliminate a certain identifiable group of people. He does not hear voices, or have visions. The mission is self-imposed
Hedonistic	Killer kills simply for the thrill of it – because he enjoys it. The thrill becomes an end in itself
Power/Control	Killer receives gratification from the complete control of the victim. This type of murderer experiences pleasure and excitement not from sexual acts carried out on the victim, but from his belief that he has the power to do whatever he wishes to another human being who is completely helpless to stop him

Source: Adapted from Holmes and Deburger, *Serial Murder* (1988).

These definitions are helpful, but not fixed – a serial killer might display aspects of more than one typology.

Other criminologists have attempted to understand the behaviour of serial killers by exploring whether their motivation to kill lies outside their personality (such as with underworld hit men), or deep within their psychological make-up. Although it would seem that most serial killers are motivated by intrinsic reasons, they might also still gain materially. Harold Shipman, for example, felt an inner compulsion to kill, but he also benefited financially from some of his victims. Ronald and Stephen Holmes, who worked with various US police departments in more than three hundred murder cases, suggest, through their interviews with a number of serial killers, that most seemed to murder for psychological reasons. They wrote:

> In interviews, many [serial killers] have told us that the principal motivating factor in their killing was that they simply enjoyed killing. Others have stated that they were motivated by the intense feeling they got out of holding the fate of other persons in their hands. The more a person kills, the greater becomes his need to experience those feelings of gratification or power. The feeling becomes more than a compulsion, it becomes an addiction.

This addiction is easy to feed if there is a ready supply of victims. In Britain between 1960 and 2006 there have been nineteen active serial killers responsible for killing at least 326 victims. This is likely to be an underestimation, for the total includes only those victims for whose murder the killer was convicted in court. It does not include those murdered by a serial killer who has never been caught, such as 'Bible John' in Glasgow, or 'Jack the Stripper' who killed prostitutes in London in the early 1960s.

Between 1960 and 2006 there have been on average two serial killers active in Britain at any one time, and on average seven people have fallen victim to a serial killer each year. These averages hide peaks and troughs, and some years – 1986, for example – produced more serial killers and more victims than others. The majority of those who are murdered by serial killers come almost exclusively from only five groups: gay men, the elderly, babies and infants, young people leaving home and moving to different parts of the country for one reason or another, and prostitutes; and

A young, happy Tania Nicol – ten years before drugs would begin to rule her life and lead her into prostitution.

One of the last photos of Tania – or 'Chantelle' as she was known by her clients in the red-light district.

Wearing her cut-off jeans and new pink stilettos, Tania is caught on CCTV walking towards the red-light area the night she disappeared.

Tania's parents Jim Duell and Kerry Nicol at a Suffolk Police press conference on 15 December. Mr Duell said all the victims were 'now at peace' and the killer could not take away their courage and fortitude.

Happier times for Gemma Adams. She later became estranged from her family after their attempts to get her off heroin had failed.

Gemma Adams stands in one of her favourite 'pitches' on West End Road. She had just returned from her first job of the night. She was reported missing by her boyfriend at 2.55 a.m. the following morning.

The brook in Hintlesham where the body of Gemma Adams was discovered on 2 December. A week later the body of Tania Nicol would be found downstream.

In memory of a friend. A tribute to Gemma tied to a lamp-post on West End Road where she often met her clients.

Last known movements. The third victim, Anneli Alderton was caught on CCTV on the Harwich to Manningtree train the night she disappeared.

Anneli was three months pregnant when she was murdered, but was yet to tell her family.

Armed with a photo of Anneli, police question train passengers to see if anyone remembered spotting her.

The eldest of the victims, twenty-nine-year-old beauty therapist and mother, Annette Nicholls planned to run her own business until drugs and prostitution took over her life.

One of the town's many CCTV cameras catch Annette on the morning of 8 December buying Christmas presents in Ipswich.

Roadside memorial. Annette's body had been dumped close to the old Felixstowe Road.

Paula Clennell put up a struggle against Wright before being murdered. Her blood was discovered in the back seat of his car.

Just days before Paula Clennell disappeared, she'd written a note to her three children who'd been taken into care.

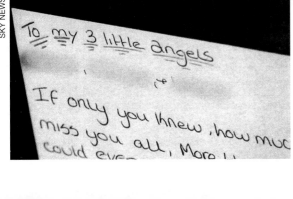

To my 3 little angels

If only you knew, how muc
miss you all, More h
could even

She told her '3 little angels' how much she missed them. She would never get the chance to post it.

Days before she was murdered, Paula Clennell told a local TV reporter that she feared she would be the killer's next victim.

Water bailiff Trevor Saunders found Gemma's naked body lying face-down in the brook as he was clearing debris left by recent flooding.

On 17 December Professor David Wilson and Paul Harrison visited all four 'deposition' sites.

females, rather than males, dominate all but the first group of victims.

Dennis Nilsen, Colin Ireland, Peter Moore and Michael Copeland killed mostly gay men; the Wests concentrated their efforts on runaways or young people who they snatched off the streets; Beverly Allitt – the only female serial killer who worked alone in this country – killed babies and infants; and Harold Shipman targeted the elderly. The typical victim of a serial killer is markedly different from the typical victim of murder. Whereas young boys are most likely to be murdered in Britain, the most likely victim of a serial killer is an elderly woman.

These broad generalisations about the victims of British serial killers can be used to help us think about the type of society we have become and the inadequacy of our protection of the poor and the vulnerable. If children, young people leaving home, gay men, the elderly and prostitutes are the prime victims of serial killers this is only because we have created a society in which these groups are also generally the victims of a social and economic system that sees no value in their lives, and routinely excludes them from the protection of the state. They can be excluded from that protection in a variety of ways, from homophobia to moralising about the way young women and men earn their living if they are involved in the sex industry. One glaring example of this lack of protection can be seen in how the police investigate crimes committed against these five groups, especially the crime of murder.

The 'Yorkshire Ripper'

Peter Sutcliffe – the 'Yorkshire Ripper' – was born in 1946, and during 1969, when he was twenty-three, he came to the attention of the police on two occasions in connection with incidents relating to women involved in prostitution. Sutcliffe had become fascinated by women involved in soliciting in Leeds and Bradford, as he was driven around by his friend Trevor Birdsall in a Reliant Robin. This fascination soon turned to violence, and one night in August, leaving Birdsall in the car, Sutcliffe attacked a woman from behind with a cosh (in this case a sock with a stone in it), and then returned to the car to brag about what he had done to his friend. His victim gave a statement to the police, which enabled them to trace Birdsall's car. Birdsall then pointed them in the direction of Sutcliffe, who was questioned about the incident. He admitted assaulting the woman, but said that they had had a fight after he had been drinking. A month later, on 29 September 1969, Sutcliffe was arrested in the red-light area of Bradford having been found in possession of a hammer.

Look again at these two incidents, both of which chime dreadfully with all that we now know of the *modus operandi* of Sutcliffe, and which would feature in his next two assaults, six years later, of Anna Rogulskyj and Olive Smelt. He frequents red-light areas, targets women involved in prostitution, and he attacks his victims from behind by hitting them over the head – usually with a hammer (as time passed and he became more confident, he would also repeatedly stab his victims). Not only this, one of his victims is able to describe the circumstances of her attack enough for the police to track Sutcliffe down, but it was Sutcliffe rather than his victim who was believed in a culture where violence towards women – especially those involved in prostitution – was the norm. We can only speculate what might have happened if these incidents had been dealt with differently, but they set in train a pattern of assaults, murders and police investigations that was to continue between 1975 and January 1981, when Sutcliffe was eventually arrested and charged with murder.

Between 1975 and 1981 Sutcliffe assaulted seven women and murdered thirteen others. As part of the ongoing police investigation he was interviewed nine times, but was never arrested as a result of those interviews. Even after the murder of Josephine Whitaker – described by the official inquiry into the police investigation of the case as a 'respectable local girl' (rather than a young woman involved in prostitution) – in April 1979, which resulted in thousands of calls from members of the public offering information that they thought might be helpful to the police, there was still no movement in the investigation. Why should this be?

One practical reason occurred in June 1979 – two months after Josephine had been murdered – when a tape was sent to the police by a man claiming to be 'Jack the Ripper', and this seems to have thrown the police off the track. Several letters purporting to be from 'Jack the Ripper' had previously been sent to the police, and now, for various reasons, detectives set great store on the tape being genuine. We now know that the tape had in fact been sent by John Humble, who at the time was twenty-three, and who in March 2006 admitted to four counts of perverting the course of justice by sending three letters and the tape to the police, as a result of which he was sentenced to eight years in prison. In court Humble was described as a 'hopeless alcoholic', who had led a 'spectacularly inadequate life' (*Guardian*, 22 March 2006).

It is helpful to look more closely at the police investigation itself, and in particular to consider the number of times Sutcliffe was interviewed by the police, and how he was able to escape detection for so long. For, while much of the subsequent debate about the police investigation of Sutcliffe centred on the administration of the investigation – whether a computer would have helped, the use of the Major Incident Room, how records were stored and cross-referenced, whether one local force shared enough information with other forces interested in the case and so on – no attempt has been made to view police handling of the Sutcliffe case through the lens of 'cop culture'. In doing so we are also assisted by the knowledge that, more than a decade after Sutcliffe was convicted, during which time the police had all the advantages of numerous technological developments and were much more experienced in sharing information, the policing failures in relation to the investigation of the murder of the black teenager Stephen Lawrence in April 1993 were related to the police's 'institutional racism', rather than to administrative failures or not having access to a computer.

'Cop Culture'

Professor Robert Reiner of the London School of Economics has been at the forefront of academic attempts in this country to try to understand if there is a distinct and identifiable set of beliefs and assumptions that determines how the police will behave operationally in the streets or while conducting investigations. He suggests that an understanding of how police officers see society and their role in it – here defined as 'cop culture' – is crucial to an analysis of what they do. In other words, 'cop culture' shapes police practice. While some might deny this conceptual bridge of saying and doing, and might be more appreciative of 'cop culture' – which is usually seen as a bad thing – we have to remember that, given the great discretionary powers that the police have over individuals, or in shaping investigations, it is not unreasonable to presume that what police officers say and how they socialise would mould their responses to what they find in the streets, or how they attempt to solve problems.

Based on extensive interviews with police officers of different ranks and in different police force areas, Reiner suggested that the main characteristics of 'cop culture' are:

- Mission–action–cynicism–pessimism.
- Suspicion.
- Isolation/solidarity.
- Conservatism.
- Machismo.
- Prejudice.
- Pragmatism.

Given the importance of such characteristics to an understanding of 'cop culture', and the impact that they might have on how the 'Yorkshire Ripper' investigation was conducted, and how this might also have had an impact on the Suffolk case, it is worth spending a little time outlining Reiner's argument.

Reiner suggests that the central characteristic of 'cop culture' is a sense of mission, that being a police officer is not just another job, but one that has the worthwhile purpose of protecting the weak from the predatory. The police are an indispensable thin blue line protecting society, and this inevitably means that they have on occasions to take action. Indeed, some police officers might want to take rather more action than is often necessary, and will pursue exciting and thrill-seeking activities, rather than repetitive, mundane or boring police tasks – such as doing paperwork. Over time, Reiner suggests, police officers will become more cynical and pessimistic – they have seen it all before, with each new development in society seen in almost apocalyptic terms, with the potential to destroy the moral world that has shaped the sense of mission that the police have developed.

So, too, the police are trained to be suspicious, but this can lead to stereotyping potential offenders, which in turn means that this stereotyping becomes a self-fulfilling prophecy. For example, a disproportionate number of young black men get stopped and searched in the streets of Britain, leading to more young black men being arrested, which in turn confirms the stereotype that more young black men than young white men are offenders. Given that police officers are often socially isolated, there is little likelihood that they will encounter young black men who play the piano, read books, or who might wish to become police officers themselves. Similarly the need to rely on one's colleagues in a tight spot means that a great deal of internal solidarity exists, which does little to erode their sense of isolation from other members of society that police officers might encounter.

Also of note, Reiner suggests that police officers tend to be both politically and morally conservative, and would thus culturally distrust those groups such as gay men and prostitutes that might be seen as challenging conventional morality. This does not mean that 'cop culture' is puritanical. Rather, it is dominated by what Reiner describes as 'old-fashioned machismo', and where there are high levels of stress, drinking and divorce. The last aspect of 'cop culture' that Reiner lists is pragmatism, by which he means the simple desire that a police officer has to get through the day as easily as possible. A police officer does not want fuss – especially paperwork – and would rather stress the practical, no-nonsense aspects of the job.

By the time the bodies of five young women were found dead in Ipswich the police knew all about 'cop culture' and how this might affect their performance. So, too, they had come to recognise their failures in the 'Yorkshire Ripper' investigation, and also the mistakes made when attempting to find the killers of Stephen Lawrence. By 2006 a great deal should have changed, and, quite apart from the latest computer technology that now exists to support a police investigation, there were also advances in forensic science and offender profiling – all of which could be harnessed to catch offenders. With the whole country focused on what was happening in Ipswich, the stakes for the police were high. Had the police learned from their past mistakes, or would history repeat itself?

Chapter Four

A Murder Investigation,
Not a TV Drama

Question:
'Do you think you're up to the job – I don't mean that in a cruel way – but there have been questions raised in the press saying this is a country force – a country cop dealing with one of the most severe criminal scenes in British policing history – there must be times when you ask yourself whether you're up to it personally?'

Answer:
'Yes, I do, but although this is Suffolk, we've done the same courses as our colleagues in larger metropolitan areas and were trained to the same standard. I've got every confidence in them [Suffolk Constabulary] that we'll find those responsible.'

Excerpt from interview between Sky News presenter Julie Etchingham and Detective Chief Superintendent Stewart Gull, 13 December 2006

DCS Gull knew that 9.30 a.m. was fast approaching. Each day up until now 11 a.m. had been, as far as the media were concerned, the most important engagement of his increasingly busy days. But today was different. No one knew what was coming, and no one yet knew just how significant it would be. Even the most resourceful of journalists hadn't a clue what to expect, though the sudden rescheduling of the morning press conference had many asking questions. Why 9.30 a.m.? What's changed since yesterday? Is there going to be a major announcement?

DCS Gull knew that once he pushed open the door that everyone in the room and across the country would be hanging on his every word. Normally, journalists would be trying to read between the lines, searching for hidden clues as to the police's progress and morale, penning the next headline and, of course, flashing the next line of breaking news.

This morning he would be serving up rather different news to the hungry pack. His statement would be short, to the point, and there would be strictly no questions afterwards. But before his papers had hit the table in front of him, before he'd even taken a quick sip of water, he was blinded by the flashing of cameras before him, their shutters clicking in unison.

Drawing his chair up to the table, DCS Gull leaned forward towards the bank of microphones, many of which had been positioned close up in front of him so as to give their radio or TV channel the maximum exposure. A brief pause, and then he began to speak.

'Detectives investigating the murder of five women in the Ipswich area have today, Monday, 18 December, arrested a man. The thirty-seven-year-old was arrested at his home address in Trimley, near Felixstowe, at approximately 7.20 a.m. this morning.' He could already sense the impact of his first few words on those facing him, but he continued to focus on the remainder of his statement.

'He has been arrested on the suspicion of murdering all five women.' He emphasised the word 'all' and then slowly read out the victims' names, pausing between each one, as if to allow reporters and viewers watching live at home a moment to digest the substance of this morning's news.

'Gemma Adams . . . Tania Nicol . . . Anneli Alderton . . . Paula Clennell . . . Annette Nicholls.' Their names were by now familiar, but this morning they had a particular resonance.

For DCS Gull and his colleagues it had been an exhausting two weeks.

The thirteenth of December. With the announcement the previous day that the fourth and fifth bodies had been discovered, the Suffolk force had seemed broken and incapable of responding to the daunting task that lay ahead. It wasn't only the number of bodies discovered that was shocking, but also the speed with which they had been found – five bodies in just ten days. The space of time between each discovery had shortened dramatically, too. Six days had passed between the discoveries of Tania Nicol and Gemma Adams, but between Tania Nicol and Anneli Alderton it was only forty-eight hours. Forty-eight hours, too, between the discovery of Anneli in the woods at Nacton and the unearthing, barely a mile away, in Levington, of the bodies of Annette Nicholls and Paula Clennell.

As well as that, the most recent discovery – that of Paula Clennell – was of a woman who'd last been seen as recently as Saturday night or early on Sunday morning. Not only did the murders seem to be picking up momentum, but the killer was committing them under the noses of the police, too.

The police were also able to establish that there had been roughly two weeks between the actual murders of Tania

Nicol and Gemma Adams, likewise for those of Gemma and Anneli Alderton. But then the killer had started to strike more quickly – he had murdered his final two victims within a week of his third. And since the most recent location in Levington now contained not one but two bodies, suddenly the workload had mushroomed to an unprecedented level for the Suffolk police. And few could be sure it wasn't about to rise again.

By this stage the murder investigation had earned its top-level rating – A plus – which meant that as many officers as possible would need to be dedicated to the case. For a small rural force, that was a tall order. Suffolk Constabulary remains one of the smallest in England and Wales, a state of affairs that didn't change even after the county's three separate constabularies, East Suffolk, West Suffolk and Ipswich Borough, amalgamated in 1967 to form its current force of just over 1300 officers. And while the homepage of their website might boast 'Your constabulary is ready to rise to the challenge of policing 21st century Suffolk', this was now one of the country's biggest ever murder investigations and some were beginning to ask whether the force's motto, 'Taking Pride in Keeping Suffolk Safe', was in danger of backfiring. There were those who felt that it already had – not least the family and friends of five dead women.

Such concerns had begun to appear in the newspapers, too:

- 'The fear among senior police figures, including officers in the 1,300-strong Suffolk Constabulary, is that the force might be overwhelmed physically, mentally and emotionally by the scale of the inquiry' (*Daily Telegraph*, 14 December).

- 'Police in Suffolk are overwhelmed by the scale of the task that has engulfed them in the last 10 days. The force, which has only 1,307 officers, is facing a complex multiple murder inquiry in which forensic evidence is proving hard to extract' (*Guardian*, 13 December).
- 'Officers throughout the country have been drafted in to help the beleaguered Suffolk police force as fears grow that the killer will strike again' (*Independent*, 13 December).

The headlines made for uncomfortable reading for those closely involved in the case, even though some secretly agreed with their conclusion. One man, however, did not.

DCS Stewart Gull had spent twenty-four of his forty-four years in Suffolk Constabulary, and had the distinction of being the only Suffolk officer to have served in every rank prior to his promotion, some six months before the murders, when he took up his new role as Head of Crime Management. His reputation spoke of a meticulous and methodical officer both in uniform and in the CID, and that had made him the obvious candidate to fill the vacancy created by a colleague's appointment as Chief Constable in Bedfordshire. His new department numbered two hundred officers and other staff focusing on covert policing, financial investigation, hi-tech crime, child protection, victim care, community safety, forensic science services and, of course, major crime investigation. Investigations didn't get much bigger than the one he was heading just now.

The 'Country Copper', as some of the press had begun to call him, was about to draw on all his twenty-four years of experience. The problem was that he now had five bodies, but no apparent crime scene and no clear suspect. If that meant DCS Gull was feeling the pressure from above, that wasn't the impression given publicly by his Chief Constable, Alastair McWhirter.

'The Suffolk force is a small rural force; how are you coping?' asked Sky's Colin Brazier.

'We're coping very well,' replied McWhirter. 'I've always said we had the capability to deal with this, just not the capacity. I'm proud of the way ACC Jacqui Cheer and DCS Gull and all the officers have so far dealt with the inquiry.' McWhirter continued:

> It doesn't matter what size you are, it's whether you have the skills. The people we have in validating what we're doing – because this is a very complicated inquiry – are telling us we're doing perfectly and have rarely seen it done better. This is not a police drama where the whole story from start to finish takes just one hour. This is real life and it's a hard slog whatever happens and we're dealing with five separate murders.

This was certainly not a police drama, but with twenty-four-hour news channels such as Sky News and BBC News 24 offering wall-to-wall coverage of events as they developed, Suffolk Constabulary knew that its own capacity – or lack of it – was a fundamental issue and would be something the media as a whole would focus on. It was an issue that needed addressing; too many mistakes had been made in high-profile murder investigations in the past for it not to be.

In 1994 the Chief Constable of Gloucester, Tony Butler, pleaded with the Home Office for more resources to lend weight to the already high-profile Cromwell Street murder inquiry. His force, like the Suffolk force now, was stretched to the limit trying to gather evidence to convict Fred and Rose West. At the time the help that he had requested wasn't forthcoming. Twelve years on, McWhirter was determined that *his* force wasn't about to suffer the same fate.

Even so, talk among his officers behind closed doors or before the press that this investigation was 'unprecedented' in the history of murder inquiries served only to portray the image of a force out of its depth. In the past there had been cases of similar magnitude and pace, even if the media spotlight hadn't been so bright. In 1986, for example, the Metropolitan Police had had to deal with the little-known case of the man dubbed the 'Stockwell Strangler' – Kenneth Erskine – who sodomised and strangled seven elderly men and women between April and July of that year, and earlier still Patrick Mackay had murdered at least five people in a matter of months in 1975. There were also the assaults and murders committed by Peter Sutcliffe.

But the Suffolk case was itself now high-profile, and that meant mistakes made in previous murder investigations had to be avoided. Few needed reminding of the many errors made in the investigation into the murders of young women at the hands of the 'Yorkshire Ripper' in the 1970s or, more recently, the damning report by Sir Michael Bichard into the 'deeply shocking' errors made by Suffolk's neighbouring forces Cambridgeshire Police and Humberside Police in relation to the Soham school caretaker Ian Huntley, who murdered ten-year-olds Holly Wells and Jessica Chapman.

The Soham investigation had also raised questions about the ability of smaller forces to handle the bigger cases, and was partly, though indirectly, responsible for Home Office plans, earlier in 2006, to reduce the number of police forces across England and Wales from forty-three to seventeen. Suffolk, Norfolk and Cambridgeshire Constabularies had been due to merge into a single East Anglian 'super' force, the idea being that these combined forces would be better able to deal with more complex investigations that required greater resources. The proposals were eventually scrapped after they proved too costly to implement.

Therefore, not only was this crunch time for a small force with limited resources, but if the investigation didn't run smoothly a beleaguered Home Office, which had come to the end of a difficult year of adverse headlines, would feel the full force of the media's criticism yet again, something it could ill afford. For all concerned, it was vitally important that Suffolk be given all the assistance it needed, though many continued to argue that help should have been given or requested much earlier than it had been.

If the investigation had become high-profile, it was matched by equally high-profile figures now making the trip to Ipswich to lend assistance. For some, the arrival at police headquarters in Martlesham Heath of the Metropolitan Police's Commander Dave Johnston marked a clear turning point for the Suffolk investigation. Drafted in primarily on an advisory basis as one of Britain's leading murder invest-igators, and Vice Chair of the Association of Chief Police Officers (ACPO) Homicide Working Group, Commander Johnston also headed Scotland Yard's Serious Crime Unit which handles around 170 murders a year – it has a success rate of more than 80 per cent.

Normal procedure or otherwise, his role in the hunt for a serial killer meant that someone had decided Suffolk Constabulary should be given all the help it needed and the force's Chief Constable was at pains to deny any suggestion that the Metropolitan Police might be asked to take over the investigation, dismissing that as an idea that 'went out in the 1930s'. Instead the 1300-strong constabulary would soon be supported by up to five hundred extra officers from forces all over the country. Some would inevitably come from neighbouring forces such as Norfolk and Cambridgeshire, with whom Suffolk operated a 'mutual aid' pact. Others would be sourced through a London-based National Police Information Centre which could find extra officers at short notice. The newly expanded constabulary was now capable of employing any means possible to catch the killer before he struck again.

But the police weren't the only ones who could help catch the killer and investigators knew that.

The world's press were assembled outside the main entrance to the police headquarters in Martlesham Heath. There were four television satellite trucks, half a dozen people carriers kitted out with edit suites, a dozen or more cars and, on the edge of the grass, close to the main entrance to the headquarters, a seemingly endless row of open-sided canopies – crammed with cameras, sound equipment, TV monitors and lights – marking out each television station's territory. Miles of interwoven, multi-coloured cables stretched out and linked millions of pounds' worth of hardware in what could increasingly be mistaken as a Hollywood movie set.

That morning, then, DCS Gull knew that in a matter of minutes he was due to take his place beneath those canopies to face interrogation by presenters under their blinding lights. The previous evening producers had bid for him to do specific slots in their morning shows and he was due on Sky News' *Sunrise* show at the top of the hour – in effect leading the programme as the main news item that day.

He'd talk as much as he felt he was able to about the progress of the investigation and deal as best he could with questions about his force's ability to handle such a high-profile case. In the light of the discovery twenty-four hours earlier of the fourth and fifth bodies, DCS Gull knew he had a busy morning ahead of him.

He knew the media's appetite for new information was voracious, but he was eager to get on with the job. The investigation was progressing well, he felt, and later at the usual 11 a.m. press conference he was keen to express his thanks to the public for their response to his appeals for information.

'More than two thousand calls were received from the public yesterday,' he told the ever-growing pack of journalists. 'The response from the public to our appeals has been massive. Our task is to sift through this vast volume of information to prioritise our inquiries into these murders.' To all intents and purposes the police knew they needed the public as their eyes and ears across the town, and it had been members of the public who'd found three of the five dead prostitutes.

'We have a significant gap between when the women were last seen and the discovery of their bodies. We need to find out where these women were between these times,' DCS Gull continued.

It might have seemed an obvious point to make, but sightings of any of the five girls in places as yet unknown to the police would give them new locations to search, at which vital forensic evidence could throw up fresh leads to the killer. For example, with the discovery of the first body – that of Gemma Adams – on 2 December, senior investigators quickly established that they were dealing with a 'deposition' site – the place where her body had been dumped but not where she had been killed. The same would be true for all the victims. They were dealing with an organised killer who disposed of his victims carefully. Crucially, this also meant that forensic evidence could be gathered only from the deposition site. And in the case of Gemma Adams and Tania Nicol, their bodies had been found some time after their death, stripped naked and submerged in fast-flowing water. Forensics would face an uphill struggle with only one location per victim from which to gather evidence; had they had the murder scene for any of the women, they would have much more to go on.

The three-hundred-page policeman's bible – *The Murder Investigation Manual 2006*, compiled by veteran officers at the National Centre for Policing Excellence in Bedford – identifies five possible scenes for forensic analysis:

1 Where the victim was last seen alive.
2 The location of initial contact between the victim and the perpetrator.
3 The site where the victim was subdued by the perpetrator.
4 The murder scene.
5 Where the body was dumped.

Point 1 they were still collating for each of the victims – friends, relations, the girls' clients and other women working the same streets would help piece that together.

Point 2 was almost certainly the red-light district of Ipswich for each of the girls, though until a specific location could be pinpointed within that area it would be of little help. Points 3 and 4 were black holes for now. Point 5 was more than apparent for each victim, but it was the only certainty the police had.

We met Tracey – again, not her real name – on 8 December, the night Tania Nicol's body was discovered in Copdock. Tracey had wandered unprompted up to us to ask what we were filming. Like many of the women who worked in the town's red-light district, she was talkative and extremely inquisitive and agreed to chat to us about the dead girls. Aware that she might be happy to say just about anything for a bit of cash, we were careful not to part with the £30 interview fee too quickly; we asked a couple of trick questions to see if she really knew Gemma and Tania.

'Wasn't Gemma the brunette who moved down here from Scotland?' was our first, deliberately inaccurate, question.

'No, stupid, Gemma's got lovely blonde hair and she's local, a bit posh, though heroin fucked her up.' Tracey later admitted that heroin had 'fucked' her up, too. It was clear she knew both girls, but we wanted to ask her a few more questions before paying her. Among other things, we wanted to know how relations were between the police and the young women who sold sex on the streets.

'I've called the police once already because I've got information I think they should know. Me and some other girls reckon we know who the killer is. They took my number and said they'd phone me back, but they 'aven't.'

It's not beyond the realms of possibility that, faced with a phone call from someone sounding as high as Tracey did and who claimed she knew who the killer was, little attention was paid to her call. But she wasn't the only prostitute to complain about the police's attitude to their offering information. It would be a mistake to disregard their calls, as these were the very women who could hold the key to the killer's identity. Even so, relations between the women and the police were clearly poor in Ipswich – in 2004 the Ipswich Crime and Disorder Reduction Partnership reported that many sex workers felt the police didn't 'give a stuff' and looked at them 'like you were dirt'. But the truth was, their situation differed little from sex workers in most other towns and cities across the country.

There had been signs that that relationship was about to

change, though not necessarily for the better as far as Tracey and her colleagues were concerned. The Home Office had invited Ipswich to become one of the six areas in England to be part of a national media campaign aimed at reducing kerb-crawling and prostitution. Councillors had welcomed the initiative and the indications were that the campaign would have started towards the end of November or early December 2006. Subsequent events put paid to that, however.

In order for the investigation to gather information about the girls' last-known whereabouts, bridges between the police and the women in the red-light district would need to be built quickly. Trust – or the apparent lack of it – would be the biggest hurdle. Many girls, fearful they could become the subject of the next headline – 'killer strikes again' – had, it appeared, decided not to venture out into the cold December nights. The streets had become eerily empty; instead, women were making contact with their regular clients by mobile phone. And despite the police increasing the number of patrols in the red-light area, the girls continued to stay away. In short, the investigation was being hampered by the absence of girls on the streets to talk to. As if to underline the lack of information available on the street, police did not even know that Anneli Alderton, the killer's third victim, was a prostitute who had gone missing. It suggested that intelligence was not being gathered quickly enough to prevent further murders. Things had to change.

As far as the police were concerned the easiest way to stop the killer attacking again was to remove his prey altogether. This came in the form of a personal appeal from Suffolk Police's most senior female officer. Assistant Chief Constable Jacqui Cheer maintained: 'The welfare of the prostitutes working in Suffolk is my priority at this time. My message to them is simple: stay off the streets. If you are out alone at night you are putting yourself in danger.'

This was much easier said than done, and ACC Cheer's statement was attacked almost immediately by people inside and outside the sex industry as unworkable. Some were incensed by the police's suggestion that Ipswich's prostitutes should stay home. These were women who, while terrified, didn't have the luxury of stopping work for a few weeks while they waited for the police to catch a killer. Would ACC Cheer have asked the same of teachers, bankers or journalists?

The faces of some of those women who did remain working while the investigation continued were becoming familiar: they were there primarily to earn money to feed their drug habits. Free alternatives, it was being suggested, would be the only way of getting them off the street. But how long would that last? 'My suppliers would be well hacked off if I stopped using them. And, anyway, when they've caught the murderer, we'd 'ave to go back to them to start scoring drugs again and they might want more money because they lost out for a few weeks. It's not as simple as just getting off the streets. We've got obligations,' Tracey said, with complete absence of irony.

In an attempt to build even better bridges, ACC Cheer declared an amnesty on the illegal activities associated with prostitution. In this way it was hoped that not only would many of the girls with outstanding warrants feel more confident about coming forward with potentially vital information, but that the police would also be able to tap into another vital source of information – the punters. For this latter group – the demand side of prostitution – there was the promise of anonymity through the use of a dedicated mobile phone number to police headquarters. The punters knew the girls well, it was reasoned: they talked to them, knew their habits and in some cases might even have been the last people to have seen the girls alive.

Meanwhile, investigators were simultaneously tracing the whereabouts of nearly four hundred registered sex offenders across the county. Even though it seemed that neither Gemma Adams nor Tania Nicol had been sexually assaulted, this suggested that officers were not leaving any stone unturned. They tried to narrow their lines of inquiry even more by trawling through the sophisticated HOLMES (Home Office Large Major Enquiry System) database, which was established in 1987, updated ten years later and then again in 2003, and which is an information storage and retrieval system that allows for all the information that emerges from a major inquiry anywhere in the country to be stored, indexed and cross-referenced.

The police were also planning ahead. Detectives had already begun gathering information for a database of prostitutes' personal features. Women were being asked to provide details of scars, tattoos, birthmarks or any other markings that would enable speedy identification should there be another victim. It was a morbid process, but it served not only as a means of warning the girls of the risks they faced – as if they needed reminding – it might also help in thawing relations between the police and those in the red-light district. This was not something that could be taken too far since the girls and their clients together made up only about two-thirds of this murky world. The police couldn't rule out the possibility that the vital clue leading them to the killer might be found among the many drug-pushing pimps who, by and large, provided the *raison d'être* for prostitution in the town. All five victims were known to have had drug habits, and the police were also aware that there seemed little evidence that any of them had struggled with their killer, possibly suggesting that the girls had been incapacitated by drugs. The police therefore needed more information about the world of the town's suppliers.

An amnesty was therefore extended to the suppliers. Because the police were focused on the murders, DCS Gull said dealers could 'present themselves with impunity'. 'Clearly, dealing Class A drugs is a serious offence,' said Gull. 'However, our priority remains finding the person responsible for the deaths of these five women. I am not interested in other offences at this time. No one has got anything to fear in coming forward and providing us with information.'

The 'come-to-us' approach, directed at the women, their clients and drug pushers, might just work. But the police decided to take the 'we'll-come-to-you' tack as well. However, to some the extra foot patrols and the endless police cars smacked of too little too late. To the women on the street, their presence was seen as an invasion of their patch. Put simply, the police were too close for comfort.

'I don't normally stand here, and it's not really what people might think is the red-light district,' said Tracey, slightly uncomfortable in her new surroundings. 'Because the police keep walking up and down around Portman Road and that, the punters are being scared away. They don't want to pick me up while the Old Bill is standing there watching, so I 'ave to come 'ere if I want any business at the moment.'

Not only did many women feel the need to ply their trade while the killer was still on the loose, but in order to do so they had to venture to unfamiliar, often badly lit territory; this was the worst-case scenario for many of the women because they felt they were being put at even greater risk.

The suggestion that the policeman on the beat in the red-light area made it hard for the girls to operate was in itself slightly illogical. For years, even before the police had begun patrolling on foot in greater numbers, women and their clients had completed their transactions in full view of the area's CCTV cameras. The last known sightings of the girls were crucial, and if they were made by an electronic eye, so much the better – CCTV images could be studied at length, printed and distributed to the media, whereas the memory of human sightings faded with time. Better still, because the girls' clothing, and the evidence it might hold, were so crucial, the images told police exactly what they were looking for.

It was also possible that the killer hadn't been fully aware of the sheer number of cameras spread out across the town and specifically within the red-light district; there was even a chance that his vehicle, its registration number or even the face of the killer himself would be captured on film. It might also give clues as to where he'd murdered the women before dumping them.

And apart from the sixteen Council-owned cameras, there were at least another thirty additional cameras surveying the exteriors of private businesses within the red-light area. The Build Centre in West End Road has seven, for example, of which two are directed on to the street and would often routinely record prostitutes getting in and out of cars.

The only problem was that more than forty cameras recording for weeks amounts to thousands of hours of 'harvested' footage – and the footage wouldn't always be of the highest quality. Fast-forwarding was not an option. The painstaking real-time analysis meant that dedicated CCTV analysts had to be brought in to do the job for the police.

That proved vital. The last confirmed image of the first

victim, Gemma Adams, was made when a camera recorded her legs as she walked past a garage in West End Road. Tania Nicol was last sighted by a CCTV camera the night she vanished as she walked past the Sainsbury's petrol station in London Road on 30 October. The images were almost immediately released to the media.

The use of CCTV footage in murder investigations wasn't new. It had played a crucial role in such high-profile cases as that of Damilola Taylor, murdered in south-east London in 2001, the Soham murders and even as far back as 1993 when ten-year-olds Jon Venables and Robert Thompson were filmed by shopping centre CCTV leading James Bulger to his death in Liverpool. But camera technology wasn't of use only within the red-light district. Detectives tracing the last known move-ments of Anneli Alderton had also released CCTV footage of her travelling on the 17.53 from Harwich to Colchester on 3 December. 'We are now confident we can begin piecing together the jigsaw of Anneli's last movements,' announced DCS Gull, apparently pleased with the investigation's latest breakthrough. 'However, we still need to know where she was after the evening of 3 December and we need to find the clothing she was wearing in the CCTV footage.' Transport CCTV was also to play a key role in the form of Automatic Number Plate Recognition (ANPR) camera footage.

The pattern now emerging was of a killer who was dumping his victims south of Ipswich. The four 'deposition' sites – Hintlesham, Copdock, Nacton and Levington – were each located within a few hundred metres of the busy A14 dual carriageway. Was the killer using this road to travel to and from his home and the red-light district? He certainly gave the impression he knew the back roads surrounding the trunk route, but did he know them well enough not to use the A14 at all? Was he savvy enough to realise that the larger, busier roads heightened the risk of being caught on camera?

Police would soon find out: the footage would be studied to try to identify suspicious cars or vans that used the A14 between Copdock and Levington on the nights the murdered women disappeared. ANPR cameras are accurate enough to read not only car number plates but tax discs as well.

However, the killer was still at large and possibly mobile. He must also have gained confidence from the fact that, while police pored over the site where Tania Nicol had been discovered in Copdock, he had already taken his third and fourth victims. Having been two steps ahead of the police then, he might now have been planning to carry out his next murder. A team of ten mobile ANPR vehicles was therefore drafted in from Merseyside Police to track the movement of vehicles in and around Ipswich.

With the cameras mounted on their roofs, the police cars were deployed at strategic locations across the town. Not only would they automatically catalogue every passing car, over time a pattern would emerge of vehicle movements in and out of the town. In an instant, registration numbers could be run through the police statbase. If a vehicle was indicated as being of interest to the police – perhaps it had been used in a previous crime or had been registered as stolen – alarm bells would ring and the vehicle would be stopped.

New resources and technology had allowed Suffolk Police to get clever and there were soon signs that the investigation was making significant progress.

The exact location of each of the five girls at the moment they met their deaths would probably not be revealed on CCTV, but to help the police narrow their investigations they could use one thing that all the girls possessed – their mobile phones.

Little did any of the girls know on the nights they disappeared that their mobiles would cease to be merely a tool of their trade but instead become a means by which the police could trace their last known movements. As ACC Jacqui Cheer explained, 'We have numbers which relate to some of the women and that enables us to get all the information we need to try and narrow the investigation.'

Mobile phone data experts were drafted in to try to locate the spot the mobile phone belonging to each girl had last been used. The so-called 'farewell signal' emitted by a phone when it is disconnected from its host network can be used to pinpoint a precise location. It was a long shot, but it might just throw up a new lead. This was, after all, a means of operating that had been used successfully to catch Ian Huntley, the Soham murderer. Detectives concerned with mapping out the last known movements of the five girls were making good progress, even if they were nowhere near to a single murder scene.

One thing that was to a degree out of the control of the police was how much the families of the girls – missing or murdered – were talking to the media. As concerns had grown for 'missing' Paula and Annette, Paula's father, Brian Clennell, had made an impassioned plea on Sky News for his daughter to make contact with the police, and – recognising what might have befallen her – also addressed his remarks to the man who might have killed her:

Paula is a wonderful girl. She cares for everyone. We all love you and you have nothing to hide. There's no repercussion coming out of it. Just say you're alive, that's all we want. We want you back safely. This is the most horrific time of my life. This man – and I'm saying this to you in front of the cameras – if you can realise what it is to lose somebody, we could all be brought back from the darkness. Nobody's asking anybody to be a Christian, just give me my daughter back. I send my heart out to the families of those that have been identified in this horrific, perverted, psycho, sicko campaign. This man must be caught.

Such emotive talk had an impact on the police, too, because suddenly families were appearing on television appealing for the killer to come forward. It made for uneasy viewing for those monitoring the news channels at police headquarters, especially as such interviews had not been stage-managed.

The pressure was on, and it was showing:

'Where do you think the girls were killed – in a car, a lock-up or at a house?' asked Sky's Chief Correspondent Stuart Ramsay at one of the police's scheduled eleven o'clock press conferences. 'We can only speculate where they met their death' was the generic response from DCS Gull. 'But what are your thoughts?' pushed Ramsay. 'They are working girls so they are going to get in a car willingly as is the nature of their work. Whether they've gone on elsewhere where they've met their death is something we're working on.' Surely that much was evident, and Gull's response was greeted by sighs of frustration. It was the sort of statement that merely highlighted to the media the intensity of the investigation and the pressure that seemed to be mounting on the shoulders of a 'country cop'.

Detectives were also looking for clues from the past, something that we had actually suggested might prove helpful at the very start of the investigation in interviews broadcast on Sky News. We noted, for example, that similarities were emerging between the bodies that had been discovered and those of unsolved murders of prostitutes in recent years, especially in Norwich. As early as 10 December, when we were broadcasting live from Copdock, we suggested that there was a 'striking resemblance' between the murders of Gemma and Tania and that of sixteen-year-old Natalie Pearman, who had been working in the red-light district outside the Ferry Boat Inn in Norwich in 1992. Like Gemma and Tania, she too had been found naked, although she had been dumped near a lay-by as opposed to being left in water.

Eventually the police would review the Pearman case and they would revisit four others, too: after Natalie's body was discovered, twenty-six-year-old prostitute Mandy Duncan from Ipswich went missing. Her body has never been discovered. In 1999 seventeen-year-old student Vicky Hall was murdered after leaving a nightclub in Felixstowe. Twelve months later, Norwich prostitute Kellie Pratt vanished from the town's red-light district. The twenty-nine-year-old has never been found, unlike twenty-two-year-old Michelle Bettles, whose strangled body was found dumped in woodland in Norfolk on Easter Sunday 2002.

For Natalie's mother, Lin, the emergence of a serial killer targeting prostitutes brought everything back, and with it a renewed hope. Interviewed on Radio 4's *Today* programme on 14 December, she said:

> I feel extremely mixed because I have no idea if there is a connection. I'm hoping there is because for fourteen years I've wanted that phone call from the police to say my daughter's killer has been found. We know there are certain similarities in the deaths. It's extremely difficult to know that these girls have met an end like Natalie's. Like it was for me, it must be very difficult for the parents of these girls who discover for the first time the path their children had taken. It's a tremendous shock and there's always the feeling of shame, and I say don't be ashamed of

them, they are still your children. At the moment my heart goes out to these families who are going through this. Their lives will never be the same again.

Meanwhile, as Lin Pearman waited for contact from the police, forensic teams were still trying to gather as much evidence as they could, although this was not always possible. In Hintlesham and Copdock, where the bodies of Gemma and Tania had been discovered a mile apart, there had been little or no police activity for some days. It had quickly become clear that there was little point in continuing the forensic-gathering exercise in either place. Tania had been missing for more than five weeks and Gemma for well over two. Stripped naked and dumped in water, their bodies had been washed by the flow of Belstead Brook and for days, if not weeks, by the falling rain. The decomposition of both bodies was relatively advanced, which is why they were quickly removed by coroner's ambulance on the day they were discovered. Nor were post-mortem examinations at Ipswich Hospital able to reveal a cause of death for either Tania or Gemma. There had been no evidence of wounds or obvious marks around the neck indicating strangulation. Police explained to the press that it could take a number of weeks to establish the exact causes of death and that both bodies would be undergoing a series of toxicology tests. Drugs might have played a significant role in their demise.

In Nacton and Levington the task of gathering crucial forensic evidence from the scenes where Anneli's, Paula's and Annette's bodies were discovered was, by comparison, much easier. Scenes of Crime Officers would have been mindful of the advice outlined in *The Murder Investigation Manual* concerning the painstaking and thorough searching of deposition sites: 'Given there is only one chance, scene examination should not be made in haste,' it urges. It was clear they were conducting the investigation quite literally by the book.

Initial analyses of the bodies of Anneli, Annette and Paula, combined with information gathered about their last-known whereabouts, indicated to police that the killer's murder spree had gathered such a pace that he was prepared to kill his victims right under their noses: the last known sighting of Anneli was 3 December, of Annette Nicholls 8 December, and Paula Clennell was last heard from on Sunday 10 December. All three had been murdered and dumped while police were making their inquiries into the murder of Gemma Adams.

Moreover, this meant that none of the three bodies had been left in the open for more than nine days. And although all three girls had been exposed to the elements for a number of days, none had this time been dumped in water. Anneli's body was left in woodland just ten metres back from the road near the entrance to Amberfield School in Nacton. Similarly Annette's and Paula's bodies were discovered a hundred metres apart in even less dense woodland barely five metres to one side of the old Felixstowe road, close to Levington. This suggested to the police that the killer was becoming less and less fussy about how well he concealed the bodies of his most recent victims.

To forensic officers that might just mean he was also becoming careless, and that he might have left forensic clues on his prey. They would therefore take their time over the bodies of Anneli, Annette and Paula and that was reflected in how long the three bodies were kept at their respective scenes before being taken away for post-mortem examinations.

So, too, the discovery of Anneli's body in woodland rather than in water would not only mean it could provide telling forensic evidence, but it also meant the killer had actually stood at that exact spot – which couldn't be said for certain about the final resting places of Gemma and Tania. Police knew that he must have carried or dragged Anneli for ten metres, which meant the extra weight he was bearing could have caused him to leave footprints – and could also help to build up a picture of the killer. But more likely, on that short journey, his clothes could quite easily have snagged on twigs and branches, leaving valuable fibres at the scene.

Because it had been raining and would probably continue to do so, a large white tent was placed over Anneli's body and the ground surrounding her to protect any evidence that might be found. It would remain in place long after the body had been taken away.

Home Office forensic pathologist Dr Nat Cary had been brought in to conduct the post-mortem on all the bodies. His involvement in some of the most notorious cases of recent years, including the investigation into the murder of Victoria Climbié in 2000 and the murders of Holly Wells and Jessica Chapman two years later, had made him one of the best known and most experienced pathologists in the country. His conclusions were quickly conveyed to the police, and the following day they decided to release limited information to the media. At the eleven o'clock press conference they confirmed Anneli's death by asphyxiation, and went on to say: 'At this stage it's not known whether Anneli had been sexually assaulted or not so further tests are still to be carried out.'

The brief statement omitted one significant fact that the police later claimed had not been made public because it wasn't 'deemed relevant' to the ongoing investigation – Anneli was three months pregnant when she was killed. However, the story had somehow been leaked to the press three days after her post-mortem and made headlines in most national newspapers the following day. The *Sun*'s that day read: 'Baby is 6th victim'.

What the police felt *was* relevant to the inquiry was that they now had their first definitive cause of death. Anneli had been strangled, although further tests would show whether other factors had contributed to her death. There had up to this point been nothing to differentiate this killer from any other, but now it was clear he had developed a taste for strangulation. From then on he was no longer simply 'the killer' or 'the murderer'. Now he had a more sinister nickname – the 'Suffolk Strangler'.

The causes of death of his last two victims, Annette Nicholls and Paula Clennell, were also eagerly awaited. News had already filtered through that once again both had been discovered naked. Had they been strangled, too? That would have to wait. Police knew Annette's body hadn't been there for longer than a week, Paula's for less than two days, so it would be some time before either body would be taken away for post-mortem examinations.

Police officers had been placed at twenty-metre intervals across the field that separated the A14 and the old Felixstowe road where the bodies had been discovered, principally to prevent the media getting close to the scene in Levington. The best vantage point had been the A14 roundabout three hundred metres away, but improved weather and daylight soon allowed various media helicopters to home in on the site for a closer inspection. Apart from the obvious proximity of the bodies to the roadside, it was also intriguing that they had been dumped a hundred metres apart. Speculation that the bodies had been deposited there at the same time would, many thought, have to be ruled out. Why would a killer drive two victims along the old Felixstowe road, get rid of one body, and then drive another hundred metres in order to dump the second?

The obvious conclusion was that, because Gemma's and Tania's bodies had been dumped so close together – as were Annette's and Paula's – this was a killer who liked to establish a procedure with which he was comfortable, a location in which he felt confident, and stick to them. The only reason he had changed location when it came to getting rid of his third victim, Anneli Alderton, was because his preferred spot was by then crawling with police; he knew Gemma's body had only just been discovered and it would be too risky to return to it.

By the afternoon of Wednesday 13 December, the day after the discoveries at Levington, both Annette's and Paula's bodies still remained *in situ*, concealed by the now depressingly familiar forensic tents. Unsurprisingly the first body to be removed from the roadside in a coroner's ambulance later that afternoon was that of Paula Clennell. Since she had been dead for only forty-eight hours or less, her body could provide the freshest clues yet as to the killer's identity. The priority was clearly Paula. Annette's body would remain the subject of meticulous forensic examination in her tent beside the old Felixstowe road for a further twenty-four hours before being taken away for post-mortem examination.

'Police have now established the cause of death for one of the women whose bodies were found near Levington,' revealed DCS Gull at that afternoon's press conference. 'We are advised by the pathologist that the woman who was recovered from the scene yesterday, died as a result of compression to the neck. Her death is being treated as murder. As we speak, formal identification of the body is taking place.' Journalists would be told the following day it was that of the missing prostitute Paula Clennell.

'Compression to the neck.' The killer was clearly developing his preference for strangulation, although once again the waters were muddied when, the following day, police announced that the post-mortem of Annette Nicholls had 'failed to reveal a clear cause of death'. However, DCS Gull made it clear that her death *was* being treated as murder and would unquestionably be linked to the other four victims. The killer had been striking with greater frequency so it was time for a different tack – to try to prevent another murder.

To some in the media it had seemed odd that DCS Gull had not yet really appealed to the killer directly, but, prompted by a journalist during a press conference, he asked the killer to give himself up following the discovery of the two bodies in Levington:

'Make contact with Suffolk Police. You have a significant problem. Give me a call and we can deal with this,' DCS Gull had pleaded, looking straight into the nearest live camera.

But the call hadn't come. Three days later, and for the first time, a family directly involved in the series of murders would sit in front of the media. Police hoped that if the killer had even the slightest remorse for the misery he'd caused so many already, perhaps an appeal from one of the families whose lives he'd wrecked, or a tribute from them to one of his victims, might persuade him to contact the constabulary – or at the very least prompt someone who knew him to come forward.

A news conference was scheduled for 1 p.m. The parents of Tania Nicol – Jim Duell and Kerry Nicol – would face the world's media and share their memories of the daughter they'd lost.

Blinking at the flash of the cameras, Kerry appeared flustered, the ordeal of recent weeks having taken its toll. No less emotional, yet more composed, Jim would make the statement. There would be no questions from the media afterwards.

Tania was a lovely daughter – she was a caring, loving and sensitive girl who would never hurt anyone. Unfortunately drugs took her away into her own secret world – a world that neither of us was aware of. Tania has been taken by someone who needs to be found. We ask for anyone who knows this person or persons to come forward and contact the police. We would like to thank all the people who have offered help so far, but ask if anyone has information however small to please tell us, even if they come forward anonymously.

That was largely the police talking. But then, almost at pains to make it clear these were his own words, Jim read out a passage he had earlier written himself. It was largely directed at the families of the other victims, but to many in the press conference it was a veiled message of defiance to a killer who would not beat them.

As if speaking for everyone, Jim said:

They can't take away our memories. They can't take away our love, our fortitude, our courage. Grieve for our daughters but not unnecessarily. Live your lives through our departed daughters, as they would want to see us getting on with our lives and not going around with our heads bowed down. A time for sadness and a time for gladness. A gladness that they belong to us. A gladness of the happy times we shared. The joy they brought to us. A thankfulness that they are now at peace.

There was a sense that the police were now very much in control. This press conference showed more than anything else that they were using the media's interest in the story to convey messages to the killer, and in doing so were maintaining the public's fascination with the story and thus their interest in helping the police with their inquiries. So the job of sifting through the increasing number of calls from the public had by now become a mammoth task. In the time leading up to the Levington discoveries on 12 December, just over two thousand calls had come in to the force hotline or Crimestoppers. By the 17th, that figure stood at over ten thousand, and they were accompanied by hundreds of e-mails to the incident room each day.

The public's response had been massive; while the killer was clearly only targeting prostitutes, the collective sense across the town was nonetheless that it was in everyone's best interests that this killer was caught soon. Even the police warned all women to be on their guard. And if anyone wondered whether their call would make a difference to the investigation, there was always the added incentive of a reward for information leading to the killer's arrest and conviction.

Fifty-two-year-old Ipswich-based businessman Graeme Kalbraier was the first to put up a reward. He explained his justification for offering a £25,000 reward, saying that while the killer was at large not only was his seventeen-year-old daughter at risk, but so were the lives of many young girls his company employed.

His offer stole a march on a second one, ten times bigger, which followed four days later. The *News of the World's* reward was £250,000. And if together the unprecedented £275,000 helped to sway people to call the police rather than not bother, it would be money well spent. However, this was a double-edged sword. Rewards also attract a small number of people with largely irrelevant information keen to tap into the small fortune just a phone call away, and that wastes police time.

Aside from timewasters, another threat to the investigation was posed by hoaxers. Few on the force, including DCS Gull, needed reminding just how much the hunt for the 'Yorkshire Ripper' was thrown off course by the tapes and letters sent in by the man known as 'Wearside Jack'. Suffolk Police were beginning to give off signals that certain suspects were in their sights. Talk among journalists was that these people numbered anything from five to fifty, and the last thing detectives needed now was to be taken on a wild goose chase fuelled by the media. But that's exactly what happened next.

Only days after the last body had been discovered, the police arrived at Jubilee Close in Trimley St Martin at 7.30 a.m. on Monday 18 December. It was close to where all five murdered women had been found and it was where Tom Stephens lived.

Tania, Gemma, Netty, Paula, Anni.
I knew some of you better than others. But I miss you all.
x Tom.

These were the words attached to a bunch of pink roses that had been tied to the lamp-post on London Road. They had been left by the man now in custody at an undisclosed police station and being questioned on suspicion of murder. Was Stephens just a sad loser, hoping for a few fleeting minutes of fame, or could he really be the killer?

The investigation changed focus and pace in the space of just a few hours. Having decided to arrest Stephens, possibly after he admitted in the *Sunday Mirror* that he knew all five girls and that he had no alibi for the times that any of the girls had gone missing, Suffolk Police now had limited time to question him and search his house for forensic clues pointing to his guilt. He would have to be charged or released by Friday afternoon.

Stephens had already been questioned by the police two days before he was arrested. He had thought they were stupid because they didn't know he had moved to Trimley. But his cockiness was mixed with a real concern too. A few of the five women had spent a lot of time at his house. Tania in particular had shaved her legs in the bath and had also slept with him in his bed. He was worried what the presence of her DNA might suggest to the police.

We quickly established that Stephens was a former Norfolk Police Special Constable from Norwich who had moved back to his birthplace of Ipswich in 1997 where he was married the following year. But within five years he and his wife were to separate and the quiet loner soon developed into a self-styled 'protector' of women selling sexual services, some of whom, he admitted in the Sunday newspaper, he had also paid for sex. Stephens had been working at the twenty-four-hour Tesco superstore just a few hundred yards from Suffolk Police headquarters in Martlesham Heath. When he wasn't at work, he was driving the girls to meet their dealers or simply giving them shelter from the cold. Often he would drive them home after they had finished for the evening. In return, he would expect no petrol money, but sometimes one of the girls would have sex with him as payment.

Stephens hadn't long been at his 1960s semi-detached home in Jubilee Close and so the locals barely knew him. He'd moved there only three months before his arrest after moving out of a house he shared with three others east of the town centre. He'd 'kept himself to himself' according to neighbours, perhaps because the girls in the red-light district had become 'family' to him. He had grown attached to two in particular – Gemma Adams and Tania Nicol. He would buy them presents, too. He bought Tania the pink glitter stilettos she had been wearing the night she disappeared.

The media quickly massing outside Tom Stephens' house in Jubilee Close needed to know more about the new focus of the investigation. A good deal would come from his own MySpace website which he had updated as recently as 27 October. According to the site his occupation was 'team leader' at Tesco 'from 1997 until they sack me'. He described himself as a fitness fanatic who loved sport – perhaps unsurprisingly, his hero was cartoon character and crime-fighting karate expert Hong Kong Phooey. He explained that his main reason for having the web page was to look for friends and a serious relationship, but admitted that, while he loved kids, they were 'not for me'. His nickname was 'The Bishop'.

Police now at Stephens' house were wasting no time. They had already taken away the purple Renault Clio he used to ferry his 'friends' to and from the red-light district.

By 7.20 a.m. on Tuesday 19 December, the first twenty-four hours of his detention by police were drawing to a close. If Ipswich police wanted more time to question Stephens they would first have to get permission from a magistrate. The force's media line would announce to the press whether that extra time would be granted to investigators. At 7.19 that phone line was engaged. Four attempts later the press officer's voice announced that police had been granted an extra twelve hours to question Stephens. It also gave forensic teams more time to search the arrested man's house. Once that time was up at 7.20 p.m., the police would again be granted extra time to question Stephens – this time they would be given a more generous thirty-six hours.

A team of forensic officers had been at the scene the previous day. The meticulous search of the property had to be carefully planned. With the preparation complete, the lights inside the house burned late into the evening as investigators searched for vital evidence. By the Tuesday, the focus of the search seemed to shift from inside the house to the small garden.

On their hands and knees, suited in white overalls, gloved, and equipped with miniature rakes, forensic teams combed the grass in the back garden for the entire morning. The first two inches of soil would be loosened and then sifted using their fingertips. Officers carrying metal detectors followed close behind. The mind boggled as to what they were looking for. Was it jewellery or clothing belonging to the girls? Officers also pored over the contents of Stephens' green garden dustbin.

To many, though, something about the arrest didn't quite add up. The murdered women had all known Tom Stephens and, from what the press was being told, they had trusted him, too. Despite admitting he was a little too persistent at times, some prostitutes couldn't speak highly enough of him. So when Stephens was arrested the women in the red-light district were quick to show their support for him. One prostitute called Paige described Stephens as a man whose sole purpose was to 'help us girls'. 'He's harmless,' she explained. 'He'd do anything for the girls and if they needed some cash or a bed for the night he'd help 'em out. There's no way he killed the girls.'

And just as television cameras prepared to zoom in on the ongoing fingertip searches in Stephens' garden from the cages of their hired cherry pickers, the focus of this now fast-moving investigation changed yet again.

Forensic officers had spent days removing DNA from the

bodies of Anneli, Annette and Paula in the hope it would yield a breakthrough. It came on 17 December. A single DNA profile had appeared on all three bodies, and was the only profile common to all three women. In an attempt to find out who it belonged to the results were passed through a police DNA database. A match: Steve Wright. He had been convicted for the theft of £84 in 2003. He was immediately placed under surveillance at his home in London Road. Two days later, on 19 December, he was arrested.

Four forty-five a.m. It was still dark when officers from Suffolk Police arrived in London Road. Pulling up outside number 79, they saw that the lights were on in Steve Wright's front room. Then they caught him peering from behind the curtains to see who was outside at that time of the morning. Ringing the doorbell, the police were quickly met by a stocky, middle-aged man dressed in blue tracksuit bottoms and a white polo shirt.

'Are you Steve Wright?' asked one officer.

'Yes,' replied the seemingly confused, greying, balding man. The TV was on, but the screen was blank.

Wright was cautioned and arrested on suspicion of committing all five murders. When he realised the police had finally caught up with him, he became unsteady on his feet. 'Let me sit down, before I fall down,' he said to the officers gathered around him.

En route to Stowmarket police station one police officer noted that Wright had begun sweating, and his eyes remained closed during most of the journey. Once at the station, and before the police were able to question him, Wright underwent a medical examination.

Nearby in Nacton, Wright's partner Pam was over halfway through her nightshift. Christmas was almost upon them, she was thinking. The tree had been decorated, a goose was in the freezer ready to be put in the oven and she had spent some time preparing the special Christmas puddings she knew Steve adored. As usual, she called home to make sure he was awake for work, but this time she got no reply. Then her supervisor approached to tell her a man and some women had come to see her. She feared the worst. Had Steve been in a car crash? Had he had a heart attack? The officers showed her their police badges and explained it could be some time before Pam would be able to return home.

At a hastily arranged 8.30 a.m. press conference which gave journalists just forty minutes' notice to get prepared, DCS Stewart Gull announced that a second man had been arrested on suspicion of the murders of all five women at five o'clock that morning. But unlike the first arrest, sources described the latest as 'significant'.

Why was this arrest different from the first? Why hadn't police quietly questioned Tom Stephens 'in connection' with, rather than 'on suspicion' of, the murders? To many it seemed that Stephens had been too vocal for his own good and, by his own admission, could be perceived as a potential suspect. By arresting Stephens, detectives knew that he couldn't talk to the press while they searched his house for clues. So, too, they understood that by arresting one credible suspect, the reactions of others could be monitored as well. If Stephens was as innocent as he maintained in his newspaper interview, the real killer might be lulled into a false sense of security and show himself.

Within the space of twenty-four hours the investigation had gone from no arrests to two.

Before long, the media had camped outside Steve Wright's house at 79 London Road, close to where Paula Clennell and

Tania Nicol had last been seen. The press was now split between the houses of two suspects. Stephens, it had been announced, would be held for a little longer, although he would have to be charged or released by Friday afternoon. In the end, he would be released on police bail, and then allowed to drift quietly back into obscurity.

However, throughout Thursday 21 December exhaustive searches continued at both addresses. At Steve Wright's home in London Road, police were seen entering the property with a crowbar – it would be used to pull up the floorboards in case anything had been concealed beneath them. No stone – or rather floorboard – was being left unturned.

Later that evening, the police announced they would be holding yet another unscheduled press conference; that the number of unscheduled press conferences seemed to be on the increase was an indication that the investigation was making serious headway. It would climax that evening. After a brief delay and endless speculation about the fate of the two men in custody, DCS Gull entered the crowded press room to make a statement, which, as before, would not be followed by any questions.

You will be aware that on Monday, as part of our investigation into the murders of five women in the Ipswich area, we arrested a suspect at his home in Trimley. The next day, Tuesday the 19th, a second suspect was arrested in Ipswich. There have been significant ongoing inquiries and interviews during the period that these men have been in custody. As a result, the thirty-seven-year-old man from Trimley was this evening released on bail, pending further inquiries. The second man, Steven Wright, from Ipswich, has been charged with the murder of all five women – Gemma Adams, Tania Nicol, Anneli Alderton, Paula Clennell and Annette Nicholls.

The police believed they had their killer, and the following day he would appear in court for the first time.

Chapter Five

Profiling: Art or Science?

'The range of opinions offered was staggering. Some thought that it was the work of Al Qaeda operatives. Others considered it a homage to the "Son of Sam" murders, to mark their 25-year anniversary. An even more exotic suggestion was that it was a re-enactment of a storyline in the television programme *Homicide*. Computer nerds, addicted to shoot-'em-up video games, were also blamed. And, inevitably, the Devil got in on the act. "This has something to do with a satanic ritual," said "holistic adviser", Zorel. "If you look at the map and connect the dots, it looks like a cross upside down, but people aren't realising it, not even the police."'

Professor David Canter, describing the Washington snipers' case

One of the new techniques that police have in their armoury is offender profiling, and it was clear that in the Ipswich case several profiles of the killer had been constructed. Offender profiling is a subject of great popular and media interest and, perhaps inevitably, also of extensive exaggeration. In films such as *The Silence of the Lambs* and *Manhunter*, in TV dramas such as *Cracker*, *Wire in the Blood*, *Millennium* and *Profiler*, and in bestselling books such as Paul Britton's *The Jigsaw Man*, the profiler emerges as one of the means (perhaps the key) by which the police solve crimes, especially those such as serial rape and murder. As if by magic, the offender (whom the police had been unable to catch) is apprehended by the gifted 'outsider' – most recently psychologists of various types – leaving the viewer or reader gasping in admiration and half expecting to be told: 'It was elementary, my dear Watson.'

What exactly is offender profiling, and how accurate is this media portrayal of the activities of the profiler? In reality, how successful is offender profiling and should profiling successes be seen as art or as a science? In other words, should we see offender profiling as something based on intuitive guesswork on the part of the profiler – and therefore limited to one or two especially gifted individuals – or does offender profiling have some scientific objectivity, relying not on intuition, but rather on a series of empirically tested techniques? How much did offender profiling actually help in the Ipswich murders, and why was the public just as interested in compiling its own profiles? Were these profiles of any use – perhaps even better than what the 'professionals' described – or were they as misguided as those that David Canter points out in relation to the case of the Washington snipers?

All these questions might seem easy enough to answer, but there are at least two major stumbling blocks to negotiate before we can separate fact from fiction, myth from reality. First, there is no consensus about what constitutes offender profiling. Indeed, 'offender profiling' is often described in various ways by different people – reflecting their backgrounds – such as 'psychological profiling' or 'crime scene analysis'. Second, profilers are often very reluctant to reveal their methods, either through fear of being plagiarised or even of being criticised in academic journals. Reputations can be made or broken in this field. Profilers tend to write about or describe their successes, and rarely discuss their failures. One recent academic review has even suggested that many profiles are clearly related to the personality and identity of the profiler.

Setting these two problems aside it is still fascinating to explore the role of profiling in the Ipswich case. We constructed a profile ourselves after the discoveries of the bodies of Gemma and Tania. The public also got in on the act, creating a '*CSI*' or '*Cracker* phenomenon', and besieged us – and the police – with theories and suspects.

Offender Profiling: A Basic Definition and Some History

The central premise of offender profiling is that the characteristics of an offender can be deduced by a careful, considered examination of the offence. As the criminologist Peter Ainsworth puts it: 'Offender profiling generally refers to the process of using all the available information about a crime, a crime scene, and a victim, in order to compose a profile of the (as yet) unknown perpetrator.' The key here is to understand that from the *offence characteristics* – how the crime was committed, why the victim was chosen and then subsequently dealt with, and so forth – we can tell something about the type of person the offender is – the *offender's characteristics*. This relationship between the offence characteristics and the offender's characteristics is at the heart of all subsequent thinking about the type of person who might be committing the crime, and is often used to drive a police investigation forward. Using this basic premise

Police set up town centre roadblocks to question drivers about possible sightings of the murdered women. The incident room handled more than twelve thousand calls from the public during the investigation.

A specialist police diving team was brought in to search Belstead Brook. Investigators were particularly keen to recover any clothing belonging to the victims.

DCS Stewart Gull held almost daily press conferences, partly to satisfy the demands of the world's media but also to keep the story in the news headlines.

The Coroner's ambulance arrives in Levington to transport the body of Paula Clennell to Ipswich Hospital where Home Office pathologist Dr Nat Cary would remove DNA belonging to Steve Wright.

A large team of scenes of crime officers (SOCO) document the 'desposition sites' in Levington after the bodies of Annette Nicholls and Paula Clennell had been removed.

Supermarket worker Tom Stephens was the first to be arrested in connection with the murders.

The self-styled 'protector' of Ipswich's prostitutes, Stephens had slept with all five victims, and regarded them as his friends. He left this message to the murdered women on a lamp-post in the red-light district.

Officers equipped with metal detectors search the back garden of Tom Stephens' house in Trimley St Martin.

Searches continue into the night, but in the absence of any evidence linking him to the murders, Tom Stephens was released.

Forty-nine-year-old Steve Wright was arrested on 19 December 2006. During more than eight hours of questioning the former pub landlord answered 'no comment' to every question put to him.

79 London Road, after Wright's arrest. He and his partner Pam had moved to the house on the edge of the red-light district just weeks before he began his killing spree.

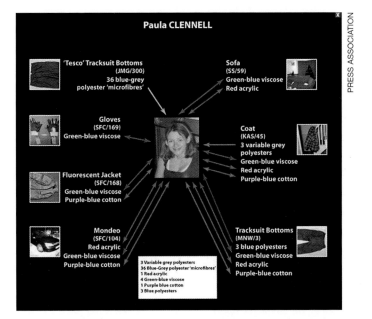

Paula CLENNELL

'Tesco' Tracksuit Bottoms
(JMG/300)
36 blue-grey
polyester 'microfibres'

Sofa
(SS/59)
Green-blue viscose
Red acrylic

Gloves
(SFC/169)
Green-blue viscose

Coat
(KAS/45)
3 variable grey
polyesters
Green-blue viscose
Red acrylic
Purple-blue cotton

Fluorescent Jacket
(SFC/168)
Green-blue viscose
Purple-blue cotton

Mondeo
(SFC/104)
Red acrylic
Green-blue viscose
Purple-blue cotton

Tracksuit Bottoms
(MNW/3)
3 blue polyesters
Green-blue viscose
Red acrylic
Purple-blue cotton

3 Variable grey polyesters
36 Blue-Grey polyester 'microfibres'
1 Red acrylic
4 Green-blue viscose
1 Purple blue cotton
3 Blue polyesters

The jury was told how fibres from Wright's clothes, car and house
had been transferred on to all five victims – this diagram shows
Wright's links to fifth victim Paula Clennell.

After he gave up his job as a steward on the *QE2*, Steve Wright ran the Ferry
Boat Inn in the heart of Norwich's red-light district. Several prostitute murders
and disappearances linked to the Norfolk city remain unsolved.

When writing to Members of Parliament please give your previous home address in order to avoid delays in your case being taken up by the M.P.

In replying to this letter, please write on the envelope:

Number ...TT6221... Name ...WRIGHT...

Wing ...H213...

H.M. PRISON BELMARSH
WESTERN WAY
THAMESMEAD
LONDON
SE28 0EP

Dear Dad
        this is a reply to your letter you are quite
right you have never seen me angry before
because I am a quite and placid person
whenever I get upset I tend to bury it deep
inside which I suppose is not a healthy thing
to do because the more I do that the more
withdrawn I become because I have seen
to much anger and violence in
my childhood to last anyone a lifetime.
        But what really makes me sad is the
fact that I thought all the family feuds
were behind me now I really thought we had
made a step forward I just wish everyone
would get along and work towards a family
unit because all the bickering and point
scoring against each other is really getting
me down it seems you are pulling me
one way and pam is pulling me the other

VF004 (F243) Printed at Leyhill N 799

Steve Wright writes to his father Conrad from his cell at HM Prison Belmarsh, in which he pleads for his family to stop 'point scoring', which he's finding hard to deal with in jail.

as their starting point, some criminologists have then gone on to suggest that the goals of offender profiling are not only to provide a social and psychological assessment of the offender, but also to consult with the police in relation to strategies for interviewing suspects. But where did these goals and the premise at the heart of profiling come from?

Modern profiling effectively starts with the FBI's Behavioral Support Unit – now known as the Investigative Support Unit – which became famous through Thomas Harris's books, notably *Red Dragon* and *The Silence of the Lambs*. The FBI wanted to find a way to use the wealth of forensic information that they were able to gather at a crime scene and to see if that evidence could suggest something about the type of person who had committed the offence. So, in part using their collective experience of investigating multiple murder and sexual assaults, and crucially through carrying out extensive interviews with thirty-six convicted serial killers, they began to discover that the personality of an offender – in cases of serial rape or murder – could be gleaned from a consideration of the following five areas:

- The crime scene.
- The nature of the attacks themselves.
- Forensic evidence.
- A medical examination of the victim.
- Victim characteristics.

On the basis of these factors the FBI suggested that offenders could be characterised as either 'organised' or 'disorganised'. Such descriptions occur regularly in profiles, and, despite the various criticisms that can be made about these categorisations, we find them useful, especially as they also suggest other personal characteristics.

An 'organised' offender, for example, is one who plans carefully – he wears gloves, brings a rope or handcuffs to incapacitate his victim, and typically is very much in control of the crime scene. Few clues, such as fingerprints, blood or semen (he will wear a condom), are left. Typically, there will have been few, if any, witnesses to the crime, because the organised offender has also planned carefully to avoid being discovered either committing the crime, or when disposing of the evidence that might incriminate him, or, indeed, the body. It is also suggested that 'organised' offenders have a specific personality type. They will typically be intelligent, sexually active and competent, and are likely to be in a relationship. They will have skilled or semi-skilled jobs, and to all intents and purposes will appear 'normal'. However, this mask of normality hides an anti-social personality. It is also suggested that 'organised' offenders follow reports of their crimes in the news, and that they are often propelled to commit a crime as a result of anger and frustration in their personal lives.

'Disorganised' offenders, on the other hand, do not plan their offending. Their crimes are sudden and random, and the offender will use whatever means he can to help him commit his offence. So, for example, he will tie up his victim using her scarf or underwear; he will stab or bludgeon using weapons that he finds in the home of his victim, or in the vicinity of the offence. There is little attempt to conceal evidence, and often the victim's body is simply abandoned, rather than hidden. More than this, the 'disorganised' offender is said to live alone – or at home with his parents – and usually offends within his home area. He will be socially and sexually immature, and will often have a history of mental illness. Finally, it is suggested that this type of offender commits his crimes while frightened or confused.

At this stage a degree of scepticism is necessary as part of our attempt to separate fact from fantasy. First, the original FBI theory that offender characteristics can be gleaned from offence characteristics is largely based on interviews with thirty-six convicted serial killers. Would serial killers necessarily tell an interviewer the truth? Might they attempt to confuse, or alternatively be over-eager in the hope of getting preferential treatment, such as parole? Second, does the fact that they were caught suggest anything about their offending, and would those who remain at large have a different approach? Finally, can we really, unquestioningly, use the evidence of American serial rapists and murderers and simply transfer these findings into different social and cultural settings?

The greatest critic of the FBI's approach is Kim Rossmo, a former police detective in Vancouver, Canada, who argues that their theory has no scientific validity whatsoever, is largely intuitive and has never been subject to rigorous academic scrutiny. He further suggests that their central finding – 'organised' or 'disorganised' – should instead be seen as a continuum, rather than as two distinct categories. We can also pursue this question of the honesty of serial offenders after they are caught by looking at what they say – or do not say – to the police or to criminal justice professionals when questioned, and a range of others who have an interest in their case.

Talking to Serial Killers

In working with serial killers and other serial offenders we have encountered two distinct groups. The first – the majority of those with whom we have spent time – had invariably developed a very robust and self-serving view as to why they had repeatedly killed. More often than not, the views and insights of these killers were very carefully constructed to suit the nature and circumstances of their arrest, conviction and imprisonment. Their explanations were rooted in the forlorn hope that, for example, they might lead to parole; or transfer to a better prison; sometimes they were given so as to maintain their self-perception, and what they thought they were entitled to.

With further investigation, however, it became clear that the sorts of explanations they gave could have come from any of us. Who has not lost a beloved parent, grandparent, uncle or aunt? Who has not felt lonely, bullied or excluded as a child, has not been saddened by the end of a close and loving relationship? Who would not like to be given a little more credit for their achievements, and a little less criticism for their failings? Would these everyday, almost prosaic, life events be enough to push us into 'killing for company', as Brian Masters claimed in respect of the serial killer Dennis Nilsen? Can such justifications account for the phenomenon of serial killing? And while some serial killers – such as Robert Black, who abducted, sexually assaulted and killed at least three young girls in the North of England and Scotland in the 1980s – have undoubtedly had appalling childhoods, filled with abandonment and abuse, is this enough to explain their crimes, especially when so many others have had similar experiences, but have not gone on to kill again and again?

These observations stem from working with serial offenders after they have been caught and imprisoned. However, even in the immediate aftermath of arrest – long before their trial and conviction – those serial killers who are prepared to talk regularly construct a picture that is often far removed from reality. After his arrest, Peter Sutcliffe gave a variety of interviews to detectives working on the case. He appeared forthcoming, but a leading expert on the murders has since commented that it is now clear that he was both deceitful and manipulative. Specifically Sutcliffe sought to hide any sexual motive for his crimes; instead he simply tried to suggest that he was mad, in the hope that this would influence every aspect of his trial and his sentence.

So, too, Fred West, who, before taking his own life, left 111 pages of autobiography. But as David Canter explains, anyone hoping for clues as to why West killed would be disappointed, for 'the journal ignores all of this'. Canter's observation would come as no surprise to John Bennett, the detective in charge of the West investigation. After his arrest, West's interviews with the police amounted to 145 tape recordings that translated into 6189 pages of transcript, but since his retirement Bennett has commented that 'West's interviews were worthless except to confirm that nothing that he said could be relied upon as anything near the truth'. Gordon Burn, one of West's most perceptive biographers, simply dismisses him as a 'bullshitting liar', who claimed, for example, to have travelled the world with the pop singer Lulu. Burn explains that West would talk 'palaver while apparently talking the truth. Laying out and simultaneously covering up.'

The second group that we have encountered was the exact opposite of the first. They never talked about the motives that drove them to murder, and they guarded their secrets carefully. For example, just after his conviction in April 2001 for the murder of fifteen of his patients, the West Yorkshire Police decided to re-interview Harold Shipman about the deaths of other patients that he had attended while practising in Todmorden. Their videotape –

which we have viewed – is very revealing, and we quote here from a transcript:

> *Police officer*: No replies are going to be given to any questions during the course of this interview and any subsequent interviews. I think it is fair to say for the purposes of the tape that we are happy that we are interviewing Harold Shipman.
> *(Officer gets up and walks round the table to place a picture in front of the face of Shipman, who has turned to face the wall.)*

> *Police officer*: To start with, if I can try to jog your memory by showing you a photograph . . . that's Elizabeth Pearce. Of the three ladies there it's the elderly lady dressed in black. For the benefit of the tape Dr Shipman's eyes are closed.
> *(Officer returns to desk and picks up two photographs.)*

> *Police officer*: Unfortunately we don't have a photograph of Mr Lingard. To try and jog your memory here is a photograph of Eagle Street and there is a photograph of where Mr Lingard lived. Just for the benefit of the tape, Dr Shipman's eyes are closed and he didn't look at all.
> *(Officer returns to desk and returns with another photograph which he places again in front of the face of Shipman.)*

> *Police officer*: Just to try and jog your memory, Dr Shipman, I have here a photograph of Lily Crossley. Just for the benefit of the tape Dr Shipman's eyes are closed and he didn't look at all.

This final comment from the police officer sums up perfectly this second group of silent, uncommunicative serial killers – 'Just for the benefit of the tape Dr Shipman's eyes are closed and he didn't look at all.' Not only did he not look, he never even spoke. Shipman refused to discuss why he killed 215 (and possibly 260) elderly people either in Todmorden or elsewhere, and ultimately, like Fred West, he chose to commit suicide, in his cell at HMP Wakefield in January 2004, rather than reveal the circumstances that led him to murder.

So, to apply Gordon Burn's phrase about Fred West more generally, we have one group of serial killers who 'lay out', and another who 'cover up'; some who talk endlessly – although not necessarily to any purpose – and others who refuse to, or indeed cannot, talk at all.

Should all this – from the difficulty of believing what caught and convicted serial killers do or do not say, to the problem of translating the findings from research conducted in the USA to Britain – mean that we simply dismiss the contributions offered by offender profilers? We believe this would be a step too far, one that would fail to acknowledge the work that profilers from very different traditions and backgrounds have done to help the police catch offenders in this country.

Canter and Britton

Look, for instance, at the very broad outlines of profiles produced by two of Britain's best-known profilers, Professor David Canter and Paul Britton. There are other advantages in doing this, especially as Canter and Britton are very much on opposing sides of the argument at the heart of what we describe in this chapter. Canter, Director of the Centre for Investigative Psychology at the University of Liverpool, has in particular promoted a scientific basis for offender profiling through what he calls 'investigative psychology'. His methods and techniques have been widely published in some twenty books and in more than 150 papers in learned journals. Britton, often described in the media as 'the real Cracker', has published two bestsellers on the subject, including *The Jigsaw Man: The Remarkable Career of Britain's Foremost Criminal Psychologist*, and in *Offender Profiling and Crime Analysis*, Peter Ainsworth assesses his contribution to offender profiling as 'personal and highly idiosyncratic'. Britton is now also perhaps best known for the part he played in the investigation of the murder of Rachel Nickell.

Starting on 1 June 1982 an offender committed a series of rapes and three murders in the Greater London area, concentrating particularly on lone women travelling by train. The police did not seem to be getting anywhere with their investigations, and almost by chance asked Canter, at the time working in the psychology department at the University of Essex, to become involved. Employing specific techniques and principles that he had developed, he sifted through the vast amount of data collected by the police about these events, eventually producing a profile of the type of person he believed had committed the crimes. He suggested that the offender would be living in the area in which the first three offences were committed, with his wife or girlfriend, but he would have no children; he'd be in his late twenties, with light hair, be five foot nine inches tall and right-handed. Canter further suggested that the offender would be an 'A secretor' (someone whose blood type shows up in body fluids such as saliva and semen), and be in semi-skilled work with little or no contact with the public. He also suggested that the offender would be quite solitary but would have one or two close male friends. Even though he would be sexually active he would not have much contact with women. He would also have a good knowledge of the railways, where most of the attacks took place.

All this allowed the police to target their activities – their interviewing of suspects, decisions on surveillance, elimination of other suspects and so on – although the profile does not say, as so often in fiction or drama, that 'so and so is the murderer'. Canter has been particularly open about the limitations of offender profiling, often admitting that the profile presented is the subjective opinion of the psychologist. He has been at the forefront of the development of what he and a colleague have termed 'investigative psychology', which champions a more scientific basis for working with the police. Canter's work would help the police in their investigation leading to the eventual arrest of John Duffy, the so-called 'Railway Rapist', indeed, the profile was considered to be central to his arrest. The story didn't end there: in February 2001 his accomplice, David Mulcahy, was also convicted of the murders, and once again Canter's original profile had pointed to there being a second offender. In all of this we can see that Duffy matches the characteristics of the 'organised' serial offender.

Paul Britton is a criminal psychologist who profiled the murderer of Caroline Osborne in Leicestershire in 1984. She had been stabbed seven times, and had had her hands and feet bound with twine. There was no evidence of robbery or sexual assault, but close to her body a drawing of a pentagram within a circle was found. This is often associated with satanic ritual. Britton suggested that the offender – and he was to commit a second offence before he was caught – was a young man in his teens to late twenties; a loner; sexually inexperienced, with few friends or girlfriends. He further argued that he would have poor social skills, be of low intelligence, likely to be a manual worker – with some experience of knives – and was probably still living at home, near the vicinity of the murder. Britton also suggested that he would have an interest in sado-masochism and would use pornography. As with the profile completed by Canter, this one was uncannily accurate. The man eventually arrested for the murder – an eighteen-year-old butcher called Paul Bostock – turned up at a police station on the advice of his grandmother, and was eventually convicted of murder in 1986. Bostock seems to match the profile of a 'disorganised' offender.

Unfortunately Paul Britton is also associated with more contentious issues. The Rachel Nickell case also serves to remind us of the limits of the profiler, and how reputations can be made or broken. Rachel Nickell was a twenty-three-year-old model who was murdered in July 1992 on Wimbledon Common while walking her dog with her two-year-old son. The police's prime suspect was Colin Stagg, but they had very little evidence against him. They turned to Britton for help, not only asking him to draw up a profile but also to help them design a covert operation based on information on the killer from the profile. Their aim, it is alleged, was to test whether the suspect would incriminate or implicate himself in the killings. An undercover policewoman began to exchange letters with Stagg, in an attempt to win his confidence and to encourage him to describe his fantasies. She succeeded in this, but Stagg did not confess to the murder, although detectives working on the case believed that he had revealed enough evidence for him to be arrested and charged. During the committal hearing Britton explained that the nature of the undercover operation had been a series of 'ladders' that Stagg would have to climb, rather than a 'slippery slope' down which a vulnerable person might slide if pushed or encouraged to jump.

At the Old Bailey the judge agreed with Stagg's defence that Britton's evidence was speculative and based solely on his intuition, and dismissed the case. He suggested that the police had shown 'excessive zeal', and that they had tried to incriminate a suspect by 'deceptive conduct of the grossest kind'. A complaint was then made by Stagg to the British Psychological Association (BPA) that Britton – in allegedly helping the police to design a 'honeytrap' operation to entrap him – had breached the BPA's Code of Conduct. This case was eventually heard in October 2002, almost a decade after the murder of Rachel Nickell, but the seven allegations against Britton were dismissed because of the delay in bringing the case against him. During the two-day hearing it emerged that the 'honeytrap' had been approved at the 'highest levels within the Metropolitan Police', and that Britton's work had been checked by the FBI's offender profiling unit at Quantico, Virginia.

Is it therefore possible to separate the reality from the myth of offender profiling? As we have indicated, this is difficult to do, especially as some profilers – and some organisations – are keen to share only their successes rather than their failures. Thus it is difficult to test empirically much of what passes as 'profiling'. But it is also clear – as with the examples provided above – that there have been profiling successes, although it is false to believe that a profile identifies a specific offender.

So could profiling help us to develop an understanding of the type of person responsible for the Ipswich murders?

What did the offence characteristics reveal about the offender's likely background and circumstances?

A Tentative Profile

We initially constructed a profile of the killer by looking at the sites where the bodies of the first two victims had been dumped. It would have been preferable if we could have analysed the crime scene itself (which has still never been established), nor did we know the order in which the first two women – Tania and Gemma – were murdered (but we have always presumed that Tania, who went missing first, was probably murdered first, although it was actually Gemma's body that was initially discovered). Indeed, discovering the time line in relation to the murders, as opposed to a time line in relation to the discovery of dead and discarded bodies, was a recurring problem of the Ipswich case. The first murder in a series of murders normally produces more clues. Why should this be so?

With the first victim the killer is still inexperienced, and with inexperience come mistakes. When he first kills, the killer does not yet know – although he may have fantasised about this on many occasions – how to subdue his victim, or what the limits of his power might be, or how he will react to the fact that he is about to take another person's life. In these circumstances killers often make mistakes and these mistakes produce the clues that the police use to direct their case, and catch their man. We also have to remember that the weather in early December 2006 was awful. It seldom seemed to stop raining, and Gemma's body was only found by accident by a water bailiff trying to clear a blockage in Belstead Brook. It seems likely that, given the swollen state of the stream, Gemma's body must have moved from where it had originally been discarded, and floated into view.

On Sunday 10 December we travelled to the two sites where the bodies had been discarded, and which, over the coming days and weeks, would eventually resemble tourist sites, with cars and even a bus disgorging its passengers to take a look at where Gemma and Tania had been found, and where others – displaying that most curious of post-modern British sensibilities – had left flowers and notes to the victims for all to see. After spending several hours looking round the sites, we had to go live on Sky, and we quote here from a transcript of the original live broadcast that we made.*

Paul Harrison [PH]: Professor David Wilson, you've been to both locations, what are your impressions?

David Wilson [DW]: There is a pattern emerging, it seems to me. Because I've been able to visit the disposal sites I would say first this is someone who has good knowledge of the highways and byways. This is someone who feels quite confident about where he can stop his car – to dispose of a body. And remember, because the first body was discovered accidentally – this is someone who has taken great care in terms of disposing of the body. So he's confident and organised. What we're seeing is an organised killer – in other words he goes through a great deal of planning. He carefully selects his victims; he finds a place to incapacitate them; and then, once he's killed them, he finds a way of disposing of them – so their bodies won't be discovered unless by accident.

There is something else. He knows this area, which

---

* The transcript is verbatim, except where we have tidied up the grammar.

either implies he lives here, has lived here, or works in this area. But for me the overwhelming factor is that nobody emerges as a double murderer as if by magic, or by chance – this is obviously a pattern in his past. He probably used prostitutes in the past; he's undoubtedly hurt prostitutes in the past – and I would suggest he's killed prostitutes in the past, too.

PH: Looking at the bodies that have been found, there are similarities . . . most obviously, both naked. The police have also stated that there are no marks on the bodies to indicate a cause of death. Does that strike you as strange?

DW: Don't forget, we may well not be being told all of the details. We don't know if there was any forensic evidence at the scenes – obviously placing the bodies in water is an example of how planned the disposal was. If I was in the police's position I would be trying to discover which punters used prostitutes in this area, and gather as much CCTV evidence as possible. I know people keep using the word 'prostitute', but that tends to stop the public from coming forward because the term implies they deserved it – they asked for it, they shouldn't have been behaving in this way. So the police should be getting as much information from the public as possible, and from the other girls in the red-light district.

PH: How common is this?

DW: There have been sixty murders of prostitutes in England and Wales in the past ten years and only sixteen arrests, so that gives you some idea of the scale we're talking about.

This basic outline – with recurring phrases related to the 'organised/disorganised' continuum; the killer's knowledge of the roads around Ipswich; his plausibility as a 'punter' with prostitutes; and the fact that no one becomes a serial killer overnight – was repeated time after time, as is the nature of a twenty-four-hour news service.

As a result of appearing on Sky we were inundated with requests for interviews, and David Wilson in particular was also asked to write articles for the newspapers. Below is an example of one such article that appeared in the *Sun* four days after the first live broadcast from Copdock, where Tania's body had been discovered, and after the bodies of three other young women had been found. The article, written by David, repeats many of the arguments that we have outlined above, but it is helpful to reproduce it here not only because it reveals how the story was being covered in the press – and in the country's best-selling tabloid – but also because it reinforces several of the ideas that we have been describing in relation to offender profiling.

With any crime I like to keep three principles in mind when thinking about the culprit – access, opportunity and motive – and these seem to me to work just as well when analysing serial crime, including the three murders that have taken place in Ipswich.

Think first about access. All five victims – two only discovered yesterday – worked in the sex industry. In other words, access was not an issue because they willingly entered into an arrangement with a client – a stranger – that immediately put them in a position which they did not control. Unsurprisingly there have been at least 60 murders of prostitutes in England and Wales in the last ten years, and arrests in only 16 of these cases. There are even four unsolved murders of young women in the Norwich/ Ipswich area dating back to the mid 1990s. In fact if you want to become a serial killer – and several people such as Colin Ireland who killed gay men set out deliberately to claim that title – targeting prostitutes is one easy way to achieve your ambition.

But what about opportunity? Our serial killer might have wanted to kill for some time, but the opportunity might never have presented itself – he might have only recently been released from jail, or perhaps he was in a relationship that he valued and which kept him occupied. And, while he might be able to gain access to prostitutes, there could have been all sorts of reasons why the opportunity to kill repeatedly might never have arisen. CCTV cameras, for example, which cover the red-light area and keep a check of the number plates of a punter's car, reduce opportunities to gain access to a suitable victim.

But there's more going on here too, for opportunity also implies thinking and planning so as to create your opportunities. That's why the Wests travelled together in their car when they picked up lone female hitch-hikers, for their victims were far more likely to trust a couple than a man on his own. I have never visited the Ipswich area before, and if it had not been for the fact that Paul Harrison – a Sky journalist – was willing to drive me from one site to another I would have been lost more than once. The major roads in this area – the A12 and the A14 – all have a variety of smaller B roads that feed onto and off of them, and unless you know the area well you are going to need sat-nav to get about. Each of the bodies that has been found – all to the south of Ipswich – was very carefully taken down a road that the killer knew would be quiet, lacking street light, and where the killer could park his car without being disturbed. Here I think that the killer is using the opportunity that his knowledge of the local roads gives him to dispose of the bodies, and which implies that he once lived, still lives or works in this area.

Then of course there is motive – and despite everyone watching *Cracker*, or *Wire in the Blood*, profiling really isn't about 'entering the mind of the killer', but has far more to do with looking at how the victims are chosen, how they are treated, what forensic evidence is left at the crime scene or on the victim's body, and how the body is disposed of. All of this usually indicates whether a killer is 'organised' – whether he has thought through what he is doing, and planned his crimes, or whether he is 'disorganised'. Killers who are disorganised are caught quite quickly, and our Suffolk killer has so far not struck me as being disorganised – he knows something about forensic science, which is why he removed the clothes of his victims and placed them in a stream; he knew which roads to travel; and was sufficiently plausible as a punter for at least five women to get into a car with him.

Of course we can also think about the motivation of other serial killers who have targeted women who work in the sex industry like Peter Sutcliffe – the Yorkshire Ripper. He claimed that he started to kill prostitutes (and then other women not involved in the sex industry) because he heard 'voices' telling him to do so, and would therefore be labelled as a 'Visionary' serial killer. Other types include 'Mission' serial killers – who don't hear the voices but set themselves up as judge and jury of the group that they want to target, or 'Power/Control' or 'Hedonistic' killers who do it for the thrill, and for the feeling of power and control that they have over their victim – the power of life or death.

But in my view we have to be careful with motivation as I worked with two distinct groups of serial offenders. The first talked endlessly about why they 'did it' but with no great insight, and some, like Fred West would lie outrageously. Others like Harold Shipman – our worst ever serial killer – never talked at all.

The police are not revealing too much information about how the first two victims were murdered, but when they do we will be able to look further at motivation based on whether, for example, he had sex with these women prior to killing them. In the meantime we need to think about the basics – who was the first girl to die, and who were her punters, her associates, what were her movements, and who did she make her last mobile call to? Concentrating on this type of information will get us much closer to stopping this serial killer than endless speculation about why he's doing what he's doing. What we do know is that he is organised, plans and is careful and has so far been able to make the most of his opportunities to take the lives of five young women. The body count is getting higher, and the time between murders much shorter – this is a man who is now capable of anything.

Theories and More Theories

The growing interest in the case was now reflected in a number of ways. Numerous print and broadcast journalists had swarmed into Ipswich and its surrounding villages, making it almost impossible to find a hotel room for the night. There were camera crews from every terrestrial broadcaster in Britain, several in Europe, and also from as far away as Japan, Canada and the USA, and every local, regional and national newspaper had a correspondent covering the story. So, too, more police arrived to support Suffolk Constabulary. And finally, having become the public faces of Sky News' coverage of the case, we became inundated with theories e-mailed by members of the public eager to share with us their views on who was murdering these young women, why he was doing so and how he could be caught. This was a very interesting development, and clearly revealed how serial killing and serial killers – or at least how they are presented in the media, especially the entertainment media – have seeped into the public's consciousness. They also revealed unspoken assumptions that some members of the public held about murder in Britain. Five examples of the hundreds of e-mails we received illustrate some of the points made (certain details have been disguised to maintain the anonymity of the sender).

- 'Have you considered that the killer may be a woman who has been infected with some sexually transmitted disease that her husband caught while visiting a prostitute?'
- 'I think that you have got this right, Professor Wilson, when you talk about the importance of the roads to this killer. And don't forget that there are ports at the end of the A12 and the A14 – Felixstowe and Harwich. I think that is significant for the killer must be a foreigner as I just can't see an Englishman doing this.'
- 'Is the fact that the first two bodies were found in water of significance? Is the killer trying to cleanse these women of their sins? I think that he is religious, and in the same

way that Ian Huntley was never off the TV in Soham
and he proved to be the killer of Holly and Jessica,
don't you think it is interesting that [names a cleric that
had been regularly interviewed] is never far from a
microphone?'

- 'Perhaps the killer still lives at home with his mother?
  He's probably very repressed because his mother hates
  sex and so he kills these young girls to win her
  approval.'

- 'Do you think that the KGB might be behind this?
  After all, ever since these bodies have been found
  Litvinenko [Alexander Litvinenko was a forty-three-
  year-old former KGB officer living in London who
  died on 26 November 2006, having been poisoned]
  has been taken off the front pages of our
  newspapers.'

These e-mails are representative of the many hundreds
that were sent to us either at Sky, or through other websites
where our contact details appeared. They are hardly a scientific sample, but they are by no means the most extreme we
received. Nor do we doubt the sincerity of many of those
who were sending us their thoughts and views – especially as
they wanted us to pass on their suggestions to the police
in the hope that it would help with their investigation. One
e-mail troubled us so much that we did pass it on to the
police, although that did beg the question why the senders
didn't e-mail the police in the first place. What were we to
make of them?

Several themes emerge from a close reading of these e-
mails. First is a recurring, underlying assumption about sex
generally and prostitution specifically, which reveals how
persistent public attitudes are towards the selling of sexual

services, and how this is often connected to religion. Prostitution is a 'sin', and hence needs to be 'cleansed'; prostitutes carry diseases which then infect 'husbands' – who also happen to be clients, but this fact is ignored by the presumably vengeful 'wife', who one e-mailer thought was seeking to avenge her partner – and presumably herself – for the sexually transmitted disease they had both caught. This should merely beg the question as to why this 'wife' did not in fact attack the 'husband' who had, after all, given her the disease. Some of these e-mails suggest that only men should be allowed to be sexual, whereas women – in the shape of the 'mother' who disapproves of sex and represses her son – play non-sexual roles. In short, sex is part of the culture of a man's world.

Second, we should note how regularly the entertainment media's love of a 'whodunit' with a twist in the tale appears in these e-mails. So, for example, it is in fact the cleric who was the killer, according to one e-mailer – conjuring up images from the board game *Cluedo* – rather than someone already known to the police. And then there is a conspiracy theory, which sees the killer(s) as Russian agents determined not to allow their president's name to be dragged through the mud. Indeed, the idea that the killer must be an 'other' – someone not like us, someone not 'British' – is most clearly revealed by the e-mailer who states quite bluntly that the killer 'must be a foreigner as I just can't see an Englishman doing this'. Here the murders have come to symbolise in the minds of cerain people something much broader about the state of Britain, where their fear and anxiety of being swamped by 'foreigners' finds an outlet in the serial murder of young women in Ipswich.

Finally, these e-mails suggest how little some people actually know about the reality of serial killing, as opposed to the media presentation of serial murder. For example, there has been only one female serial killer in this country who has acted alone (Beverly Allitt), which made it statistically unlikely that the killer in this case was a woman. There seems also to be a lack of awareness that the most prominent serial killers of young women involved in the sex industry in this country have been, like Peter Sutcliffe, Englishmen. More generally our e-mailers did not seem to appreciate that no one becomes a serial killer overnight, that they will probably have a history which the police will be aware of and be able to use in their investigations. It is almost as if our correspondents wanted the killer to emerge fully formed – suddenly, frighteningly, unexpectedly, with no prior history of violence or of other offending behaviour. This idea, too, surely comes from the narrative drive of the books, TV programmes and films in which tension and suspense comes from the unexpected and the out of the ordinary, rather than from the sad, banal reality of serial killers and serial murder.

Profiles and Profilers: Any Use?

As the police made abundantly clear at almost every press conference, they used a 'variety of experts, including profilers' in their search for the Ipswich killer. However, they were reluctant to identify an individual profiler (and didn't at any point during the investigation, or after its conclusion) and the careful way they explained that they were employing a 'range of experts' suggests a great deal about how profilers are now employed in the wake of the Rachel Nickell murder. In other words, the police no longer use an individual profiler (if they ever did) who is able to direct the investigation, but rather engage a series of experts who they think might be of assistance in the particular circumstances of the case. One of the key decisions made in Ipswich was to call in the services of the Forensic Science Service (FSS), an executive agency of the Home Office, at an early stage of the investigation. These experts work on the basis of there being an 'interchange' between the offender and the victim, and that interchange ensures – in the phrase made famous by the French scientist Edmund Locard, director of the world's first crime laboratory in Lyon in the early twentieth century – that 'every contact leaves a trace', and so these experts might include those with a background in, for example, bloodspatter patterns, DNA, firearms, clothing, guns and bite marks. And whereas in the past profilers have come from a variety of backgrounds (although perhaps mostly academic) the police are now more likely to access accredited profilers via the National Crime Faculty in Bramshill, Hampshire. Finally, there is now a whole series of national databases that the police have at their disposal for complex investigations, including the Homicide Index (HI), CATCHEM (Centralised Analytical Team Collating Homicide Expertise and Management), CCA (Comparative Case Analysis), BADMAN (Behavioural Analysis Data Management Auto-Indexing Network) and SCAS (Serious Crime Analysis Section).

All this might suggest that the science of profiling – especially forensic science – has overtaken the art. Forensic science after all implies certainty, self-discipline, objectivity, truth and justice all rolled into one, and in so doing effortlessly accommodates much-heralded successes, as well as the more rarely mentioned failures. Hardly a day goes by without news of some offender being caught by yet another new DNA profiling technique that allows a cold case to be solved years after it was opened. James Lloyd, the rapist and shoe fetishist who preyed on women in Rotherham and Barnsley between 1983 and 1986, and who was convicted in September 2006 on new DNA evidence, is one such example. Even so, on the very same day that Lloyd was sent down, a juror in the Barry George case – he was given a life sentence in 2001 for the murder of the journalist Jill Dando – broke her silence to say that she had felt 'tricked' into convicting George. She would find support from a number of forensic scientists who are now claiming that the forensic evidence on which George's conviction rested – which related to gunpowder residue – is suspect and being dismissed as 'unreliable'. Indeed, as a result of a decision by the Criminal Cases Review Commission in June 2007, George's case has now been referred to the Court of Appeal.

It is doubtful whether many of us have ever questioned what forensic science is, or looked too deeply at how and when scientific principles come to be applied within the criminal justice and legal systems, and so tried to understand what forensic science can or cannot do. The key word here is 'science'. After years of almost inexorable academic and popular ascendancy it has lost much of its cachet either (according to its defenders) because it is too 'hard' for the new schools curriculum, or (for its critics) because the so-called principles under which it operates are seen to be less rigorous than scientists had previously led us to believe, and are just as likely to be the result of conjecture, prejudice and error as anything else.

There were also major problems in the Ipswich case that no amount of forensic science could overcome. Consider once more Locard's famous phrase – 'every contact leaves a trace'. As noted previously, *The Murder Investigation Manual* identifies five possible significant scenes that require some level of forensic analysis:

- Last seen Alive.
- Initial Contact.
- Attack Site.
- Murder Site.
- Body Dump Site.

In Ipswich the police were never able to establish either the 'attack site', the 'murder site' or where the initial contact was made, although they concluded, quite reasonably, that the latter was the red-light area of the town. They only had two out of five of these significant scenes, which was why trying to recreate the final movements of the five victims was vital, and why a great deal of police energy was devoted to this aspect of the investigation. It also explains why the sites where the bodies were found became so crucial. Even so, the absence of the two outstanding significant scenes was a major problem, and, as a result, forensic science was only ever going to get the police so far – despite the desperation of some forensic scientists who seemed to want to maintain that anything was possible and others who claim that there is 'zero error' tolerance in their discipline. The latter simply cannot be sustained in the face of mounting evidence.

Take the hapless Brandon Mayfield, for example. Brandon is a Portland lawyer who was arrested and held for two weeks in Madrid in 2004 in the wake of a terrorist attack on the city's train system. The FBI insisted that they had found his fingerprints – that staple of forensic science since Francis Galton and Alphonse Bertillon – on several crucial pieces of evidence, only for the Spanish authorities to disagree and release Brandon without charge. We could also cite the case of Shirley McKie, the Scottish police officer, who, in 1997, was wrongly placed at the scene of a murder by her 'fingerprints', which were eventually shown to belong to someone else. Or the case of Jimmy Ray Bromgard, who was convicted of raping an eight-year-old girl in 1987 in Montana, after the state's chief forensic scientist wrongly claimed that pubic hair found on the victim's bed sheets matched Bromgard, and would match less than one in 10,000 people in a given population. All nonsense, and Bromgard has since been released and exonerated. Indeed, several states in the USA, such as Texas, have now become so concerned about 'junk forensic science' that they have set up special Forensic Science Commissions to investigate crime lab problems which might lead to miscarriages of justice.

In the Ipswich case the police, profilers and other experts would, in the absence of two significant scenes, have to make an imaginative leap with the evidence they had. They would have to use conjecture to develop hypotheses about the offender that they would have to test out. Inevitably some within the investigation would have more power – both formal and informal – than others working on the case, and they would be able to use that power to push their hypotheses more forcefully. This might have enabled them to pursue particular lines of inquiry at the expense of others that might have proved more fruitful, or to brief the FSS in a particular way that suited the hypothesis that they wanted to be tested. So, in the end, there would be just as much error, prejudice, guesswork and personal judgement in this process as in all processes where people are involved, all of which gets masked by the word 'science'. But this should not blind us to the reality that mistakes are made in murder investigations – when the wrong person gets arrested, or where mistakes ensure that the case remains unsolved. Were the profilers at Ipswich of any use? The answer is undoubtedly 'yes', even if we are unable to say with any certainty whether or not pro-filing is simply intuitive guesswork – an art rather than a science. This lack of certainty is partly created by the media and by the way profiling and profilers have been presented and dramatised, but in an age of wall-to-wall news coverage, no one can doubt that the media influences, shapes and at times can also prompt how murders are investigated.

Chapter Six

The Media: Breaking News

'I can confirm that this afternoon, two bodies have been found near Ipswich. We received a call at 15.05. This is shocking news . . . We've got this to you as "breaking news" . . . we were planning for the worst in relation to this – the teams looking at the disappearance of Paula Clennell and Annette Nicholls will now become murder investigations.'

Detective Chief Superintendent Stewart Gull at the press conference on 12 December

'We were due to talk to you about resources but due to the fast-moving nature of this inquiry we now have some "breaking news" for you.'

Suffolk Chief Constable Alastair McWhirter live on Sky News, Tuesday 12 December

4.15 p.m., 12 December. It had been more than ten minutes since the Sky News team had got the tip-off about new police activity on the outskirts of Ipswich.

The information we'd been given soon began to look more and more credible and before long other media outlets would be making for the location to which we were heading. We weren't there yet. To reach our destination we had to follow narrow country roads; it was dark and raining and the going was treacherous. There was pressure to get there first, to beat the other lot – the competition – but we had to get there in one piece and without forgetting that what lay at our destination wasn't a photo opportunity but the body of a murder victim.

Ten minutes earlier we had been standing on the edge of Belstead Brook in Hintlesham following a team of police divers in wetsuits as they searched the shallow waters for evidence such as items of clothing. Three naked bodies had been found so far within a week and the absence of clothing belonging to the girls was hindering the progress of the investigation.

Hoping to film the moment officers pulled a shoe, a coat or any other item from the water, we wanted to follow the divers up the snaking tributary, which meant walking across the sodden farmland laden with camera equipment. To avoid clogging up the only road that ran through Hintlesham, the Sky News uPod – a van with a satellite dish attached to the roof – had parked just off the road inside the gate of the nearest farmyard. The uPod would allow us to bring to the viewers live the search for clues as it happened. But there were a few hurdles to overcome first, one of which was persuading the put-upon farmer to allow us to park on his land. We promised to shut the gate when we left.

Meanwhile, the search had gathered pace. The team of divers were now a few hundred metres upstream so we'd have to be quick to catch them. The brook eventually took the officers along the bottom of a garden belonging to a large house. We made a point of not climbing any fences and instead decided to follow the banks of the brook on to the land belonging to the house. Then the team of divers were suddenly out of the water – had they discovered something? Couldn't they go any further? A glance in the direction of the house provided the answer. Walking towards us was a woman carrying a tray of tea and biscuits. She'd seen the divers and decided they needed a morale boost. But she hadn't seen us and when she did she wasn't pleased.

'This is private property. Please leave now, and I mean *now*.'

She was clearly in no mood for discussion, so we did as she asked. It was a good thing, too. As we approached the uPod our mobiles started ringing. It was the news desk. A tip-off suggested there was a lot of police activity close to the small village of Levington, south of Ipswich.

'We're not sure yet whether it's anything significant, but how long will it take to get there?' asked the news editor.

'We could be there in less than ten minutes.' It would take the uPod a while to stow its satellite dish, so our car would go on ahead. Two minutes later, as we headed towards the A14, the phone rang again. 'It's definitely another body – we've not got any more details other than that, but let us know when you're getting close.' The adrenalin levels were clearly rising in the newsroom, not least because the main evening bulletin, *Live at Five*, was fast approaching and the possible discovery of yet another body meant a last-minute change of scripts and programme content.

Soon we were driving through Nacton. By now it was a place we knew quite well and the fact that the sat nav said Levington was only a mile away sent the obvious thoughts racing through our minds. This was the road we had been taking for the past two days to the place where the third body had been discovered. If it was another body, the killer was using this area again, just as he had done with the first two victims.

Sat nav directed us to the pub in Levington; one U-turn later we were outside it, but there was no blue police light and no police cordon in sight. We'd have to ask in the pub. It would prove to be the third encounter with someone less than pleased to see us in the space of an hour. The man who popped his head out of the pub store room didn't seem to know about any police activity, but at the same time he didn't look surprised to see us either. Before we had the chance to ask him anything else, another man approached us.

'Who are you?' he asked abruptly. We explained we were from Sky News and that we understood the police had set up a cordon nearby because another body had been discovered. Could he point us in the right direction?

'Journalists, yeuch, can't stand 'em' was his response, so we left.

Confrontations with local people unhappy about the presence of journalists were by now quite commonplace. Suddenly, the lives of private individuals were in the full glare of the news media, and the reason for that was hardly one that anybody wanted to be advertised.

'While it did not seem Ipswich was being portrayed as the hub of the sex industry in Britain, it did become the face of prostitution and a microcosm of the problems every town and city in the country has, no matter how much people wish to ignore its existence,' explained Ipswich's *Evening Star* assistant editor Colin Adwent, on duty from the moment the first body was discovered.

What was to some an invasion of privacy was to others an unexpected pre-Christmas boost to business. There were three hundred or so extra police in town from forces around the country to help out Suffolk Constabulary and about the same number of journalists. And they all needed somewhere to sleep. At the height of the investigation there wasn't a hotel vacancy for up to twenty miles around Ipswich, and that would not change until Steve Wright was charged. Hotels and B & Bs were raking it in, and though we weren't personally aware that prices were being hiked up, it was pretty obvious they were. Sky News had been in Ipswich from the beginning and so our rooms were block-booked for two weeks. Others less fortunate were forced to drive for up to an hour just to get four hours' sleep.

The media circus had come to town, but it didn't turn up in dribs and drabs. The entire extravaganza seemed to arrive overnight. It was almost too much for this provincial town to bear.

A Local Story Goes Global

Throughout November the disappearance first of Tania Nicol and then, two weeks later, of Gemma Adams attracted predominantly local and regional television, radio and newspaper coverage. There was at this stage little, if any, interest from the national media. And the effect on the lives of the people of Ipswich during this period was minimal, as a report in the *Evening Star*, one week after the disappearance of Gemma Adams, suggested:

> Gemma Adams is one of two young vice girls to have vanished in Ipswich in recent weeks. Officers spoke to pedestrians and motorists near to the BMW garage on the junction of West End Road and Handford Road, an area Miss Adams was last seen at about 1.15am on November 15. Tania Nicol left her home in Woolverstone Close, at about 10.30pm on Monday, October 30, with

the intention of going into town to work as a prostitute. Do you feel concerned by the disappearances? Do you know either of the girls? Write to Your Letters in the *Evening Star*.

'Between Tania vanishing and Gemma going missing, appeals were put out by police and the *Evening Star* put out posters around the town in the hope of helping to find her,' explained Colin Adwent. 'We were already covering the story strongly with front pages and inside leads.' He described how the story grew:

Locally it became a big story and made a few paragraphs in the nationals. Realistically, most people believed then it would only be a matter of time before Tania's body would be found, although the hope was this belief would be unfounded.

National media began to get really interested after Tania was found, but things really became surreal when Anneli's body was discovered near the entrance to Amberfield School in Nacton two days later, especially as there had been nothing to say publicly that she had been missing. The arrival of the national and international media only made it more competitive and created problems when it left bad feeling in its wake, which – to be fair – seemed rare. At one stage some national papers had as many journalists working on the story as our whole reporting staff. We had reporters who worked twenty out of twenty-one days so they could cover the story properly. Everyone volunteered for extra hours because of the sheer enormity of the story. We made a conscious decision very early on to treat the memory of those who died as victims and not as people whose lives

were any less precious because of what they did or their
drug addiction. This is why we set up a memorial appeal –
Someone's Daughter – almost immediately, when the scale
of the killings was becoming apparent. Five women are
dead, five families will never fully recover from their
loss and five children will never be able to see their mothers again. We have the luxury of only being able to
imagine their suffering. Their families will have to live
with their loss for the remainder of their lives.

But until the body of Gemma Adams was discovered this
had simply been a story about the disappearance of two
women who worked in Ipswich's red-light district and so
was far from national headline news. For many readers and
viewers these were women who had chosen to take to the
streets and knew the potential danger they were placing
themselves in. Some even felt they only had themselves to
blame, that they had it coming.

And as far as the red-light district was concerned, that was
a place far away from their own day-to-day lives and didn't
impact on them at all. More to the point, because Tania and
Gemma were prostitutes, if someone had harmed or attacked
them it was clear that whoever it was was only targeting
prostitutes. That meant that no other women in Ipswich
were at risk. Any such false sense of security would disappear once it became clear a serial killer was on the loose,
even more so on 12 December when the police began warning all women to be on their guard.

Suddenly every woman in Ipswich was being told that she
could be a potential target. As well as bringing them closer to
the story, many women also felt it created an unnecessary climate of fear. Others were more circumspect: if women were
more careful, it would inevitably reduce the killer's ability to

attack outside his normal target group. But it was a statement broadcast by the scores of national media organisations that had some days earlier finally woken them up to the enormity of the story.

Sky News quickly saw the story's potential. From the moment the body of Gemma Adams was discovered, news editor Mark Evans and managing editor Simon Cole had begun pushing it. 'We first came to the story after the discovery of the first body and while one girl was missing I didn't think we should send a team quite yet,' explained Evans. He continued: 'Simon Cole was very interested in the story and mentioned it to the morning meeting. After the meeting he and I agreed we would send Paul Harrison to Ipswich at the weekend. The idea was that he could spend some time within the town's red-light district talking to prostitutes and punters about their fears, thus giving us a way into the story.

'But even as the first Sky News team prepared to head for Ipswich the story took an unpredictable turn with the discovery of a second body, barely two miles from the first. So what was intended as a pre-shoot – we would film overnight solely for a report to be broadcast the following morning – suddenly became a "live" moving story.

'We diverted Paul from Portman Road in Ipswich where women would soon start appearing on the streets, heading instead to the new crime scene in Copdock to provide live pictures and interviews late into the evening.

'Like the BBC, the Sky News team on the ground was small but nonetheless sufficient for that weekend's coverage. Saturday saw police confirm the second body was indeed that of Tania Nicol and Sky reported that, in the light of the second discovery, prostitutes in the red-light district were operating in a heightened sense of fear. But to keep the story

alive the following day, we decided to enlist the help of criminologist Professor David Wilson to construct a profile of a
potential single killer.'

There had so far been little information from the police
about the investigation and by early evening the decision
was made to pull the team out of Ipswich and see where the
story went. No one was expecting the news that was to
follow later that evening.

'Paul, we're going to have to get you back up live in a
place called Nacton as soon as possible,' said Mark Evans
just as he was ending his shift. The Suffolk Police's media
phone line had announced that the body of a third woman
had been discovered in woodland and Sky's Martin Brunt
was already live on the phone elaborating on what the police
were telling us, using his contacts within the police. It meant
I would be live all evening, but it also suggested that the
way we intended to cover the developing story would need a
radical rethink. Clearly this would be the only story in town
and all news organisations would begin to 'monster' the
story.

'Monday's morning meeting was hugely taken by the
story and even more people were sent to Ipswich as it
became increasingly clear that not much else would make air
for some time,' said Mark Evans. He also stated that there
was a 'little disagreement':

. . . about how the story should be covered between input
and output – as is usually the case when a big story hits. It
was decided early on that the dead women would be
treated with respect in death and that derogatory terms
such as 'hooker' had no place on Sky but also neither
would we accept euphemisms such as 'working girls' or
'sex workers'. The women worked as prostitutes and that

had to be referred to in our output because it was absolutely intrinsic to the story. But it was not a point that needed labouring, as they were women, mothers and partners as well.

Evans also recognised that 'The story was quite similar to Soham in the sense that it gripped the nation and was followed on a minute-by-minute basis by the news networks. New technologies mean that we can have a number of dishes and therefore live locations within one relatively small geographical area.'

The sprawling media village had grown tenfold almost overnight and some even reckoned the press sent to Ipswich outnumbered the police on the investigation itself. They were probably right.

With any story the media tend to congregate where they are able to tap into the best source of information – in Ipswich it was to be at police headquarters in Martlesham Heath. With three bodies having been discovered in just eight days, the press pack was in for the long haul. The killer might, after all, strike again and then there'd be no knowing how long it would take to catch him.

So the media took root, and four-tonne satellite trucks lowered their jacks for stability in heavy winds. Coffee and biscuits were available round the clock. Awnings were erected and tables and chairs laid out, and satellite dishes were deployed for live broadcasts. Like an army on manoeuvre, in a matter of hours television channels, radio stations and cars full of newspaper reporters and photographers glued to laptops had crammed themselves into the space of a five-a-side football pitch. Food could be got from the police canteen or the ubiquitous burger van.

The close proximity of the media teams to each other

brought other difficulties. Cameras stood cheek by jowl; reporters and presenters had to compete with each other to get their voices heard as their respective channels crossed live to them at the top of the hour. Even in the most dismal circumstances, a certain camaraderie always exists between the media, but it is one counterbalanced by healthy competition and suspicion. A competitor in need of a cable or cassette, or power to run an edit van will be helped out, no questions asked. Contacts and tips-offs, on the other hand, are closely guarded, camaraderie or no camaraderie.

And such close proximity means that little goes on without your competitors knowing about it. Chinese whispers begin, and paranoia sets in. Why is that team packing up at short notice? Where are they going and why? Have they heard something we haven't?

Arrests and Developments

The media wasn't located only at police headquarters. By 12 December the bodies of the murdered women had all been taken to Ipswich Hospital, which meant another location had to be covered, and, not long after that, the houses of the two suspects, Tom Stephens and Steve Wright, would become the focus of the investigation. With resources spread so thinly, the teams had to be prepared to leave at a moment's notice. Monday 18 December was one such day when we had to move quickly.

The morning had started differently from any other day so far in Ipswich. First, no five o'clock wake-up call to be on location ready to go live on *Sunrise* with Eamonn Holmes. This time we were to be at a location by 8 a.m. which until now had been of little significance in the hunt for a serial killer – Ipswich Crown Court.

On 6 December, it had been the place where a coroner had held an inquest into the death of Gemma Adams, the first of the women to be discovered. At that stage none of the other women's bodies had been found, so you could be forgiven for thinking this was an isolated incident. The naked body had shown no signs of sexual assault and the cause of death was as yet unknown, meaning that further tests would need to be conducted. The case was adjourned.

Now, twelve days later, journalists had begun arriving back at the Crown Court. This time the coroner was to hold inquests into the four other deaths that had occurred subsequently, but the day did not go as planned. By 9 a.m. rumours that the inquest would be postponed were confirmed, and minutes later the police called an unscheduled press conference at which a statement would be read. No questions would be taken from the media. Something was happening, so we were ready to up and leave.

The 'Obvious Suspect'

The moment the police announced that thirty-seven-year-old Tom Stephens had been arrested on suspicion of all five murders, it only took a quick bit of detective work by the news desk to find his address; we were soon in the car heading in the direction sat nav was telling us to go. Eighteen minutes to our destination it said, but we would have to be there quicker than that.

By the time we arrived the police had already blocked off the road, allowing only local residents through. We were closely followed by the uPod van, whose engineer would within minutes have us ready to go to air live. Our team was again in its state of semi-permanence at our new location, but we knew police would want to question Stephens possibly for days and his house would need to be thoroughly searched by forensic teams. That, too, could take days. If the police were going to keep the media back at the end of the road, we'd have to bring in some hardware to counteract that.

The Sky News helicopter had proved its worth since the start of the Ipswich investigation. Cameras at ground level two hundred metres away won't capture significant detail or depth, but one mounted on the front of a helicopter hovering over a crime scene gives viewers a bird's-eye shot of what's happening. American TV networks have used helicopters for news coverage for years and seldom to greater effect than whey they tracked the flight of O. J. Simpson on the LA Freeway in June 1994.

The helicopter would now serve its purpose at the house of Tom Stephens, too, but helicopters can't stay airborne 24/7, so a more permanent solution was needed if we were to be able to see what forensic work was going on at the house. For £500 a day a thirty-foot cherry picker enabled our cameras to offer a live 'top shot' of activity at Stephens' house. And ours wasn't the only one. Alongside the steadily increasing number of satellite vehicles were three more cherry pickers.

Jubilee Close in the quiet village of Trimley St Martin was soon flooded by the media. Some organisations had paid families overlooking the house for the use of their living rooms as studios. Others had – for a price – taken over local residents' drives in which to park their edit vehicles. Dave, who owned a house fifty yards along the street, allowed us to use his toilet – which meant we no longer had to use the nearest field. Dave also invited us to take refuge from the cold in between live interviews in his living room. For the more extravagant media organisations, Winnebagos obviated the need to rely on the generosity of neighbours who'd woken up to discover that not only did the police's main suspect in the Ipswich murder inquiry live next door, but that the media had moved in and taken over their street as well.

While some residents saw the presence of the media as an imposition or a chance to make a quick buck, Dave wasn't one of them: 'Oh, don't worry about money, so long as it helps you lot catch the bugger who did this.' Dave, like many others, felt he was doing his bit. He was also savvy enough to know that the man whose house police were searching along his street might well *not* be the killer. Dave saw the media as an extension of the police, there to report on the hunt for a serial killer and also to help catch him.

The arrest of Tom Stephens that morning had taken place largely as a result of a very candid interview Stephens had given to the *Sunday Mirror* the previous day. Although police had questioned Stephens several times before, his comments to *Sunday Mirror* journalist Michael Duffy were strong enough to lead to his arrest: 'I'm a friend of all the girls. I was closest to Tania. And Gemma as well. I was close to others as well. But I should have been there to watch over them,' he told Duffy on 17 December.

From the police profiling it does look like me – white male between 25 and 40, knows the area, works strange hours. The bodies have got close to my house. I know that I'm innocent. But I don't have alibis for some of the times – actually I'm not entirely sure I have tight alibis for any of the times. If new information, coincidental information, crops up, I could get arrested, [adding] I know I am innocent and I am completely confident it won't go as far as me being charged.

The media was also quick to broadcast a radio interview Tom Stephens did with a BBC radio journalist:

I've known Gemma for about eighteen months which is kind of about as long as I've known any of the girls. Tania I've only known about six months but in the end I got to know her better that Gemma. I didn't know Anneli at all – I only spoke to her since Gemma and Tania went missing and that was partly to say 'if you know anything please talk to police and if you won't talk to police then talk to me and I'll talk to police', and also trying to say 'are you OK?' and I don't know what I was trying to say.

To some, the arrest of Tom Stephens looked like a knee-jerk reaction: was the media ahead of the game and so calling the shots? Was the police investigation slow off the mark? Far from it. The police knew who Stephens was and about his relationship with prostitutes well before any of the women were murdered

On 12 October, eighteen days before Tania Nicol disappeared, police had stopped Stephens in his car with the nineteen-year-old sitting beside him. He explained he was giving her a lift. The reality was that he saw her most nights of the week and would do small jobs for her – like taking her to score drugs or giving her a lift home after a night working in the red-light area. He had similar arrangements with other girls, but he felt Tania was the most reliable and honest.

Then on 1 November, just after Tania was reported missing, Tom Stephens phoned the police to say he had 'confidential material' about her. He told police he thought he knew where she was going on the night she disappeared. He refused to give any details over the phone and asked police to call him back – he gave officers his number, describing himself as 'a friend' of the girl.

On 7 and 8 November Stephens made further calls to the police and the very next day he was made a subject of a surveillance operation.

A week later, on 16 November, the day after the disappearance of Gemma Adams, Tom went again to the police, accompanied by another prostitute called Tracy. He told an officer that the prostitutes he knew had such an overwhelming addiction to drugs that they would take irrational risks. He told investigators he'd warned the girls that if they went out to work then one of them would be murdered.

Less than a week after that, on 21 November, Stephens called the police and said he didn't want to be seen as 'another Ian Huntley' and wanted to help the police. He was back on the phone three days later, checking on the progress of the missing person's inquiry. He offered to go into massage parlours on a fact-finding mission for them. Suffolk Police declined his offer.

Then, at the height of the investigation on the evening of 11 December, Stephens spoke to the police about the deceased women. By this stage the bodies of Tania, Gemma and Anneli had been found and Annette and Paula were known to be missing. He said the girls were 'all on drugs and would do anything for drugs . . . If it had been me, I would have strangled them'. The statement shocked the police, so they decided to keep tabs on his every movement.

On 13 December he had a meeting with a journalist at a pub in Levington – close to where the last two bodies had by now been discovered. Police were watching when Stephens left the pub after his meeting. He turned left along the old Felixstowe Road in the direction of the locations where the two bodies had been dumped. But as he approached the police cordon in the distance, he stopped and performed a U-turn just short of the flashing police lights. Later that night Stephens was seen in the red-light area of Ipswich having discussions with police officers on the streets.

The following day Tom Stephens again approached the police to say he was concerned that DNA might be found in his car and in his house.

On 17 December, he made yet another trip to the police station, this time carrying a copy of a national newspaper which named him as a suspect, and said he'd thought about committing suicide. But later, after Stephens phoned police to say he was worried about whether he had a 'split personality' and feared he was doing things that he didn't know about, then going back to his 'normal personality', he was arrested. DNA samples were taken and analysed and police spent more than twenty-four hours searching his house, garden and car for forensic evidence.

Tom Stephens was never charged with any of the murders, yet his arrest on 18 December and twenty-four hours in custody took up much police time and resources. He was the obvious suspect at the time, so what did he make of his whole experience?

Tom's mobile rang just a couple of times before he answered. His mobile number was, he said, the 'holy grail', implying that everyone wanted to get their hands on it. He agreed to meet us but on condition we did so at a location a short distance from his house. We would then take him to a pub of his choice, where he felt relaxed. It was September 2007 and he hadn't long been home. When he had been released from custody on police bail, it was considered too early to send him home, not only for fear of reprisals (even though he hadn't been charged) but because the police had turned his house upside down looking for evidence and it would be some time before it was habitable again. For a while home for Tom would be a police 'safe house'.

'They turned over my house, took my laptop and phone. There were some pictures on it you wouldn't want to show the vicar, but I was quite hurt when police seemed confused that they hadn't found anything more serious on it. There was a silver film over everything still when I moved back in – probably from finger printing, but actually the place was tidier than before I was arrested. I think they'd hoovered everywhere, probably looking for evidence.'

Tom admitted this wasn't the first time police had searched his house. The first visit had been after Gemma Adams was reported missing on 15 November.

'The police were a little bit like lions led by donkeys. I was put into a paper suit to start with, I assume because they wanted to take a look at my clothes. The officers who interviewed me were much lower than Stewart Gull and were quite good, I thought. They sent one particular man to arrest me and he treated me OK – in fact the police who were involved with me handled it all very well. I did wonder whether they kept me in for longer than they needed to because that might make the real killer feel safe and encourage him to make a mistake.'

Some months after his release, and once police had made it clear no charges would be brought against Tom, he was allowed home. But he still felt people were whispering about him and viewed him with suspicion, so he continued to fear he was in danger. It was hardly surprising given that, for days since the morning of his arrest, his neighbours had to put up with hundreds of journalists blocking roads, running noisy generators from six in the morning, climbing walls, parking up cherry pickers, using their toilets and putting their homes on national television and in the tabloids – and all because of Tom. It made him feel deeply uncomfortable.

'For a few days I was the most hated man in Britain – more than Ian Huntley. I was walking home the other day and a couple was walking past me on the pavement. I heard them whispering under their breath. I do worry about being recognised and being beaten up. I did wonder about leaving Ipswich, just to get away, but how would that have looked to people and the police?'

After taking a sip of bitter, Tom conceded that he was staying put for the moment, but now that he had no car – the police had seen to that: they had taken it apart looking for evidence and had not returned it, despite his not being charged – he had to resort to cycling to and from Ipswich. It had been his car that most of the girls he'd befriended in the red-light area had often been so pleased to see. The self-styled 'protector' of many girls working on the streets, he knew all five of the victims well, some of them intimately. He'd get calls at all hours asking for lifts either to score drugs or for lifts home. He'd help out when he could.

It wasn't just Tom's car that was attractive to the girls. He worked full-time at Tesco and so had money and a house. Many girls had been to his house. By his own admission all five who'd been murdered had at some stage been there, which made the police's job all the more difficult. Tom was quite candid about how well he knew the girls.

'Tania was really petite. She said she wanted a boob job, but any breast enlargement would have looked wrong. She was pretty, but I didn't fancy her.' In fact, as far as he was concerned the five murdered girls were among the best-looking girls who worked the streets of Ipswich, and Tom felt that was the reason the killer had targeted them.

'I made a few mistakes while the investigation was going on – I put my foot in my mouth once talking to a Sunday newspaper and I'm the kind of person who'd do it a second and a third time. I spoke out because I wanted to help rather than just watch the girls I knew being killed.

'I'd lend the girls money, too. I trusted them to pay me back and often it would take a while. Sometimes they'd pay me back more than I lent them. I gave one girl £20. Some time later she gave me back £50, knowing I'd keep the £20 and hold on to the £30 for when she needed it – usually until the next night. I think if she had kept hold of that £30 herself, she would have spent it on drugs straight away and had nothing left for later. Also because I owed them I had to drive it to them. They would then ask for a lift somewhere.'

Tom hated the drug dealers. 'I can't tell you how much I hate them. Taking the girls off the streets is not going to solve the whole issue of the red-light district, because other girls will just take their place. Taking the dealers out of the equation is the answer.'

Tom seemed lonely and you couldn't help but wonder who he would be friends with now that more and more girls were being helped off the streets. He had lost five 'friends' in the space of six weeks to a killer and he questioned whether he could have done more to prevent their deaths.

'Could I have done more? The girls were making me promise not to talk to their families, but had I done so maybe they'd be alive today. Certainly they'd have ended our friendship if I had. And then, when the girls started going missing, I would tell the police as much as I knew. Sometimes in the middle of the night I'd remember something and call them with the most minute detail, which in hindsight was probably not relevant. I just felt I had to try something.'

Tom looked different from many of the photographs in the papers and on TV at the time of his arrest. The biggest difference was that he was now clean-shaven. By the look of it he'd only shaved that afternoon.

'With beard or without?' he asked. Tom had an issue about the way he looked. He wanted to know if he was ugly, if he had a good physique and why he didn't have a girl-friend. He certainly wanted to be in a relationship, yet the idea of joining a health club or going away on a singles holi-day worried him.

'I'd be scared that people would find out who I was. And why get into a relationship and close to someone when they would eventually find out and leave me?'

Tom was at his lowest point after being released from police custody. When he had no one to talk to he'd sometimes cycle down to the red-light area and chat with whoever was there. Quite often, though, he'd be asked to make himself scarce – picking up a punter with him around wasn't always easy.

Interviews and More Interviews

The media falling into the role of detective is easily done. No one should underestimate the possibility that, with so many police and journalists in town, someone could unwittingly meet the killer and talk to him. At the back of our minds was the 2002 interview with Soham murderer Ian Huntley con-ducted by Sky News' Jeremy Thompson.

During a live broadcast outside the Soham caretaker's house, Huntley had looked Thompson straight in the eye and said: 'They just seemed like normal happy kids. Chatty and cheerful. They seemed fine.' A few minutes later Thompson had interviewed Huntley's girlfriend, Maxine Carr, who showed live on air a card Holly had made her on the last day of term. He and his producers were struck by how Carr referred to Holly in the past tense: 'She was lovely, just really lovely.'

Twenty-four hours later Huntley would be interviewed again, this time by the police.

To illustrate this point in the Suffolk investigation, where interviews with key figures had already begun to take place, among the prostitutes interviewed by the media was Paula Clennell. Despite the discovery of the bodies of Gemma Adams and Tania Nicol, the twenty-four-year-old was still out in the red-light district touting for business. It made her not only a target for a serial killer still on the loose but for the media, too, keen for a reaction to the announcement that the latest body was indeed that of Tania Nicol. And on Saturday 5 December, before becoming the next victim of the serial killer, Paula would give an interview to Anglia TV in which she admitted she was taking a real risk by continuing to work on the streets. She needed the money, she said. It was the last interview she would give.

Even before Tom Stephens' arrest we began building up a profile of the killer and found ourselves scrutinising people more carefully to see if they fitted the profile. One afternoon we looked perhaps a little bit too hard.

It was Saturday 16 December – two weeks since the first body had been discovered. There were now five bodies and no one had been arrested. The investigation was fully underway. In a bid to try to refresh people's memories, we decided to revisit all four scenes live, one per hour and in the order the bodies had been found. We started at Hintlesham, arriving in Copdock, just two miles away, an hour later.

Standing in Copdock we realised that someone must have known the area well enough to know there was a brook running under the old A12. At night, if you weren't familiar with the area, you wouldn't know it was there. The killer, we speculated, might come here regularly because he needed to. There was an animal feed wholesaler's adjacent to the brook. Perhaps the killer had something to do with animals. We decided to check if the Amberfield School, whose entrance was just a hundred yards from where the third body was discovered in Nacton, kept any horses. Nothing showed up online, so we thought little more of it and headed to Nacton.

The police cordon was still in place and we were kept about a hundred metres back from where Anneli Alderton's body had been found. We were just packing up after the live, and about to head to our fourth and final location in Levington, when a man appeared with a couple of dogs. We half-joked about the dogs and the link to the animal feed wholesaler's in Copdock. But we decided to try to find out what he was doing there.

'Sad, isn't it?' we said to him. The man had been reading the message attached to flowers left by someone at the top of the road who seemed to have known Anneli.

The man agreed that what had happened to the girls was terrible, admitting a family member had once had connections with the red-light district. We probed further. He lived locally, he told us, and said he had come to pick up the friend he brought there once a week to feed the horses.

Our minds began racing. He was a local to the area, and knew someone with connections to the red-light district. Moreover, he had a reason to come to this particular location in Nacton and *if* he regularly brought horse feed, this might also take him to Copdock next to the brook where the second body was discovered.

For a split second we wondered whether we had inadvertently stumbled upon the killer. We hadn't, of course, but only realised this after the information we'd given the police came to nothing. We joked that we were getting too imaginative, too close to the story, but hoped we hadn't been wasting police time by playing detective – albeit by accident and with the best of intentions.

What Should Be Private?

On other occasions information the police deemed either private to the victims' families, irrelevant to the investigation, or both, made it into the public domain. For example, the *Sun* article on 16 December read: 'One of the Suffolk Strangler's victims was pregnant, the *Sun* can reveal. Vice girl Anneli Alderton, 24, was around three months into her pregnancy, cops confirmed last night.'

The police's reaction to the Tom Stephens interview in the *Sunday Mirror*, and their annoyance that Anneli's pregnancy had made it into the national press, clearly demonstrated that they were following the national and local coverage. And they were watching television news as well. In fact, unable to get the coffee machine to work in the police canteen, one WPC remarked to us in exasperation: 'Oh, you can profile a killer, but you can't even get a coffee!'

But though the media may sometimes have been seen as a nuisance, the police appreciated their usefulness in both getting information out to the public and helping them engage the people of Ipswich in catching the killer. The media had plenty of pages and hours to fill, and the police were happy to benefit from that. Sometimes you felt that officers were watching so much twenty-four-hour TV news coverage that they were beginning to sound like presenters themselves. Moments after the discovery of the bodies of Annette Nicholls and Paula Clennell, for example, Suffolk Constabulary's Chief Constable Alastair McWhirter and DCS Stewart Gull both used the expression 'breaking news'. While it sounded awkward coming from them, and made a few of us journalists smile, the news they delivered quickly wiped the grins off our faces.

While providing some of the information the media needed, press conferences didn't offer nearly enough for the hundreds of journalists who'd gathered in Ipswich. ACC Jacqui Cheer had admitted to Sky News that we were only being allowed to see the tip of the iceberg.

There was a lot of information out there and plenty of people to provide it and it often meant that the hunt for a story or new line would move out of Ipswich. Close relations of the victims in the Ipswich area were difficult to get to because police were protecting them from press intrusion, but up to and beyond the point Steve Wright was charged, his family and friends were fair game.

On 20 December the *Hartlepool Mail* gained exclusive access to the former wife of Steve Wright, fifty-two-year-old Diane Cole, the name she had adopted by deed poll following the break-up of the marriage. She had met Wright while working on board the *QE2* cruise ship as a window dresser and they were married in 1987. Together they eventually ran the Ferry Boat Inn, a pub in Norwich. Diane Cole said: 'It's been an absolute nightmare. I couldn't believe it when I saw his name on the telly. I'm curious about the whole thing like everyone else but I'm curious in a different way because I know the person.'

She also told the *Mail* that their relationship had been 'a total disaster' and a 'nightmare'. 'Our marriage didn't even last a year and he went off with someone else,' she said. She also revealed: 'I've had journalists and national newspapers offering me money but I've been scared to talk to anyone. The *Mail* are the only ones I've let in.'

After her break-up with Wright, Diane had tried to make a fresh start. The *Hartlepool Mail*'s interview with her had been made possible partly because the paper had spoken to her before and had struck up a good relationship. Diane had suffered from meningitis and blood poisoning, as a result of which she had both legs amputated. Her move back to her roots in Hartlepool was covered extensively by the paper.

Out-of-town journalists, if they were unable to speak face to face with those close to the story, would often use their friends as a mouthpiece. Through one of Steve Wright's closest friends, forty-nine-year-old builder Pat Keohane, for example, the *People* was able to voice the supposed feelings of Steve Wright's girlfriend Pamela Goodman hours after he was charged. Keohane explained to the paper that the forty-eight-year-old girlfriend of six years had said: 'I will always love Steve no matter what happens. I'm sure he's innocent. I don't know why they're doing this to him. When this is all over we will be back together again and start a new life.'

According to Keohane, Goodman was also reported to have said: 'During our time together he's always been a perfect gentleman to me. I can't imagine a future without him.' She continued:

'I know people will be talking but nobody knows Steve like I do. Our love for each other will get us through this nightmare. We just have to be strong. You don't stay with someone for five years only to walk out when they need you most. I hope to see Steve again soon to let him know I'm there for him in whatever way I can be. If he thinks I've turned against him then he will have nothing left. I'm just praying I will get him back. I've hardly eaten for three days.'

Walking the Streets: Media Whores

In order for news organisations to get to know the red-light district, reporters had to speak to the women who worked there and discover more about the serial killer's victims. This meant that journalists had to start work at the same time as the prostitutes. Most organisations had to operate a night shift so that, as one team finished work at 6 p.m., another would only just be starting.

We had already spent several evenings in the Portman Road area, but had not been there since the discovery of the last two victims in Levington. Cruising along Sir Alf Ramsey Way, we felt more conspicuous than ever. Almost at walking pace we had turned left into Portmans Walk from West End Road in search of a prostitute willing to talk to us about the girls. As a result the cars behind us had been forced to slow down to the same speed as us, and, as one overtook, the driver peered into our car as if to try to catch a glimpse of a kerb-crawler who might just be the killer. The look of disgust on his face made us sink into our seats. It was a hugely uncomfortable feeling and it made us realise just why business in the red-light district was at a low point.

And because business was at a low point, the women there had to find other means of making money. Many had caught on very quickly to the fact that they had something the media wanted – and this time it wouldn't involve sex, even if it still involved a certain amount of roadside negotiating. They had information, and the press with their deep pockets would have to pay for it. Not only that but some were so good at talking to the press and passing on their mobile phone numbers, that their faces became well known, almost gaining them celebrity status among their peers. One such prostitute was Lou.

At twenty-eight, Lou looked ten years older. Her £150-a-day heroin habit had clearly taken its toll on one of the older women working the streets of Ipswich. The mother of three children in care explained that normally she wouldn't ask for money, but because she was working, if we wanted to talk to her then it would cost us £40. It struck us that the cost of a five-minute interview had gone up in less than a week. The first time we filmed in the red-light area, girls would willingly talk for £20–£30, depending on how hard you haggled. We seldom had to haggle since it was clear these girls had fallen on hard times; the only minor concern was how to claim the expenses at work. It wasn't so much that you couldn't exactly ask for a receipt, more the look on your boss's face when he saw the claim for 'Prostitutes × 2 = £60' on your expense sheet.

By now Lou knew how much she was worth. She had been friends with the victims and, despite the damage drugs had done to her, she remained remarkably lucid. Over the course of a few days she had done interviews for most of the main television channels and national newspapers. This was her third for Sky. 'Media whore' is a term used to describe someone who loves being interviewed on TV, radio or by the print media. The double entendre was not lost on us.

Sometimes Lou would turn up during the day and offer herself for interviews.

'I don't want to be on the streets, especially at the moment with that man around, but I've got to if I'm to keep going. I could get the cash for my drugs by shoplifting and things like that but I'd go to prison,' she told Sky News. She continued:

Me and the girls that are still out each night are trying to be careful. We're staying close together and watching after each other. We try and take all the punters' reg numbers and I only go with those clients I know. I know Annette and I also knew Gemma Adams and Tania Nicol. They worked with us and they were also great fun. Netty and I went to school together. She was a laugh and really lovely to be with. I saw Paula on the Saturday she went missing in a car with a punter. She seemed OK then. It's a nightmare – I just can't believe that it has happened again. The police have got to get this guy quickly before he strikes again. It's really scary out there – you worry about who might be next.

The One That Got Away

'He seemed really nice. He looked like a businessman and he smelled nice too. The first time he picked me up he was the most decent bloke. It was the middle of winter and I was freezing when he pulled up. He took me to McDonald's and bought me a burger and coffee. When he saw how cold I was he put his jacket around me. He didn't even want to sleep with me that night but still paid me £60 and dropped me back at home. He was a very different man when he picked me up late last year.'

Lisa – her name has been changed – feels lucky to be alive. One night in December 2006, unbeknown to her, she was to come face to face with the killer, and, had it not been for one moment of panic, she could well have become victim number six.

'I'm not dumb. I know it can be really dangerous. I'd been picking up punters for about four years. The first week I worked I got raped. I've even gone with a bloke who's raped me before. You're scared, but you've got to do it and hope he gives you the money before you're attacked. You cross your fingers and say to yourself "Please be nice, please be nice." It doesn't help to be naive. You learn quick, like taking advice from the other girls. There was this bloke the girls had warned me about in a van. But when I saw him he offered me £60 up front. I'd already been waiting two hours so I thought, stuff it, I'll go with him. He battered me and raped me three times in the same night. He dropped me off and gave me an extra £20 to keep quiet.'

But Lisa was smarter now and she had learned which punters to trust and which not to trust.

'The second time I saw the businessman guy I did sleep with him – in his car. Again he was a nice guy. I'd stand on the corner of West End Road and he'd picked me up. We'd go to the Tesco car park in Copdock, he'd do what he had to do and then drop me off near London Road. Sometimes he could be really gentle, but when he wanted to be rough, he could be really rough. I told him a couple of times to back off and he would. He would always spend about an hour with me. I know he used to see Gemma, Paula and Annette. Actually, he was a regular to a lot of the girls. But I can't say if he knew Anneli and Tania.

'I didn't see him for a while and then in December last year he resurfaced. I can't remember exactly when it was but it was after Gemma had gone missing. But this time he was different. It was different. He was really scruffy, he looked trampy, was sweating lots and he smelt too. This time he took me to his house on London Road which he had never done before and instead of spending an hour with me, it was just fifteen minutes. Acting really strange, he went to open the door and then called me to follow him inside. He told me to take my clothes off and put them in a pile. His mind was somewhere else. He said he had family problems but wouldn't say what they were. I didn't know he had a wife and the flat didn't look like anyone else lived there. He'd keep moving about like he was nervous and looking out of the window all the time. I just wanted to get on with it. The problem was he couldn't get hard, and that had never happened before. Then he started pushing on me so hard that I couldn't get up and it scared me. Then someone in a car came back to the house – he looked out of the window and panicked. It was like I was with his evil twin brother.'

'You've got to leave now,' the man barked at her. She was glad to leave. She never saw him again, that is until his picture appeared in the paper.

The fact was, not only was the press covering a story that people wanted to read and watch with growing fascination, but it was bringing a social issue to the top of the news agenda. Suddenly people were being forced to ask why these five women, and potentially more, were being targeted. Why were they vulnerable? Who was supplying the drugs? How were they able to slide into such a desperate and sad situation? The media provided a platform upon which the debate could take place. Experts in the fields of drugs and prostitution were suddenly thrust into the spotlight, with bulletins being watched by millions each night and newspaper columns read by hundreds of thousands each day. They had an audience, and that audience was captivated.

And that forced politicians to get involved, too. In the House of Commons Tony Blair pledged his full support for the police in tackling the murders and at the same time condemned the horrific killings: 'We will do everything we can to support the police in the difficult and challenging work they do and I've every confidence they will perform their task well,' he said.

Not to be outdone, Conservative leader David Cameron followed suit: 'We all want this monster to be caught and locked up.' But perhaps it was the Liberal Democrat leader Menzies Campbell who summed up the problem better than most: 'Once again we have exposed the link between poverty, drug abuse and prostitution. We have to look at the law to see whether that adds to these women's vulnerability.'

Rightly or wrongly, the media had delved into the depths of each suspect's past, and the extent to and manner in which that had been done had clearly begun to frustrate the police, so much so that they brought it to the attention of the Attorney General. They expressed concern that press coverage was damaging their inquiry, and Lord Goldsmith appealed to editors to 'exercise restraint' in reporting developments in the investigation, warning that media organisations could find themselves in breach of the Contempt of Court Act which might prejudice and therefore jeopardise a criminal trial. 'The wide media and public interest in this police investigation is wholly understandable. However, in view of the concerns that some coverage may impede the police investigations, the Attorney General asks all parties to exercise restraint in their reporting' read the statement from the Attorney General's office. It continued:

Editors must avoid the publication of materials which may impede or prejudice the complex and ongoing investigations by the police and avoid the risk of prejudicing potential prosecutions or prejudging their outcome. Depending on the circumstances and information, this could include speculation or information relating to suspects' connections or other activities, or details of their background. In particular, the Attorney General urges all parties to take note of the risks in publishing material that asserts or assumes, expressly or implicitly, the guilt of any individual.

What did Steve Wright make of everything going on around him? Not only was the public able to watch the whole story being played out in the media, but Steve Wright was watching, too. He would buy local and national newspapers. He had multi-channel television. Was he in fact using the media to help keep one step ahead of the police? Was he using the information we were broadcasting – including press conferences at police headquarters where DCS Gull was being pushed by reporters to divulge all he knew – to make sure he wasn't caught? Was he smiling to himself each time the police discovered a new body, closely followed by the media? Was he watching us as we hunted evil? And was he enjoying his new-found notoriety – did he like his new nickname the 'Suffolk Strangler'? If he did, that enjoyment would be short-lived. For soon Wright would be in custody and within three days charged with five counts of murder.

Chapter Seven

Mondeo Man

Tony Blair, then just a normal MP met the owner of a house cleaning his new car, a Ford Mondeo. Tony Blair asked the man if he intended to vote Labour. 'No way,' he exclaimed, puffing out his chest, 'I'm voting Tory.' Blair could tell by his accent that he came from a working-class background, and he asked him why he wouldn't vote Labour. He replied, 'I used to vote Labour, but now I am successful. I've got a nice house. I go on good holidays. I've got this new Ford Mondeo. Why would I want to vote Labour?'

As reported in www.fordmondeoownersclub.co.uk

What motivates someone to kill and kill again? There is no simple answer. We have described how difficult it is to rely upon the statements of serial killers themselves – when, that is, they are prepared to speak at all about why they killed – and, indeed, how hard it is even to define the term 'serial killer'. There is a tendency, too, to pore over the early lives of serial killers in the hope that the clues to their later murderous careers can be found in, for example, their relationship with their father, their mother, their siblings, or as a result of the physical, mental or sexual abuse that they might have suffered when growing up.

This search for clues in the killers' distant past to explain why they 'did it' is understandable because it might well reveal some insights into why they kill, but it is probably never going to provide complete answers. Serial killers are only able to kill repeatedly if they target individuals from within groups that are vulnerable in some way, and young women involved in the sex industry are made vulnerable by inappropriate policing, as well as by a more widespread moralising about how they earn a living. The serial killer knows, too, that if he selects high-profile targets – captains of industry or politicians, for example – he's less likely to get away with it. The deaths of such individuals would be big news and thus put pressure on the police to catch the killer. In selecting less prominent, more vulnerable groups, the killer knows that the police may devote less time and resources to tracking him down.

It is still possible to make tentative suggestions about what motivates serial killers without having to dig too deeply into their childhoods. If we harness what is known about the killer's psyche, his sexual or offending history (where this is known), his work habits or his relationships more generally to the various typologies that we outlined in Chapter Three (Table 1, p. 81), it is possible to suggest what drove him to kill. We can, after all, explain many of the things that motivate us in life, and they are often put down to the influence that family or friends have had on us throughout our lives, or to the cultural values that surround us in society and which make certain types of behaviour preferred, or desirable.

We have not been able to interview Steve Wright, but, as we have argued, this is not necessarily a disadvantage now that we know how some serial killers respond. On the other hand, we have interviewed many people who knew him, including several young women who once worked in the sex industry. Some of these individuals prefer to remain anonymous, so we have taken care not to identify our sources. We have read virtually everything that has been written about Wright, although much of it was not always reliable or verifiable. For example, one website claimed that Wright was a member of the British National Party (BNP), but we could find no evidence to support this assertion. We also have the evidence that Wright left behind in the way that he killed and then disposed of his victims.

In Search of Wright's Life

Steve Gerald James Wright was born in Norfolk on 24 April 1958 – the day after St George's day – in married quarters at RAF West Beckham. His father, Conrad, was a corporal in the military police. The small West Beckham radar base had provided a long-range early warning system against enemy aircraft for north East Anglia and the area of the Wash, along with the approaches to the Midlands during the Second World War. The Wrights' house stood just yards from the base's entry gate where Steve Wright's father would stand at his security post. From there, he could see into the garden of the house.

'All I can remember was a cheeky, boisterous little boy running around the house. He was a big softie, really,' explained Conrad Wright, Steve's father, as he carried over two cups of piping hot coffee.

At the time of Wright's birth Conrad was in the RAF and he was to reach the rank of corporal before leaving for a career in the police. Wright's mother, Patricia, later divorced Conrad after she ran off with another man, but not before the marriage produced another son and two daughters. Steve Wright was eight when he watched his parents separate.

'I didn't think she would go through with it, but she did. That was the last I ever saw of her,' explained Conrad.

Eventually all four children went to live with their father. Social services offered him the choice of placing the children up for adoption since holding down his job as a policeman on the docks in Felixstowe while looking after four children was practically impossible.

'I couldn't just give them up. They were just little and Steve was old enough to remember what was going on. So that's when Valerie came in. She was the babysitter living next door.'

Soon she had moved in and began helping bring up Steve and his brother and sisters. Valerie and Conrad eventually married and had two children of their own, but Conrad's children would never accept Valerie as their mother. Far from it.

Because his father was in the RAF, Steve Wright moved around the world with him – wherever he was stationed – and went to school in countries like Malta and Singapore. After leaving school in England at sixteen with no qualifications, he began training for his Silver Service certificate at a hotel in Aldeburgh in Suffolk. Within a year the seventeen-year-old had joined the merchant navy and started working as a kitchen pot-washer on ferries sailing in and out of Felixstowe. Through a friend at that time, Wright met his first wife Angela O'Donovan from Milford Haven. The couple married in 1978, when Wright was just twenty, and together they moved to Wales. Within two years, the couple had a child. Wright was by now employed as a waiter in the

Queen's Grill on the transatlantic cruise liner the *QE2*.

Respite from the gruelling schedule on board came with trips ashore in countries all over the world. One favourite with the young, mostly male, crew was Thailand. For twenty-five-year-old Steve Wright, as for many other staff on the ship, this would be his first taste of the sex industry. And with so much time away, his marriage fell apart. But it was on the liner that he was to meet his second wife. Diane Cassell (who later changed her name by deed poll to Diane Cole) was working on board as a window dresser. Wright divorced Angela and in 1987 he married Diane in Braintree, Essex, largely because they wanted to run a pub and the brewery insisted on having married couples as tenants. The marriage was tempestuous and the couple continually rowed with one another. Diane described it as a 'total disaster and a nightmare'. Even so, they succeeded in getting a pub to run – the Ferry Boat Inn, in King Street, in the centre of the red-light area of Norwich.

Wright's work experience on the *QE2* seems to have impressed Greene King, the brewery that took over the Ferry Boat Inn after almost a decade of the pub being a free house. Wright was to be licensee of the pub for only a few months – between May and September 1988 – but over ten years later he also found work behind the bar at the Brook Hotel in Felixstowe, although he was fired for stealing from the till. Wright had other jobs too. He worked in a bingo hall as a caller, as a fork-lift truck driver for a company on the Hadleigh industrial estate in Ipswich and at the time of his arrest he worked dockside in Felixstowe.

Wright's passions were golf and gambling. He played golf at three different clubs – The Seckford Golf Club, Hintlesham Golf Club and he was a member of a golfing society based in the Brook Hotel in Felixstowe (from where he had been sacked), which went by the rather grand title of 'The Brook Residents International Golf and Notable Delinquents Society' (in other words, the Brigands). Friends at the Seckford remember him dressed entirely in black, and mingling with senior police officers on golf days. Wright liked to gamble, and one friend commented: 'All his money went on the horses – he's got a bit of a gambling problem'. His love of betting no doubt helps to explain why he didn't seem to last too long as an employee where he could have access to a till full of money and quite apart from being sacked from the Brook Hotel, he was asked to leave the bingo hall for the same reason.

'When Steve and Diane broke up he came and lived here with us again. There wasn't room upstairs so he just crashed here,' said Conrad, pointing to the rug in the middle of the living-room floor. 'I got him a job working in the ship mooring team down at the Felixstowe docks. And after a bit I helped him get a flat around the corner and fitted it out with furniture – you know, to help him get back on his feet. Then one day I get a call from work wondering where he was – he hadn't been seen for a while.'

Steve had in fact left the flat in Felixstowe, sold all the furniture and moved to Ipswich. Then one day Conrad received a call from his son pleading for him to come to Ipswich because 'they wouldn't let him have his things back'. Steve had been thrown out of his new flat, because he hadn't been keeping up with his rent and the landlord was refusing to let him have his belongings back until he paid up. In the end his father paid the outstanding £130 bill. This wasn't Steve's only debt. In all he owed around £40,000 to various people and soon found himself in the bankruptcy court. These were unhappy times for Steve Wright. His father explained that his son had twice tried to commit suicide.

'The first time it was the hose pipe into the car exhaust. When they found him he was close to death and was quickly taken to hospital. The second time he just swallowed a load of pills.'

After leaving the country for a brief spell in Thailand – during which time it appeared he'd married a Thai girl – he returned to Ipswich where he met, but did not marry, his current partner Pamela Goodman. They shared the same surname – Wright was her maiden name.

'It all changed when he met Pam,' explained Conrad.

When Wright was arrested he and Pam had been together for six years and were living in London Road, in the red-light area of Ipswich, after having moved there from a flat in Bell Close in the town. Neighbours there remembered that there was always a lot of 'banging about' in the flat, and that there had been complaints about the noise. There were problems in their relationship. Pam had a son who'd sometimes visit, but he and Steve didn't get on, which meant there was a lot of friction. Friends said they disliked each other so much that Pam even considered leaving Steve because they couldn't get on.

But that wasn't the only difficulty in the relationship. Until the beginning of 2006, their working lives allowed the couple to spend a good deal of time with each other. But when Pam started working nights the couple began passing like ships in the night. The only time they were together was the early part of the evening – and that meant their sex life was pretty non-existent. Steve Wright was already no stranger to the sex trade of Ipswich, but now that his sexual appetite wasn't being satisfied, he would turn more and more to the red-light district. And since his sexual needs were being met late at night in secluded areas of Ipswich or in the surrounding countryside, that left him more time to improve his golf handicap, which he'd got down to fifteen. The only real quality time the couple had together was at weekends – but instead he'd go out and play golf. That annoyed Pam, so she would ignore him for days on end.

Before they moved from Bell Close, Wright explained to his former neighbours that they were leaving the flat because they had 'come into money', and so he and Pam were going to live in a larger house.

'They had been talking about leaving Ipswich altogether. You know, move out of Suffolk. I think Pam came into money because of a death in the family, but something made them decide to move just a short distance to London Road,' explained a close friend of Steve and Pam who asked not to be named. 'Before they moved I would see them all the time at Uncle Tom's Cabin. She would come in on Sunday morning and he would go off and play golf. By three or four o'clock he'd be back. He would always look a bit out of place in the pub. It was a working man's pub really and he was always very smartly dressed. Immaculately ironed shirts, smart trousers and polished shoes. Pam said she always had to iron creases down the sleeves of his shirts because that's what he wanted. Lots of people used to feel he wanted everyone to think he had a better job than he did. And that's exactly what people did think, because so few people got close to him to find out he was a fork-lift truck driver.

'Pam would sometimes have one too many drinks in the afternoon, but Steve would always be in control. He'd have a couple of cigarettes and one or two pints of Carlsberg, but not get drunk. He'd stand, arms folded with his back to the bar, watching what everyone else was doing. If anyone walked in you would think he was the landlord. He was very private, and didn't seem to let anyone get close to him. You'd ask him how his day was. He'd say 'fine'. Ask if he'd been busy at work, and you'd get a 'yes' or 'no'. Ask if he wanted to play a game of pool, and his answer would be 'yeah, OK' or 'not now'. He and I played pool all the time, but there also wasn't much conversation from him. It wasn't that different when I went to their flat in Bell Close for dinner. Their place was really tidy and there was always lots of chocolate around to eat. Pam would cook and set the table and at dinner she did most of the talking while he sat and listened.'

Wright was also publicly fond of women, even if privately he seems to have harboured a great deal of anger about several women in his life. Married twice, and in a common-law relationship with Pam at the time of his arrest, he was described by the landlady of Uncle Tom's Cabin in Ipswich as 'a real ladies' man. Very attractive and well dressed. But something always made me feel a bit uncomfortable about Steve because he was a bit smarmy.' Another interviewee at the Brook Hotel remembered that Wright was 'popular behind the bar and was always up for a chat – especially with the ladies'. In other words, Wright was – at least initially – superficially charming, persuasive and seductive. Despite that, we know that his long-term relationships with his partners (and with his mother and stepmother) tended to break down – the marriage was a 'disaster' and a 'nightmare', according to his second wife, and it does not seem too fanciful to suggest that the noise that neighbours heard coming from their flat in Bell Close was related to arguments and disagreement. Nonetheless, one former male friend thought that Wright was a 'nice, lovely guy ... I thought, well, if he did it, how come he manages to hide something like that so well? We drink together, play golf together, go on holiday together. It's unbelievable – I've known him for years.'

Wright's past was 'unbelievable' to this friend because he was experienced at hiding certain aspects of his life, especially his fondness for young women who worked in the sex industry.

'When I walked into Uncle Tom's Cabin the day of Steve's arrest, I thought that a company was having its Christmas party in there because everyone was wearing suits. Then I saw all the cameras,' explained Steve's friend. 'Someone I knew came up to me and said: "Your mate Steve's been arrested for the murder of the five women." I couldn't believe it at first, but then, when you think back to what he was like, of all the people who came to the pub he was the person you knew least about. Pam was upstairs in pieces, crying and saying she didn't believe it was true. I went out and bought a newspaper that night and stayed with her until the morning. We did the crossword, but she just kept breaking down. Pam was given some medication to calm her down. All the time the media were downstairs, but she didn't want to talk to them.

'The police took away the pub landlord's van, which at the time I thought was odd. But then I remembered that Steve had borrowed it in the couple of weeks before he was arrested. He told the landlord he needed to move some rubbish so he gave Steve the keys. When he brought it back it didn't look like he'd been using it to move rubbish. In fact, it looked really clean. There had been some blue telephone cable in the back when Steve borrowed the van and the landlord remarked it was now missing. The police had found my, the landlord's and Steve's fingerprints inside so they wanted to eliminate us from their inquiries. They wanted to know all about the telephone cable which had gone missing. It makes you think, what did he use it for?

'Meanwhile, Pam wanted to see Steve. But she had to make do at first with a phone call. Officers had taken her mobile phone away so they gave her a police one – she was allowed a few minutes on the phone, but that was it. What she really wanted was to go and see him. It took weeks before they let her visit.'

Prostitutes who worked the streets in Norwich described Steve Wright as a 'regular client' in the 1980s and 1990s, and here we should remember that the red-light area of Norwich is concentrated around the Ferry Boat Inn, the pub that Wright briefly ran. Even up to a few weeks before his arrest prostitutes in Ipswich would describe a typical encounter with Wright in the following way:

I charged him the full £40 for straight sex. I'd describe him as a regular customer, someone who has been picking up girls for the last eight months or so. You often see him driving around in his blue Mondeo looking for girls even if he had picked you the night before. He didn't strike me as weird and never gave me any reason to believe that I was in danger. He'd just pick me up and then we'd go back to his house. Sometimes we'd go in the front door and other times through the patio doors at the back. It would just be a discussion about how much, the range of services and whatever he wanted. It was always straight sex – nothing out of the ordinary. The last time I saw him was three weeks ago. He picked me up off the street and took me back for sex. Then I saw him driving around the area the next night in the Mondeo. He appeared to be looking for other girls to pick up. I would say that he was confident. He never struck me as nervous with the girls.

However, not every prostitute was as matter-of-fact as this young woman, and another commented: 'I didn't want to get in the car with him and would never have got in the car with him. Most of the girls never got in the car with him. I never did business with him – he freaked me out so much.' Another said: 'The police were aware of him because he sometimes scared the girls that much – he did get narked when you didn't get in the car.' Part of the fear that these young women are describing seems to have something to do with the fact that, quite apart from his fondness for camouflage trousers, Wright sometimes liked to try and pick them up wearing high heels, a PVC skirt and a 'black woman's wig'. Several noted that he liked to cross-dress, enjoyed rough sex, and one or two said that they also called him the 'Silverback Gorilla' – because he was strong and stocky and they dreaded seeing him coming.

Father and Son

'Do you think your son murdered the five girls?' we asked Conrad Wright.

'If I could look him in the eyes, I would be able to tell straight away. Just one look in his eyes and I'd know.'

Conrad had travelled down to Belmarsh Prison in south-east London where Steve Wright was being held on remand awaiting his trial. He wasn't allowed to mix with the other prisoners, but he was allowed visitors. A planned trip south from Ipswich to visit his son had been delayed for twenty-four hours. He was told Steve wanted Pam to visit first.

'I felt like I was the prisoner,' said Conrad as he explained how his visit had gone. 'They made me stand in a square and checked inside my mouth, my hair and practically made me strip. I was then taken into a room and expected to talk to

Steve through glass. I sat and waited, until eventually someone came to tell me that Steve had decided he didn't want to
see me. I asked why not and whether they could go and ask
him again to see if he'd change his mind, and they told me it
was his right not to see me.'

Conrad didn't know why his son had a last-minute change
of heart, though he suspected that Pam's visit the previous
day had something to do with it. He hadn't enjoyed being
there anyway and was quite glad of an early exit.

'I just can't see Steve murdering those girls. He's a bloody
softie, and couldn't harm a rabbit. Look, does he seem like a
killer to you?' He showed us a photograph of him and Steve
standing shoulder to shoulder at his daughter's wedding.
'But he always seemed to be in the right place. He had a pub
in Norwich where those other girls were killed and he was
on the *QE2* with that Suzy Lamplugh – makes you wonder,
doesn't it? But I can't see how he could have killed the girls
in Ipswich without someone else's help. Really, I feel more
for the five girls' families than I do for my own son. I mean,
how can anyone murder someone like that and just throw
them over the hedge like that?'

Conrad said his children blamed Valerie for the way Steve
turned out, and so now most of the former RAF serviceman's
family has little or nothing to do with him. He fears also that
one or two relatives may refuse to turn up to his funeral. As
tears welled up in his eyes Conrad left the room.

Trying to Make Sense of a Life

What should we conclude from the picture that emerges from
these fragments of Wright's life, fragments only offered after
the high-profile arrest and conviction of a man for the murder

of five young women? Those interviewed were naturally inclined to look back to see if the person they were talking about really was just a friend, a golfing partner, a client – or a serial killer. In such circumstances some wanted to exonerate themselves – he was a 'nice, lovely guy' – while others wanted to impress us that they always knew something wasn't quite right – 'he freaked me out so much'. Yet Wright will not be the first or the last client of a prostitute who wants to cross-dress, or who likes it 'rough', and the psyche of the serial killer is fascinating precisely because he is able to present one face in public, but quite another in private. In short, serial killers are accomplished liars, capable of being charming golfing or holiday companions, while all the time keeping a secret – maintaining a façade – which they will never reveal. It's as if they are inhabiting a parallel universe.

Such a dual world was inhabited by Dennis Nilsen – the serial murderer of at least fifteen young men between 1979 and 1983 – and by Peter Moore, who killed four men in as many months in 1995. Moore owned a string of cinemas in North Wales, and regularly appeared on BBC Wales, the very model of a successful local businessman. He was interviewed by the BBC about his latest venture just three days before killing his first victim in September 1995. Nilsen was a former soldier, policeman and, at the time of his arrest, a civil servant working at the Kentish Town Job Centre, where it is also likely that he gained access to many of the young men he eventually murdered. According to Nilsen's biographer the detectives who eventually arrested him were shocked by 'the fact that it was possible to kill undetected for four years in a London suburb', which explains how well a 'successful' serial killer can inhabit this dual world by presenting one face to the public – to friends, colleagues and neighbours – and another in private. There was another reason to explain Nilsen's success (something shared by Peter Moore) at remaining undetected for as long as he did, and which sheds some light on Wright. Nilsen and Moore largely targeted young gay men, whose disappearances were often simply not noted, or, if they were, subsequent police invest-igations were less than satisfactory. Indeed, Nilsen was not finally caught because the police put a stop to his activities, but because other tenants in the house that he shared called out Dyno-Rod to unblock the drains. Nilsen had been dis-posing of the dismembered body parts of his victims down the lavatory.

Is it possible to make some sense of what we know about Wright, and see how this might help us to make observations about his possible motivation? Even if we exclude some of the more extreme comments made about him, we are still left with some clues worth pursuing.

First, the description that he was 'smarmy': obsessively flattering, unpleasantly suave; too smooth and sophisticated. No doubt Wright was well-practised at using such techniques to chat up women he was interested in, which perhaps relates to the role he played and which was developed on the QE2. Wright was never 'nervous with the girls' – he was an experi-enced and plausible punter who knew what he wanted and how to go about conducting business with a prostitute. In all of this he was presenting a face to the world that seemed knowledgeable and experienced – even trustworthy. Yet we also know that his second marriage was a disaster, and that when the smarm didn't work – when women chose not to be impressed by his smoothness – he could get 'narked'. Narked is a good old-fashioned English description for being annoyed, upset, irritated, and it probably also explains why neighbours in Bell Close complained about the noise and 'banging about' they heard between Pam and Wright.

Perhaps it also explains why he liked it 'rough' with the young women he paid for sexual services; having it 'rough' with them was also a way to relieve his stress when things weren't going his way, and when his gambling got out of control and Pam had to ask for money. When he was narked his anger at women was also at its most obvious.

Several people commented that Wright was 'well dressed', and his former golfing friends remembered him as being dressed 'all in black'. Clothes were clearly very important to Wright; they were the means by which he could fit in, and also engage in his fantasies. He was both a soldier in his combat fatigues (surely also another form of fantasy?), while at the same time he wanted to cross-dress, wear women's wigs and a PVC skirt. Clothes allowed him to feel that he was connected to a more formal world of ocean liners and golfing societies and also to a more basic one of punters and hand jobs, blow jobs and straight sex. Peter Moore also used to dress all in black – although in his case black leather – both to frighten his victims but also to give himself a sense of power that comes from wearing another's skin. Wearing black leather gave Moore all the inherited cultural iconography of motorbikes, leather jackets, sado-masochism and a more private world of 'tops' and 'bottoms', while wearing the right golfing clothes gave Wright a certain legitimacy, a sense of having a place in society and of being accepted.

But Wright was never satisfied with this place, even if he was accepted, for he knew that, despite wearing the right clothes, it was all a sham. He was not the person he was pretending to be, and the lies he told himself and others couldn't mask the reality of the life that he was living, the stresses that it brought, and the anger that he felt. We also know that, while most of his violence was taken out on others, Wright had attempted suicide twice – the last time in 2000 when he was found in a shabby Ipswich hotel having taken an overdose. And his explanation for his and Pam's departure from Bell Close – that they'd 'come into money' and so were looking for a bigger place to live in – is interesting. The phrase 'come into money' smacks of old-fashioned inheritances and wills being read, as much as it does a win on the horses. Was either explanation true? Probably not. It is just as likely that a combination of everyday circumstances eventually forced Pam and Wright to find new accommodation, but the point is surely that he felt he needed to give an explanation, and one that was out of the ordinary. We would venture that Wright was not happy with being ordinary. He wanted to be extraordinary; he wanted to inhabit a world in which he had status and power (perhaps like the people he met cruising the world on the *QE2*); a world in which he could be a somebody rather than a nobody, and where the banality of his sad, failing life could be given meaning.

This desire to be extraordinary is the final point that emerges from listening to those who knew and described Wright to us, and it is consistent with all we know about other serial killers. There is a tension between the person Wright wants to be and the person he is, and what he had become. In his 'dual world' he is attractive, well-dressed, smooth and sophisticated; women fall for his charms and he plays golf (sometimes with police officers), and he is sophisticated enough to belong to a club that joshingly, and rather pretentiously, calls itself 'The Brook Residents International Golf and Notable Delinquents Society', a title redolent of old-fashioned refinement, where the words 'residents', 'international', 'notable' and 'society' rub shoulders with the playful but slightly self-congratulatory 'delinquents' – suggesting a carefree world of money and leisure. This is the world Wright wanted to inhabit.

His real world is one of gambling debts, suicide attempts in shabby hotels, failed relationships and visits to prostitutes in a PVC skirt. His real world is filled with secrets and pretences, but he still can't wait for Pam to go out to work so that he can bring young women home to have sex with him, because it is then, and only then, that he feels important, powerful, feels that he has the status he believes he deserves. It is then, and only then, that he feels alive, although that life – the life that he craves – brings with it death.

Biography and Unsolved Murders

Natalie Pearman has been described as a 'walking portrait of an ordinary girl', and in truth she did not stand out as anyone out of the ordinary. Her background was similar to those of Gemma Adams and Tania Nicol, and of Julie, our first guide to the red-light district of Ipswich. She had four brothers and sisters, a cat named Lucy, and she lived with her mother and stepfather in a neat council house on the edge of the village of Mundesley, half an hour's drive north of Norwich. Natalie took ballet lessons, liked drawing and had wanted to join the RAF, but a part-time job she took at fourteen in the village's takeaway burger bar proved to be her passport into a completely different world.

Within a year Natalie was in care, and within two – when she was sixteen – she had changed her name to Maria, dyed her hair blonde and was working the streets in 'the Block' in Norwich. Her patch was outside the Ferry Boat Inn, where she charged £15 for a hand job, £20 for a blow job and £30 for straight sex. Her killer has never been caught, but

Natalie/Maria's naked body was found dumped in a lay-by just outside the town's boundaries in 1992.

What was it that propelled this ordinary girl with dreams of a career in the RAF to turn to prostitution? How did she come to fall out of the bottom of village life and find her way to the nearest big town, where she changed her name and her destiny? Was it just the self-indulgence and self-destruction of youth, or were there stronger forces at work? And, more than this, who was her killer?

The campaigning journalist Nick Davies of the *Guardian* has no doubt about what happened to Natalie, or the root cause. For him, the key is to remember that the Pearmans were 'poor . . . they were trapped at the bottom of the financial cliff. They had enough to get by, but no more.' Natalie had no money for Brownies, or to go on school trips, and, gradually, as one crisis after another hit the family she had to stop ballet lessons, too. Prostitution provided her with the sort of money that she could barely have dreamed of, and while the short life it gave her was a grotesque parody of the life that Natalie had wanted, she wasn't poor any more. For Davies this wasn't a question of Natalie being forced to do something that she didn't want to, but rather a conscious choice that she had made. For, when she looked at her life:

> She saw that she was trapped and when she looked at her future, it was even worse – getting pregnant, getting married, getting a house and stewing slowly in front of a television for forty years. What else was there?

We do not need to agree with Davies's conclusion that Natalie made a conscious choice to become a prostitute to accept that many young people drift from one place to another as they reach adolescence, and in doing so make themselves vulnerable in various ways and that some will turn to prostitution. However, what Davies does reveal through his very sympathetic and tragic portrayal of Natalie is, once again, the dangers faced by women who turn to prostitution in Norwich and elsewhere, and the ability of their attackers to escape justice.

Natalie wasn't the only young woman involved in prostitution to have been murdered in Norwich. Michelle Bettles was murdered in similar circumstances in 2002, and Kelly Pratt has never been seen again since arranging to meet a client in a pub in Norwich in 2000.

Their deaths and the links to Wright's profile seem to be more than mere coincidence. Wright was at one point the landlord of the pub at the centre of Norwich's red-light district, and we also know that he continued to travel to and from Norwich to buy sex. Several of the young women we spoke to claimed that he was a 'regular' client throughout the 1980s and 1990s, perhaps visiting them as often as twice a week. Also, just after the murder of Natalie Pearman in Norwich, Mandy Duncan disappeared from the red-light area of Ipswich in 1993 and, like Kelly Pratt, her body has never been found. Six years later the naked body of Vicky Hall – who had lived in the Suffolk village of Trimley St Mary (a short distance from Ipswich) – was found in a ditch near Stowmarket. Trimley St Mary is within a few minutes' drive of the A14 that runs between Cambridge and Felixstowe.

Some might argue that linking Wright with these murders is unfair, that many men use prostitutes both in Ipswich and Norwich, and that some of these punters would also have legitimate reasons for travelling back and forth across Suffolk. After all, the two ports at the extremity of the

Home comforts at number 79. Wright liked nothing better than partner Pam's home-cooked lasagna, followed by a Mars bar or a Toffee Crisp.

Wright's kitchen at his London Road home after the police had searched for any evidence linking him with the five victims.

Wright enjoyed a night in front of the television watching soap operas. He'd later slip on his trainers and take Pam to work.

Cushions removed for forensic examination, Wright's sofa stands on its end after thorough police searches.

Wright admitted he'd had sex with one prostitute on his bed, but claiming he feared Pam might detect their scent on the sheets, said he'd insisted on having sex with girls only on the floor.

Wright is captured on CCTV kerb-crawling in the red-light district on 30 October shortly before 11 p.m. on the night Tania Nicol disappeared.

Carpet fibres taken from the foot-well of Wright's Ford Mondeo were found in Tania Nicol's hair. Seven flecks of Paula Clennell's blood were found on the back seat.

A trace amount of semen DNA gave low level DNA that could have originated from Wright

Police found bloodstains on Steve Wright's reflective jacket that matched Annette Nicholls' and Paula Clennell's DNA profile. It suggested Wright had become sloppy.

Wright used industrial type gloves to get rid of his victims. Police found three identical pairs in the driver's door pocket.

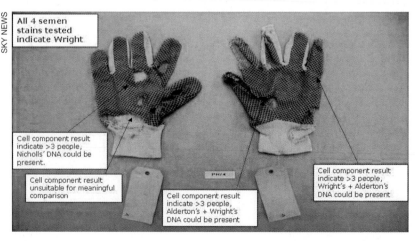

All 4 semen stains tested indicate Wright

Cell component result indicate >3 people, Nicholls' DNA could be present.

Cell component result unsuitable for meaningful comparison

Cell component result indicate >3 people, Alderton's + Wright's DNA could be present

Cell component result indicate >3 people, Wright's + Alderton's DNA could be present

Steve Wright kept partner, Pam Wright, in the dark about his use of Ipswich's prostitutes. While she worked nights, he began to kill.

Steve Wright's father Conrad attended court each day. He claimed that if he could look his son in the eye, he would know if he was telling the truth.

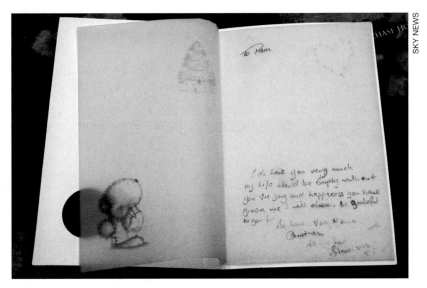

In a Christmas card to Pam, Steve Wright explains how happy she had made him. He'd already killed by the time she received it.

Courtroom Number One, on the move. The jury of nine men and three women visited Wright's house, and the four countryside locations where the bodies were found.

The jury stand beside Belstead Brook in Hintlesham where the body of Gemma Adams was discovered.

Wright at a family wedding. His smile conceals the unhappiness inside, which led to him twice attempting to commit suicide.

Wright is driven from Ipswich Crown Court. To the left of the police officer, his eyes can be seen peering out at the jeering crowds as he begins life behind bars.

Flowers mark the spot where the body of final victim Paula Clennell was found just one hundred metres from that of Annette Nicholls. Police said it appeared she had been tossed aside carelessly and in haste.

county – Harwich and Felixstowe – are specifically designed to cater for commercial traffic travelling to the Continent. However, we would suggest that this is more than just the everyday habits of the everyday Suffolk punter who wants to travel to the red-light areas of another town or city. Peter Sutcliffe visited the red-light areas of several different northern towns, especially when the police were busy in a particular red-light area following the discovery of another of his victims. Their activity meant that he murdered elsewhere, and we should remember that distance between murder scenes also prevents the police from linking up a series of murders – at least initially. But we cannot ignore the fact that Ipswich and Felixstowe are within the boundaries of the same police force, and that there is an element of chance that comes with travel. A committed serial killer experienced in his murderous trade begins to vary the places in which he murders, depending on the opportunities that might present themselves. He begins to push the geographic boundaries of his killing zone and the circumstances in which he might kill. This in turn gives him an even greater sense of satisfaction and power.

There are other links beyond geography, between these unsolved and historical murders and the five murders in Ipswich. For example, it seems significant that many of these unsolved murders involved strangulation, and that those bodies discovered were naked or semi-naked. Vicky Hall's clothes, for example, have never been found and this serves to reduce the amount of forensic evidence available to the police. And several bodies – notably those of Mandy Duncan and Kelly Pratt – have never been found at all. Clearly their killer knew how to dispose of a body without being observed, and what it took for that body to remain undetected. In short, their killer was 'organised', rather than 'disorganised'. It is more than mere chance that the bodies of Gemma and Tania were very carefully discarded – in other circumstances they might never have been found – and that the bodies of all five of the Ipswich victims were naked, and that strangulation was the most likely cause of death.

Wright's relationship to these historical and unsolved murders also helps to answer one of the questions that we were asked by almost everyone interested in the case from the beginning of the police investigation – 'why now?' Why did the killings start in late 2006? As we have emphasised, in our experience no one wakes up one night, decides to become a serial killer and then acts upon that decision. There is a history to the making of a serial killer, and this history also explains why the killer is more often than not already known to the police for one reason or another. We first speculated that the Ipswich killer might have just been released from prison, and was resuming a violent past that had been interrupted by his imprisonment. However, it would seem that Wright was simply good at what he did, chose his target group well and was knowledgeable enough about forensics to avoid detection for as long as he did. Attributing these other murders to Wright may seem unjust, but we should also remember that just about every serial killer who has been apprehended in Britain is suspected of having committed many more murders than those for which he was eventually charged. The cases of Harold Shipman, Peter Sutcliffe and Fred and Rosemary West, to name just a handful, illustrate this point.

We do not, however, link Wright to the disappearance of twenty-five-year-old Suzy Lamplugh (a name mentioned in conversation by Wright's father, Conrad) in July 1986. Suzy was an estate agent working in Fulham who left her office to show a 'Mr Kipper' a house in Shorrolds Road. She was never seen again, and her body has never been found. There has been some speculation that Wright may have been connected with her murder, because, prior to taking up a job as an estate agent, Suzy had been a beautician on the *QE2*, and would have come into contact with Wright. A former steward who knew them both told the *Sun*: 'Steve knew Suzy pretty well.'

While there are similarities between Suzy's disappearance and Wright's *modus operandi* – most obviously that her body has never been found – there are simply too many dissimilarities to tie Wright into her disappearance. As we have established, Wright's preferred target group was young, vulnerable women working in the sex industry in Norfolk and Suffolk, rather than young estate agents working in London. It is unlikely that Wright would have felt comfortable killing in this environment, and we should remember, too, how important geography was to him for the disposal of the bodies of his victims.

The Motivation Question

Looking again at the four classic types of serial killer discussed in Chapter Three (Table 1, p. 81), we can immediately eliminate the first two – visionary and mission. This is because there is no evidence either that Wright heard voices – from God, the Devil or anyone else encouraging him to rid the world of prostitutes – or that he was on some self-appointed mission to do so. His impulse to kill was neither a result of mental illness nor a feeling that somehow the world was a poorer place because young women worked as prostitutes. Quite the reverse. Wright had been a regular client of young women who sold sexual services, many of them for several years.

Nor does Wright's motivation seem to have been extrinsic. In other words, he was not killing, for example, because he was being paid to do so, as if he was a hit man, and nor were these murders linked to some wider political point that he might have been trying to make. The murders seem to have been intrinsically motivated – linked to Wright's psychological make-up – and we therefore have to consider the psychological benefits that he gained from committing these crimes, which brings us to the remaining two types of serial killers that we have discussed.

But before considering these final two 'classic' types of serial killer – power/control and hedonistic – it is also worth considering whether Wright was 'act'- or 'process'-focused, based on what we know about how he killed. By 'act'-focused we mean that the killings were done swiftly. In other words, it was important for the killer to achieve the death of his victim. In such a case death would be immediate, decisive and swift, and the killer would not need a reaction from the victim – such as pleading for her life – prior to taking the victim's life. On the other hand if the killer is 'process'-focused, certain words would have to be said, or acts performed, before the killer actually wanted to kill. Thus the process-focused killer enjoys the terror the victim experiences, and so he kills slowly – he'll stab, for example, parts of the body that will cause pain, but not death; he'll strangle but revive the victim so that he can do it again, and again. Even after death has occurred the process-focused killer continues with the removal of, for example, clothing, pieces of jewellery or certain body parts – often the sexual organs.

And we also know that there are various phases in a serial murder, and, while the killer does not need to go through each of these phases, a consideration of whether they did (or, indeed, which phases they ignored) also helps to throw some light upon the killer's motivation. The five phases in a serial murder are: fantasy, stalk, abduction, kill and, finally, disposal of the body.

However, just as we warn that a killer might display behaviours of different types of serial killers, so we should bear in mind that some serial killers will also vary the way they kill depending on the circumstances in which they find themselves. For example, a killer might not be able to dispose of his victim's body in the preferred way, through fear of being observed, and so might simply abandon the victim's body at the first opportunity.

While a killer might not necessarily go through each of these phases, what is more certain is that in all cases of serial killing there is a fantasy phase – for example, sexual, demonic or acquisitive. Fantasy is an integral part of the killing process and is shaped and developed over time. The fantasy matures and it is often the basis for the killer's masturbatory behaviour. This is a very powerful phase, as the fantasy propels the killer into murder, because that fantasy mirrors the needs, motivations or hoped-for gains the killer expects to achieve through the killing itself. Think again about how a serial killer will often inhabit what we have described as a 'dual world'.

Here you should also remember our warning that the killer might not go through each phase in a serial murder. For example, whether the killer goes through the stalking phase varies, depending on time or opportunity. The killer might simply see a victim who fits his fantasy, but he will not have the time to stalk her; alternatively, the opportunity to abduct this victim presents itself and so he simply moves from fantasy to abduction. Stalking too is often an associated feature of the organised killer. What is of interest here is that, in conversation with serial killers, it is usually during this phase that the killer begins to objectify his victim. The victim is no longer seen as a human being but becomes an object divorced from the reality of the killer's world, seen as some 'thing' to be used. Indeed, in talking to some serial killers they still describe their victims as objects; they rarely, in our experience, use the names of their victims, but instead refer to, for example, 'the third time I killed', or 'the last one', or 'the Scottish woman' – if, that is, they speak at all.

The third phase in a serial murder is abduction, but here we should also remember that not all serial killers have to abduct. Dennis Nilsen, for example, was able to entice his victims home with him, as were the Wests. Robert Black, however, carefully planned his abductions of young girls. We know how he operated because a few of his victims survived an attempted abduction. Teresa Ann Thornhill was attacked on 28 April 1988. She was fifteen at the time – outside Black's normal target range of pre-pubescent girls – but she was slight and small, and looked much younger than her age. In their 1995 book *The Murder of Childhood*, Ray Wyre and Tim Tait describe how Teresa was walking back to her house in Nottingham when a blue transit van passed her:

> I saw the driver get out and open the bonnet of the engine. As I walked level with the van the man shouted 'oi' to me. I looked towards him to make sure he was talking to me. I couldn't see anybody else about. I ignored him, looked away and carried on walking. Then he shouted 'can you fix engines?' I replied 'no, I can't' . . . I suddenly felt the man grab me from behind. I screamed and tried to struggle free. He picked me up and carried me across the road to the big blue van. I was still screaming and fighting to get away . . . he then put his big hand over my mouth, covering my nose. With his hand over my face I felt as if I was going to pass

out, so I bit him on his hand. This forced him to release his hand from my face. I then bit him on the arm and screamed again . . . I think that it was at this point that I knocked his glasses off. As he held me he opened the driver's door of the van and tried to bundle me inside. I fought with all my strength and used . . . my feet to push backwards and stop him from getting me inside. I think he said something like 'get in, you bitch,' as we were struggling.

This attack is very interesting for several reasons. First, it suggests that Black planned what he was doing, and that he had developed a method for overcoming a child whom he saw as a suitable victim. For example, he believed (incorrectly, as it happens) that Teresa was younger than she was, and, crucially, that she was alone. In fact a boyfriend heard Teresa's screams and came to her aid. Second, we can also see that Black tried to engage Teresa's sympathies (a technique also used by Myra Hindley) and asked her to help him overcome a problem – his engine – although this was merely an excuse to get her closer to the van so that he could bundle her inside. Finally, it reveals something of the bravery of Teresa and her strategy for overcoming her assailant. She screamed, she bit, she knocked his glasses off, she used her feet and her strength to prevent Black getting her inside his van, and we can see in Black's response to her – 'get in, you bitch' – his frustration at his inability to overcome Teresa, and thus achieve his objective.

The fourth phase is the murder – and we have already drawn attention to whether the killer was 'act'- or 'process'-focused, while the fifth and final phase is disposal. In other words, how did the killer dispose of the body? Was it hidden or buried, making the body difficult to discover, or did the killer simply leave the scene and abandon the body so that it was in full view and therefore likely to be spotted relatively easily?

Let's consider Wright from these perspectives. Was he 'act'- or 'process'-focused, and what phases did he go through prior to killing and abandoning the bodies of his victims? What more can we say in relation to his likely motivation based on the remaining two types of serial killers – power/control and hedonistic?

We know that Wright disposed carefully of the bodies of his victims; that he did not need to abduct – he was a 'punter' and a client and so he did not need to go through the same planning as Black did when trying to snatch a victim like Teresa. Further, we know that fantasy – dressing up – played an important part in his behaviour. (Was he perhaps fantasising about becoming a prostitute too, so that when he killed he was in effect attempting to kill this fantasy?) We might also speculate that he carefully watched the many young women involved in the sex industry in Ipswich and Norwich, trying to identify those who were most vulnerable and who best fitted his needs; noting who was new to the streets, how they looked and what they were addicted to (and which he might well have been able to supply). In other words, his victims were likely to have been part of his fantasy life before he murdered them.

However, there are also some gaps in our knowledge. We do not know the precise time between the young women getting into the car with Wright and when they were eventually murdered, and nor do we know where the murders took place. Did he keep them for a long time, or were their deaths quick? This makes it difficult to determine whether he was act- or process-focused, although we might reasonably conclude that to have kept his victims for some time he would have needed access to a house, garage or lock-up where he could indulge in the killing process for a longer period of time. And while we know that Pam worked nights, thus giving Wright the opportunity to take prostitutes back to the house, there were neighbours to consider, and of course Pam would return in the morning. However, we do know that his victims were often strangled. Strangulation can be a particularly personal form of death, with the killer literally feeling and experiencing life being squeezed out of his victims, sometimes even watching the look on his victim's face as this is being done. Did Wright strangle and then revive his victim so as to be able to 'kill' again and again?

This might seem like the stuff of movies, but we know, for example, from statements he made to the police, that Peter Moore, as a process-focused killer, kept his second victim Edward Carthy in a constant state of fear prior to his murder. Moore took Edward to an isolated forest in Wales (where they would not be observed or disturbed) and then ordered him out of his car. He had Edward strip and then showed him the knife with which he would eventually kill him, before stabbing him repeatedly about the body, but not anywhere that would be fatal; he talked to him all the time and clearly enjoyed the power and control he was able to exercise. And while, as we have shown, we must never take the statements of serial killers at face value, we can perhaps accept Moore's version of events in this case; without his testimony the police would never have known that Edward had been killed at all, or where his body could be found.

A forest in remote North Wales is far more isolated than the network of small villages clustered around Ipswich, and it is therefore unlikely that Wright would have risked toying with his victims for as long as Moore seems to have toyed with Edward. We also have to remember that all Wright's five Ipswich victims were drug addicts, and it may well be that their addiction offered him other opportunities to prolong the killing process.

What might he have gained from doing so? With serial killers each victim fulfils a psychological need. For example, Nilsen suggested to his biographer that he wanted company, and not to feel abandoned or lonely in the morning, when the young men who were his targets would leave. He wanted to have sex with his victims, too, but their deaths also made easier for him the sad, stark reality that they would remain with him in his flat for ever. Their deaths made him feel connected to a world in which people had friends, shared a drink at the end of the working day – in other words to a normal world.

We discuss below the broader psychological needs that the deaths of Wright's victims fulfilled for him, but more immediately the deaths of his victims would seem to have been related to his anger and his feelings of worth and inadequacy – about who he was and what he had achieved. Their deaths were a way of gaining power and status in his life, because they allowed him to be in charge, to call the shots. Tragically, in these circumstances it is more than likely that he would have prolonged their suffering for as long as possible, depending on the specific circumstances he found himself in with each victim, and his confidence about whether or not he was going to be disturbed. In short, he would seem to have been process- rather than act-focused, although it is still impossible to say with any certainty how long this process would have lasted, or to describe the specific circumstances in which he killed.

Putting aside such speculation, we can say with greater certainty that Wright disposed of the bodies of several of his victims very carefully. The bodies of Gemma Adams and Tania Nicol were not meant to be found. It is true that the bodies of Paula Clennell and especially Anneli Alderton and Annette Nicholls were discovered much more quickly – almost as if Wright wanted them to be found (and which also suggests that he wanted to be caught and stopped) – but even so the care with which all of the bodies were stripped of forensic evidence suggests that Wright exercised some control and organisation over their disposal. He also posed two of the bodies in a crucifix position – perhaps to deflect attention away from himself. This is likely to have been prompted by media speculation about the bodies of Tania and Gemma being found in water, which might imply that the killer had religious motives. As far as we are aware their clothes were not removed as 'trophies', but rather as a way of preventing their murders being connected forensically to Wright. It is perfectly feasible that some items of his victims' clothing were kept and hidden by Wright, but at the moment this is no more than speculation.

At several police press conferences we asked if there was any evidence of sexual activity on the bodies of Wright's victims, as opposed to evidence of sexual assault. No doubt this would be difficult to determine, as we also have to remember how these vulnerable young women earned their living. Unsurprisingly, therefore, the police were unable to answer this question, although from the evidence we have been able to gather it would seem that Wright was sexually competent. In other words, while some of the young women who had sex with Wright described how he sometimes liked it 'rough', none of them suggested that he wasn't able to achieve penetration or ejaculation. It is therefore safe to conclude that sexual activity, in whatever guise, took place between Wright and his victims.

All this might suggest that sex was at the root of Wright's behaviour, but such a conclusion, while plausible, misses the point about what motivated him to murder. Based on what we have described above, sex was not in itself enough for Wright to get what he wanted. For that his victims had to die (not, we have suggested, a quick process), although we would also argue that he does not fit the category of a hedonistic serial killer – killing for the thrill of it. Rather, we should see Wright as a power/control serial killer, and conclude that the power/control that he desired through these young women's murders is rooted in the dual world that had become his life.

Wright – by killing his victims, by evading the police for as long as he did, by creating an insatiable media interest in this case, by becoming a serial killer – was in effect putting meaning, power and status back into a life that he felt had been denied all these things – with every failed marriage, every sacking from another job, and every bad bet on the horses. Through the deaths of Gemma, Tania, Paula, Anneli and Annette – and, as we have argued the deaths of (at the very least) Natalie, Michelle, Kelly, Mandy and Vicky – Wright became the man he always wanted to be. In their murders he was at his most 'smarmy' (and narked), and through their murders he was able to become the sophisticated, well-travelled man in charge of his own destiny – like the men he had met on the QE2, or the men that he played golf with and went on holiday with. The deaths of these sad, vulnerable young women allowed him to feel in his own eyes 'notable', 'international' and a 'resident' who was rightly a member of 'society'. Their deaths allowed him to think for a moment that his life wasn't after all banal and ordinary. Their deaths made him feel as he had always wanted to feel – powerful and extraordinary. Of course, these murders have also made him a 'delinquent' of a quite infamous kind, and in a completely different way from that which the Brook Residents International Golf and Notable Delinquents Society had intended.

Chapter Eight

Justice – But Few Answers

'Why, after all, can't lawyers act as sensible people?' demanded Mr Justice Darling . . .

'It would be difficult to believe,' persisted counsel, 'that the same number could come up at a roulette table five times in succession, but if it happened you would not be entitled to convict the croupier as a dishonest man.'

'If I saw it happen,' observed the Lord Chief Justice, 'and the same people were at the table all the time I should grow suspicious.'

Exchange between Lord Chief Justice Darling and Mr Marshall Hall in the appeal of George Joseph Smith, July 1915

George Joseph Smith, aka Oliver George Love, Charles Oliver James, Henry Williams and John Lloyd, was found guilty of the murders of Bessie Mundy, who was found dead in her bath in 1912, Alice Burnham, who died in similar circumstances in Blackpool the following year, and Margaret Lofty, who was also found dead in her bath in Highgate in December 1914. All three women had gone through a form of marriage with Smith (who was in fact already married), and had then made a will in favour of their 'husband' before tragically drowning in their baths – a result, claimed Smith, of each woman suffering from an epileptic fit. Smith, who never confessed to any of the murders, was nonetheless found guilty at his trial – despite the absence of actual physical evidence to convict him – but the jury was asked simply to come to a conclusion about the awful, tragic pattern of what happened to Smith's 'wives'. He was duly convicted.

At his appeal in front of the Lord Chief Justice, Smith's counsel, Mr Marshall Hall, claimed that what is now known as 'similar fact evidence' about the deaths of Bessie, Alice and Margaret should not have been introduced into the original trial and that therefore Smith should have been found not guilty.

The Lord Chief Justice was incredulous about Mr Hall's lack of 'sense', and, using the example provided by Smith's counsel, remained convinced that if the same number did indeed come up at a roulette table five times in succession he at least would be 'suspicious', no matter what Mr Hall argued. Try putting yourself in the same position as the Lord Chief Justice. How would you react if the same numbers cropped up on five consecutive weeks in the National Lottery? Would you find this unusual and outside the boundaries of chance, or simply a remarkable coincidence, just one of those things? How would you have analysed the deaths of three new brides, all of whom seemed to have drowned in their baths shortly after they were married? In any event, Smith's appeal was dismissed and he was hanged shortly after, and to this day *Rex v. Smith (1915)* is still used to allow evidence of similar crimes – or a pattern of crimes – to be introduced as evidence in court.

More than ninety years later another serial killer would deny his involvement in murder, this time the deaths of five young women. Like George Joseph Smith, he would have had us believe that the fact that his DNA was found on the bodies of three of his victims and that there was other evidence that connected him to all five did not imply his guilt in their murder, but was, rather, simply a coincidence. Steve Wright made no secret of the fact that he bought sexual services from these women (with the exception of Tania Nicol, whose acne, he claimed, 'put him off'), which would explain why his DNA and fibre evidence were found on their bodies. And, as Timothy Langdale QC, who was defending Wright, explained, 'the defence challenges the assertion made that these findings suggest he [Wright] was responsible for their deaths as opposed to someone who had contact with them as a prostitute'. In other words, the fact that Wright paid for sex with the five women did not make him a killer; in much the same way, George Joseph Smith had argued that his wives' drowning in the bath was as a result of their medical conditions and not down to him. In both cases, it would be for the prosecution to prove that this was not so and to convince a jury 'beyond reasonable doubt' that the women were murdered, despite the absence of a confession and evidence for the prosecution that the defence would be characterised as 'circumstantial.

Innocent Until Proven Guilty

We counted twelve, but there might have been more. One in a hoist, several on raised ground, more at street level, not to mention those attached to helicopters circling overhead. Strategically positioned around the vehicle entrance to Ipswich Crown Court, television cameras waited for the arrival of defendant Steve Wright on the first day of his trial. As the roar of helicopter rotor blades grew louder, we knew that the police-escorted prison van was close by, having made the short journey from HMP Chelmsford, just along the A12. Wright had been moved to Chelmsford because transporting him every day from HMP Belmarsh in south-east London, where he'd been held on remand for the past twelve months, would have been impractical.

A burst from a police siren and the white van turned the corner in front of the bank of waiting journalists, newspaper photographers and live TV cameras. The gates to the parking area beneath the court eased open and the van passed slowly through. Wright would be allowed to alight from the van out of sight of the media glare. He was now just minutes away from coming face to face with the families of the women he was accused of killing.

The demand for seating in courtroom number one – where the trial would take place – had been so great that court officials had had to set aside courtroom number two as an extension or annexe to the main court. As a result there were a number of court cameras pointing at the judge, the witness box and the backs of the heads of the defence and prosecution teams in the main court, which fed pictures upstairs to the annexe. At times there were up to fifty journalists watching and listening to proceedings. And because seats were at a premium, each media organisation, regardless of its size or the extent of its coverage, was given only one pass to Court One and most of the journalists ended up working from the annexe.

Shortly after 10.30 a.m. on Monday 14 January 2008, the door to the dock in Court One clicked open and Wright was brought in, flanked by four prison guards. From where they were sitting, the victims' families couldn't look straight at Wright, who was just yards from them, but behind one-inch-thick glass. Their view had been deliberately obscured by frosted glass, but one or two stood up to peer over at the man dressed respectably in a dark suit, dark tie and white shirt. Not once did he turn to look at them.

'Are you Steve Gerald James Wright?' he was asked.

'Yes,' came the reply.

The families of Tania, Gemma, Anneli, Annette and Paula would soon learn how their loved ones had met their deaths, although none of that distressing evidence could be heard before a jury of twelve had been selected. That was the sole priority for the first day of the trial. There were 114 potential jurors. Each was required to fill out a questionnaire so that their suitability could be assessed. If they had known any of the victims or if they believed they had any connection with the witnesses in the case, they would be excused jury service. By the end of the day a jury of ten men and two women had been selected, but it was dismissed the following day – for reasons that were never explained – and a second jury of nine men and three women replaced it. Via video link, the judge, Mr Justice Gross, told the jury to ignore any media reports they saw or read, and warned them not to do their own research into the case. And with that, the man accused of five counts of murder was ready to be tried.

Opening Statements

The opening statements at a trial are not only the windows through which the jury comes to see the prosecution and defence cases; they are also the frames that shape the evidence and the arguments that are subsequently presented. A good opening statement sets the tone for what will follow, and prepares the jury for the journey that they must take before they weigh up the evidence and reach a decision. Peter

Wright QC – who had previously prosecuted Harold Shipman – opened for the prosecution in the simple, down-to-earth manner that would become the hallmark of his advocacy throughout the case:

> 'During a period of six and a half weeks from late October to early December 2006 five women went missing in and around Ipswich. It is the prosecution case that each of them was murdered by this man.'

Then, running through the details and circumstances of the women who had been killed, he insisted that they had been 'systematically selected and murdered' by Wright, whom he described as:

> 'A user of prostitutes; a local resident of Ipswich; a man with transport and also the wherewithal not only to pick up prostitutes in the red-light area of Ipswich, but also to transport and dispose of their bodies after killing them.'

As evidence for this conclusion, Mr Wright indicated not only that Steve Wright had had the opportunity to kill these women, but also that there were a number of links between the deaths of the women and Wright which 'pointed unerringly' to his guilt. These links included CCTV and Automatic Number Plate Recognition (ANPR) evidence which would place Wright's Ford Mondeo in the red-light area when the women disappeared, and his and his partner Pam's work schedules, which demonstrated that when Pam worked nights Wright took the opportunity to pick up prostitutes and bring them back to the house they shared in London Road. There was also DNA evidence on the bodies of Annette, Anneli and Paula that matched Wright's profile, and the likelihood of that match being obtained by chance was calculated to be something like one in a billion.

Here the prosecution – recognising that these women sold sex to finance their drug habits and therefore second-guessing what the jury might be thinking – revealed that low-level DNA results of other people had also been obtained, but only Wright's was common to all three of the women in question. And semen stains had been found on two pairs of gardening, or 'industrial', gloves belonging to Wright, and, as the prosecution put it:

> 'The wearing of semen-stained gloves by the defendant when he was in contact with these women is highly unusual to say the least; unless, of course, he was wearing gloves having murdered the women and was about to dispose of their bodies.'

There had been little likelihood of obtaining DNA evidence from Tania and Gemma, the first two victims, given that their bodies had been left in water and had not been discovered until several weeks after their deaths. However, minute fragments of textile fibres from Wright's car, his lumberjack coat and a pair of his tracksuit trousers had also been found on the bodies of all five women and these linked him inextricably to their deaths. For example, a single black nylon fibre was found on Tania that matched the carpet from the passenger footwell of Wright's car, and other fibres that came from his driver's seat, the sofa in his flat, his reflective jacket and from his tracksuit bottoms were found on Gemma's body. That these fibres found in the head hair or, as it was described, the 'debris' of Tania's or Gemma's bodies might have been transferred by chance from the running water in which they had been found was considered so remote that it was excluded as a possibility. Even more fibres from Wright's clothes, his house and car were found on the bodies of Annette, Anneli and Paula.

Mr Wright closed his opening statement by admitting 'we may never know' what had driven Wright to kill these women, but that on 'the evidence you hear you can and will be driven to conclude that each of these women was indeed murdered and that the common denominator in each of their deaths and the disposal of their bodies was the defendant'.

Alone or with Another or Others?

What might have driven Wright to kill was not the only matter that Mr Wright acknowledged he neither understood nor had a clear view about. He also admitted the possibility that Wright might have acted 'either alone or with another or others'. This conclusion seemed to be based on three factors. First, the fact that one witness, Jane Leighton, had seen Tania Nicol on the night she disappeared talking to a man in a car in Handford Road at about the time she went missing. Ms Leighton thought that there might have been more than one man in the car. The absence of scratches or marks on the bodies of any of the victims also suggested that they had been carried to the place in which they were dumped, rather than dragged along the ground. This might imply that their bodies had been wrapped in something before they were abandoned, or that Wright had help in carrying them to the place where they were ultimately discovered. Even so, we should also remember that all five women were very thin, and therefore that Wright, adrenalin pumping through his veins, should have been able to carry them unaided. Finally, another witness had seen two cars in the area where the bodies of Annette and Paula had been found, which again might have indicated that someone else had been involved with Wright in these murders.

Suggesting that there might have been another person jointly responsible for some, if not all, of these crimes gave an opening to Wright's defence that over the course of the trial they were eager to exploit. As we have already learned, Wright was not the first man to be arrested for the murders of Tania, Gemma, Anneli, Annette and Paula. That dubious honour fell to Tom Stephens, the thirty-seven-year-old local man who described himself in his MySpace profile as 'The Bishop'. Stephens was originally arrested for the murders on Monday 18 December 2006, probably as a result of an interview that he gave to Michael Duffy in the *Sunday Mirror* in which he claimed that he knew all the five victims, often gave them lifts in his car and did not have an alibi for the nights that they went missing. He also said that he was particularly close to Gemma and Tania, and when Tania's mother Kerry Nicol gave evidence, Mr Langdale (defending Wright) was quick to question her about a call that Stephens had made to her on 10 November 2006, long before Tania's body was discovered. Kerry Nicol stated that Stephens had asked her: 'Will the girls still go out and do what they do if one of them has been murdered?'

The conclusion that Mr Langdale wanted the jury to draw was plain for all to see, but in any event, shortly after Wright was arrested for all five murders on 19 December 2006, Stephens was released on police bail without charge. There was no evidence to link him to these murders – no fibres, no DNA, no CCTV, no ANPR. We interviewed Stephens on a number of occasions and while we would agree that although some people might find him odd, and sometimes attention-seeking, there was actually nothing to connect him with the murders, even though he had known all five women. Nonetheless, Stephens offered the defence a useful way of deflecting attention away from Wright, and issues relating to Stephens were the last piece of evidence they introduced into court before the defence rested.

Evidence relating to Stephens was still eighteen days away when Mr Langdale opened the defence with a brief statement – he spoke for no more than fifteen minutes – in which he acknowledged that his client did not deny having sex with four of the five women, and, as a consequence:

'You will not be hearing very much in the way of cross-examination by the defence. It's not likely that you will be hearing the defence suggest to prosecution witnesses that they are lying or deliberately trying to mislead you. In particular, you will not hear that suggestion being made in relation to the scientific evidence in the case. For example, with regard to the DNA and fibres, it's not the case that the defence suggests that the scientific findings are wrong . . . the defence case is Steve Wright was somebody in October, November and December 2006, when he was living at 79 London Road, who availed himself of the services of prostitutes in the red-light area of Ipswich. Amongst those whom he encountered in that way were those five young women. His case is that he had full sexual intercourse with four of them, either in his car or at his home address.'

In other words, it was for the prosecution to prove that the DNA and fibre evidence revealed that Wright had killed these women as opposed to simply having had sex with them, and Mr Langdale finished by maintaining that his client 'was not the "person or persons" responsible for the murder of the women and the disposal of their bodies'. However, as the trial progressed, Mr Langdale did not allow the prosecution's scientific evidence to go entirely unchallenged as he had indicated he would, and several days were spent cross-examining forensic experts about the tests they conducted – or in some cases did not conduct – on the DNA and fibre evidence.

Court Number One: On the Move

The prosecution's opening statement had taken Peter Wright QC the best part of two days to complete and the document itself ran to more than sixty pages, too much information for a jury to whom Belstead Brook, London Road, Nacton and Levington were mere locations on a map. And so on the fifth day of the trial, on 21 January (the court did not sit at weekends, and sometimes not on certain weekdays either), the nine men and three women of the jury were driven first to Wright's home in London Road. Had they requested to go inside, they could have done so, but none had thought to ask. Then, in a bus owned by a company called Forget Me Not, the jury was given a tour of the red-light district before visiting all the sites at which the bodies of the women had been found. Wearing winter coats and carrying umbrellas, the twenty-seven-strong court party stopped first at Hintlesham. They were shown how Gemma had been found on a bend in the brook near two fishing lakes. A 'Pink Delight' buddleia – a bush which attracts butterflies – had been planted nearby and bore a label which read 'Gemma's Tree'.

Jurors then moved on to Copdock and Nacton until finally they inspected the woodland at Levington, where the bodies of Paula and Annette had been found only a hundred

metres apart. There had been fears that the press would
follow the convoy of vehicles, perhaps leading to a media
scrum which might put the jury's anonymity at risk. In the
end resources from TV, print and radio media were pooled;
although care was taken not to identify jurors, some of them
expressed their concern the following day.

Such local colour and insight were vital to the Crown's
case, and so the prosecution had perhaps already won an
early victory by preventing the trial from being moved out of
Ipswich, as had been favoured by Wright's defence. Several
months before the start of the trial, on a May day in 2007,
the world's media had first descended on the new glass building formally known as The Crown Court at Ipswich, which
had only been opened in April 2004, to hear Wright's 'not
guilty' plea to the charges of murder. It seemed a perfect
example of what Mr Langdale described as 'the widespread
and at times sensationalist press', and as a result he suggested to the judge that there was a 'heightened risk of
prejudice of a fair trial' and so favoured a 'more neutral and
dispassionate location'. The judge for these pleas – the
Honourable Mr Justice Calvert-Smith (as we have seen, the
trial itself would be presided over by the Honourable Mr
Justice Gross, a South African-born former Rhodes
Scholar) – was not persuaded by Mr Langdale, and was in
part helped by Mr Wright pointing out that there had been
'no baying crowd, and no lynch mob' when Wright had been
arrested and that the people of Ipswich seemed to have a
'healthy, dispassionate disregard for events thus far'.

Throughout the course of the trial, in fact, very few members of the public actually attended court, and the public seats
that were available were almost exclusively occupied by the
media, the families of the murdered women, Alecky Blythe (a
playwright from the National Theatre who specialises in

recording day-to-day speech and turning it into documentary theatre), and Wright's father and half-brother. One local man who did attend, Roger Kirkham, kept a blog of the trial, and he suggested to us that the lack of local interest was a result of the period of time between the murders and the trial itself, and also because since Wright's arrest the murders had stopped. Locally, he maintained, this was seen as an indication that the police had got their man. The trial stayed in Ipswich, a stone's throw from the red-light area from which Tania, Gemma, Anneli, Annette and Paula had disappeared. Roger reflects on the irony of this in his blog as he describes the walk from his house to the court:

> If you were to wander from one side of the town to the other, you'd find that Ipswich is a surprisingly large place, but an accident of geography means the Crown Court is right next door to the red-light area. To get to it from my house meant walking down London Road, walking down Handford Road past the corner with Burlington Road where so many of the victims stood waiting for the next punter, and then down Portman Road – the outer edge of the red-light area. Cross into Sir Alf Ramsey Way (another favourite spot for hookers), take a left past the old football training ground and you're pretty much there.

Five Downward Spirals

From early on in the trial the prosecution felt it important to get the jury into the mindset that these women weren't 'hookers' but ordinary young women who, for some reason or another, had become addicted to drugs and were then forced to fund that addiction through prostitution. How best to do that? One way would be to allow their close relations to explain how five promising futures had been destroyed by heroin. But that meant three mothers giving evidence from the witness box in front of the man they believed had murdered their daughters. It wasn't as if they had even seen inside court number one, let alone had a chance to become accustomed to its almost surreal environment. Given that each was a witness for the prosecution, none was allowed into court prior to giving evidence.

In turn and over two days Tania Nicol's mother, Kerry, Anneli Alderton's mother, Maire, and Gemma Adams' mother, Gail, all entered the witness box to answer questions about the daughters they had lost, the daughters they had been unable to steer away from a life working on the streets.

Kerry Nicol's voice cracked with emotion as she described how she had 'no idea' until after her death that her daughter had been selling sex on the streets of Ipswich. She had accepted the offer for her to give evidence from behind a screen, thus shielding her from Steve Wright. 'She said she had a job and was managing all right,' Ms Nicol told the jury. 'She told me a few different things. She was a hairdresser at one point. Another time she said she worked behind a bar in a pub.' She was also asked to confirm to the jury that the woman seen on CCTV being picked up in the red-light district by Steve Wright was her daughter.

Sitting just yards from Wright, Gail Adams was the next into the witness box. Clutching a handkerchief behind her back, she told how her daughter had become estranged from her family because of her drug addiction and that they hadn't talked to her in the months before she died. The woman seen touting for business on the streets in different sections of CCTV footage at the time Gemma disappeared, she told the jury, was indeed her daughter.

Anneli Alderton's mother, Maire, also fought back tears as Peter Wright QC asked her if drugs had accelerated her daughter's downward spiral. 'Was it your fear she was engaging in prostitution at that time?' he asked.

'Yes,' she replied.

'Did you attempt to get her away from life on the street?' he asked. She nodded, too upset to speak.

Thanks to written evidence from Annette Nicholls' sister, Stacey, and a friend of Paula Clennell, the jury had now begun to understand the true extent of the trauma suffered by five families whose lives had been changed for ever. They were also presented with posthumous evidence from one of the dead women. Jurors heard a statement from Paula Clennell, which she'd given to police a month before her own body was discovered naked in Levington. On 13 November, two weeks after the disappearance of her friend Tania Nicol and two days before Gemma Adams would be reported missing, Paula told police she was standing one hundred yards from Tania when she saw her climb into a car at about 1 a.m. on 31 October. 'I was working as normal,' she told officers. 'Tania was standing in her usual place. I only know Tania through work. Occasionally we have a cigarette and a chat but that's about it. I can describe her as nice, harmless. She didn't speak to me about anyone bothering her. As she got in the car she looked over to me and said: "Are you OK?" That was the last time I saw her.'

Deoxyribonucleic Acid and Fibres

Deoxyribonucleic acid is more commonly known as DNA, the genetic material of a cell. Since DNA is unique within any species, and to any individual within that species, it can be used as a form of identification. This process is sometimes called 'DNA profiling' or 'DNA fingerprinting', and it was first used to catch a killer in 1987. At the time Leicestershire Police were trying to catch the killer of fifteen-year-old Lynda Mann, who had been found raped and strangled in the village of Narborough in 1983, and also the person responsible for the murder of another fifteen-year-old, Dawn Ashworth, discovered strangled and sexually assaulted in a village close to Narborough three years later. Having exhausted most of their leads, the police contacted Professor Alec Jeffreys, a geneticist at Leicester University, who claimed to have identified a technique (called restriction fragment length polymorphism, or RFLP) that could create an individual's genetic fingerprint from an adequate sample of that person's DNA, such as from blood, saliva, hair or semen.

Semen had been found on the bodies of Lynda and Dawn and this was used to create the DNA profile of their killer. The police then asked all the men in the local area between the ages of sixteen and thirty-four to provide a DNA sample – drawn from their blood – which could then be compared with the killer's. In August 1987 the police received information from a woman working in a local bakery that one of her co-workers, Ian Kelly, had taken the blood test for another employee called Colin Pitchfork. Apparently Pitchfork had convinced Kelly that he had already taken the blood test to help out another friend who had a criminal record, and that he didn't want to take another for fear of being arrested for deception. In any event the police acted on this information and tracked Pitchfork down. Pitchfork – who had a criminal record for exposing himself – readily confessed to the double murders when questioned by the police. He was sentenced to life imprisonment in January 1988.

Since Colin Pitchfork's conviction the science of DNA profiling has advanced greatly, and has become a standard weapon in the police's armoury to fight crime. And while in 1987 a considerable quantity of cellular material was needed for the RFLP technique to create an individual's profile, today only the smallest traces of saliva, blood, hair, sweat or semen are necessary. These would include allele-specific testing, and short tandem repeats (STRs), which, allied with the process of polymerase chain reaction (PCR), can identify an individual from a very small amount of cellular material. The latest technique is called low copy number (LCN) DNA evidence. This has been in development only since 1999, but allows forensic scientists to link DNA to a person even if only minute amounts of cellular evidence are present. However, this technique has to be used with some care, especially as such small samples can often become contaminated.

While scientific techniques have been developing quickly since Pitchfork's conviction in 1988, so, too, has the national database of DNA samples. Established in 1995, Britain has the oldest national DNA database in the world, with some five million people registered on it. When it was first established only those with a criminal record were added to the database, but now anyone who is arrested for an offence which might lead to imprisonment is subject to a mouth swab, the results of which will then be added to the database. This has also led to some notable convictions, including that of James Lloyd, the 'Shoe Rapist', who assaulted a number of women between 1983 and 1986 in Rotherham and Barnsley. Lloyd's DNA was not actually on the database, but when his sister was later arrested and charged with a drink-driving offence her DNA was added, and when the police reopened the shoe-rapist case nearly twenty years later this 'familial DNA' linked Lloyd to semen taken from the women who had been raped.

In the case of the Suffolk murders, Steve Wright's DNA was on the national database as a result of his having been arrested and convicted of stealing £84 from his employer five years earlier, when he was working as a barman at the Brook Hotel in Felixstowe. Little did he realise then just how important that theft would become, and how it would help convict him of murder.

Forensic Science Cross-Examined

Forensic science dominated the narrative and course of Wright's trial almost from the opening day until the close. You might even say it was the star witness. Hardly a day passed without evidence from one scientific expert being offered, and we almost began to feel sympathy for the jury who had to get their heads round just what was being objected to, explained or argued about without the benefit of a chemistry degree. But perhaps our sympathy was misplaced. If the jury had been even remotely interested in popular culture, forensic science and forensic scientists would have become very familiar to them through television, cinema, newspapers and magazines. It seemed to be everywhere.

There was danger here for Wright's defence. In popular culture forensic science suggests glamour, certainty, self-discipline, objectivity, truth and justice all rolled into one, although whether anyone has ever bothered to question what it really is, or looked too deeply at how and when scientific principles come to be applied within the criminal justice and legal systems, is rather doubtful. But what is 'science', and are these scientific principles robust and vigorous, or just as likely to be influenced by the all too human failings of error, prejudice and omission? And herein is a clue as to how Mr Langdale would run Wright's defence. Let's look further at what he said in his opening statement:

> '. . . it is not the case that the defence suggests the scientific findings are wrong [. . .] The defence challenge the assertion that these findings illustrate that [Wright] was responsible for their deaths as opposed to someone who had sex with them . . . You will have noted more than once in the case of the opening speech, the prosecution counsel suggested that another person or others may, they say, in addition have been involved in the deaths and disposals. This is a matter to which you will no doubt pay close attention. You will have to consider the evidence, for example, from the scientists as to the real possibility of someone being able to kill the victims without leaving any trace on the bodies of the victims.'

Mr Langdale was not so much implying that the scientists had got things wrong, rather that they had placed too much emphasis on certain findings, and had not paid enough attention to other possibilities. He was less concerned with prejudice, conjecture and error, but much more with omission. Specifically, that the forensic scientists had not paid enough attention to the possibility that Tania, Gemma, Anneli, Annette and Paula had been killed by someone else.

One of the key exchanges which revealed Mr Langdale's defence strategy came on the twelfth day of the trial – 31 January – when he challenged the prosecution's forensic expert, Dr Peter Hau, about DNA that had been found in blood and semen stains on Wright's reflective jacket and which belonged to Wright and Paula Clennell. Mr Langdale asked Dr Hau, who seemed ill at ease, if he had conducted further tests on other, low-level DNA that had been found on the same jacket. Dr Hau answered that he had not and was promptly asked by Mr Langdale if he could rule out that DNA from 'unknown contributors' was also present, to which Dr Hau replied 'Maybe, maybe not', hardly a ringing endorsement of his scientific conclusions. So, too, in turning to DNA found on a pair of Wright's gloves, Mr Langdale suggested to Dr Hau that his results indicated another possible component – apart from Wright and Paula – and which 'could indicate a third contributor'. Dr Hau was asked why this wasn't investigated further, to which he replied: 'It hasn't been ignored, it has been considered. In this instance it was just so low-level. In my opinion it was not worth scientifically doing.'

What Mr Langdale was trying to do was to create doubt – reasonable doubt – in the jury's minds that there might have been another person involved; someone who had escaped detection because they had taken more care than Wright, and who had thus been able to evade scientific discovery. At all times Mr Langdale reassured the jury that what he was doing was 'not a criticism from me', but in truth that is exactly what it was, and Dr Hau looked mightily relieved when he eventually left the witness box.

Roy Palmer, the prosecution's expert on fibre analysis, was more robust in the witness box than Dr Hau, and his evidence was just as significant. Specifically, he suggested that a single black nylon fibre found in the hair of Tania Nicol implied that she had been in 'forceful or sustained' contact with the car owned by Wright, for the fibre that he found matched the carpet in the front passenger footwell of Wright's Mondeo. Mr Palmer went on to say that nylon carpets found in cars were designed to be 'tough and durable' and therefore did not shed their fibres easily, all of which suggested that 'some force' was needed to break the fibres before they could be transferred to another surface.

Mr Wright asked: 'What are you able to conclude in respect of this single carpet fibre in her hair?' to which Mr Palmer replied: 'The findings in my opinion represent a more forceful or sustained contact with the carpet of the car or items in Steve Wright's home environment at or around the time of her disappearance rather than a brief contact.'

Quite apart from fibres found in Tania's hair, Mr Palmer was able to demonstrate links between fibres found on the bodies of all five women and the home, car or clothing of Wright, and that these findings would 'not occur by chance'.

This was powerful evidence for the prosecution, and Mr Langdale had to work hard to put up a defence. He stuck to the procedure that he had adopted when cross-examining Dr Hau, which was not so much to dispute the scientific findings themselves but to ask about omissions. So he asked Mr Palmer how many other Ford cars had similar carpets to Wright's and Mr Palmer was forced to concede that he did not know. This prompted him to put to Mr Palmer: 'So there is nothing to say, bearing in mind these girls' lifestyles, that she did not pick up a carpet fibre from a vehicle other than this?', to which Mr Palmer replied: 'I cannot rule that out.' Here was the familiar tactic of trying to plant doubt in the jury's mind that someone other than Wright was guilty of the murders. Even so, when redirected by the prosecution, Mr Palmer concluded that the chances of finding fibres linked to Wright on just one of the bodies of the five women were 'very small', and of finding fibres that linked Wright to them all were 'even smaller'.

'No Comment'

To all intents and purposes the end of the prosecution case came on the fifteenth day of the trial, on Wednesday 6 February, although the prosecution itself did not formally end until the following day. However, on the 6th we learned that Wright had been interviewed on ten different occasions between 19 and 21 December 2006 and that these interviews had lasted just over eight hours altogether. Prior to being charged by DC Richard Ford for murder 'at 21.50 hours on Thursday 21 December 2006 at Stowmarket Police Station' it was revealed that Wright had been asked a series of questions, among them: did he know any of the five girls? Had they ever been to his house, or in his car? Did he use any of these girls as prostitutes? Had he ever been to Nacton, Copdock or Hintlesham? Did he suffer from insomnia? How could he account for the fact that his DNA was found on the bodies of Annette Nicholls, Paula Clennell and Anneli Alderton? And did Pam know that he used prostitutes?

To all these questions Wright had replied: 'No comment', and the prosecution reminded the jury of the police caution: 'You do not have to say anything, but it may harm your defence if you do not mention when questioned something which you later rely on at court. Anything you do say may be given in evidence.' And, with that, Mr Wright and Mr Langdale suggested to the judge that it would be a good point to finish for the day, and that the defence would begin tomorrow.

Slowly, but with the feeling that they had an easy day ahead of them, the journalists started to file out of the court laughing and joking, and comparing notes. As they did so few noticed

Wright's father, Conrad, and half-brother, Keith, hurrying solemnly ahead. What had they made of these questions, and Wright's answer of 'No comment'? We knew from our own sources that Wright had not wanted to see his father while on remand in HMP Belmarsh. At the very least this implied that Wright had something to hide, especially as his father had travelled all the way from his home only to be turned away by his son at the very gates of the prison. Perhaps Wright simply couldn't face his father – didn't want to look him in the eye – when asked the obvious question: 'Did you do it?' (Here, it is interesting to speculate whether Wright had looked Tania, Gemma, Anneli, Annette and Paula in the eye as he squeezed their life out of them – or was he ashamed of that too?) Conrad must have suspected that this was the case: our sources suggested that he and Steve had always been close until his partner, Pam, entered the equation, and so he must have reasoned that his son not wanting to see him now was at the very least suspicious. Wright would subsequently write to his father from HMP Belmarsh to explain his feelings.

Dear Dad,

This is a reply to your letter. You are right you have never seen me angry before because I am quite a placid person. Whenever I get angry I tend to bury it deep inside, which I suppose is not a healthy thing to do because the more I do that, the more withdrawn I become, because I have seen too much anger and violence in my childhood to last anyone a lifetime.

But what really makes me sad is the fact that I thought all the family feuds were behind me now, I really thought we had made a step forward. I just wish everyone would get along and work towards a family unit because all the bickering and point scoring against each other is really getting me down. It seems you are pulling me one way and Pam is pulling me the other, and in the end something will give and it just seems to me that person will be me and that is the last thing I want at the moment as I am sure you do as well because if I start to fall apart at the seams I don't think I could cope in here. I need to be strong to cope with this nightmare, like that bit you said in the paper that when you looked in my eyes, you would know whether I was guilty or not. That really hurt me. It was like a knife in the heart for you to even contemplate that I could even be capable of such a terrible crime.

You say that you want to help me, the only way that will happen is if you make the effort to work together, because all this 'he said, she said', you must understand, is not doing my frame of mind any good. I just want it to stop. I do love you Dad, but you must understand that Pam is my life now and I will always stick by her, like she had by me. She is having a rough time of it at the moment. She has lost loads of weight and is on all sorts of tablets. When I saw her on Tuesday I was shocked, her face looked so withdrawn, she looked really ill, so she is my main concern at the moment.

She has made me the happiest I have been all my life. She has pulled me out of myself, it seems her only aim in life is to make me happy and vice versa, so I will not tolerate anything bad said against her.

I would like to see you but I need to be sure you are behind me 100% and that there are no hidden agendas.

Pam is making no money from the press, so where you got that from I don't know. For one thing, she is not allowed to talk to the press because she is a potential prosecution witness, not that I am worried about that at all because everyone that knows me is a potential prosecution witness, even you!

My head seems to be all over the place at the moment, so please try and sort this out. I know you are a proud man and don't like backing down, but you are the only one that can sort this out. You say you want to help, so please do that one thing for me.

Love
Steve

Whether he wanted to see them or not, Conrad and Keith (and other Wright family members, too) turned up each day at court – Conrad always neatly dressed – both keeping their thoughts to themselves and trying to show respect to the families of the victims who also attended. It couldn't have been easy listening to the evidence that was presented each day, with the prosecution case gradually being built up against their son and half-brother and the inevitable realisation that there was a serial killer in their family. We believe that Conrad was especially distressed, that his background as an RAF policeman had done nothing to prepare him for what he was now having to listen to and come to terms with. Did he really still believe that his son was innocent?

We had other questions, too, but on that bright February morning the biggest of them all was whether or not Wright would go into the witness box in an attempt to maintain his innocence, or did he believe that Mr Langdale had already planted enough 'reasonable doubt' in the minds of the jury? No doubt Mr Langdale had also explained to Wright that there were dangers if he did give evidence – not only would he be vigorously cross-examined but he would also expose the families of his victims, and indeed his own family, to further distress. There were real doubts as to what would happen the next day when the court was in session again.

The Sixteenth Day

Any doubts were quickly dispelled the following morning as Mr Langdale called Wright to the witness box. There was a moment's hushed anticipation in the courtroom, and then, as Wright rose, one of the victim's relations hissed 'murderer' as he made his way forward. Once again neatly dressed in suit and tie, he looked every inch the man next door – Mondeo Man, Middle England, the neighbour you could rely on to look after your house when you went away on holiday; the man you could play a round of golf with; the colleague who would cover for you in a crisis. This was exactly the image that Wright wanted to present – Mr Average, Mr Normal, just like me and you, ladies and, especially, gentlemen of the jury, and not at all like a man who used prostitutes, or who would cheat on his wife, or be a serial killer. He needed to show himself as a man who was vulnerable, too. Mr Langdale helped with that by asking if Wright wished to stand or sit in the witness box. The forty-nine-year-old said he'd rather sit. He had given the defendant the choice, Mr Langdale told the jury, because Wright suffered from stress. He explained that when Wright had been a prosecution witness in a court case some years earlier – undoubtedly a tactic to imply that his client was on the right side of the law – he had nearly fainted under the pressure. He reminded the jury that when he was arrested, Wright had asked officers if he could sit down. He invited the jury to imagine how he must have felt when the police knocked on his door to tell him he was being arrested on five counts of murder.

But Wright must have realised that going into the witness box was a high-risk strategy. He surely reasoned that its success depended on his ability to explain away all those little things that didn't quite match the image of himself that he now wanted to cultivate.

First Mr Langdale asked him about his use of prostitutes, and his sex life in general. Wright explained that he had started paying for sex when he was in the merchant navy at about the age of twenty-five – it was 'normal' to do so among the crew, he suggested – and that they would all visit brothels when they went ashore. He explained that he only ever had 'normal sexual intercourse', and that when he came back to England he would only use prostitutes 'intermittently'. Here Wright was trying to 'normalise' his use of prostitutes and in doing so 'neutralise' any moral scruples the jury might have had about such practices. He was simply a young sailor, doing what other young sailors did when they were far from home.

But what about much later when he left the merchant navy and returned to England? Wright explained that in Ipswich he would frequent massage parlours – particularly Cleopatra's and Oasis – but again insisted that he would only ever have 'normal' sex, and that he would wear a condom supplied by the massage parlour. You could sense the careful consideration that Mr Langdale must have put into preparing Wright for this moment, for the jury would also have remembered that Wright had a partner while all of this was going on. Wasn't this some form of betrayal of Pam? Again Wright had thought through an answer. Ever since Pam had started to work nights, they were 'like two ships passing in the night' and as a result their sex life was 'almost nonexistent'. Rather uncharitably he also pointed out that Pam was nine years older than him, almost as if to imply that she no longer wanted to be sexually active. Even so, Wright explained that Pam would have left him if she had discovered that he had been seeing prostitutes.

Mr Langdale carefully moved on to the subject of the dead women, and whether or not Wright had paid for sex with them. He admitted that he had, with the exception of Tania Nicol: her acne had put him off. Nonetheless, he admitted that it was indeed he who had been spotted by the CCTV camera in his car picking her up on the corner of Handford Road and Burlington Road, but that it was when she had got into the car that he had noticed her complexion. Wright then claimed that he didn't pluck up the courage to tell Tania that he couldn't go through with having sex with her until he had parked up in Portman Road, and then, after failing to persuade him to change his mind, she had simply got out of the car and Wright had gone home. Mr Langdale then asked about his car being spotted heading out of Ipswich at 1.39 a.m. on 31 October, and asked – as had been suggested by the prosecution – whether or not this was because Wright was in the process of disposing of Tania's body. Wright simply replied 'No way', and explained that he suffered from insomnia and was going for a drive.

Even so, Wright did admit that he regularly used prostitutes and that he would normally pick them up in his car, in which they would have sex. He explained that they would have 'normal' sex, and that he would always use a condom which would be supplied by the prostitute herself. Then he explained that he would use a glove to remove the condom after he had finished having sex. 'Why not use your hand?' Mr Langdale asked – no doubt expressing the thoughts of everyone else – to which Wright answered: 'Because I found it distasteful', even going so far as to suggest that he would 'gag' if he removed the condom without gloves. He'd then throw the condom out of the window, and put the gloves back in the side-door pocket.

Wright claimed that he had never put pressure on the neck of any prostitute with whom he was having sex – once again stressing that he only ever had 'normal' sex – but he did admit that he had taken as many as six girls back to his flat while Pam was at work. However, he claimed that he had only ever had sex with one of these girls on his bed, and that he didn't like to have sex with them on his bedroom floor because it was dirty, and because of that he would place his reflective jacket on the carpet for them to lie on. This would explain, he suggested, why DNA from the dead women was found on his jacket. Wright also said that he was worried that Pam would 'smell them' – the prostitutes – after they had had sex and when she returned home. He again mentioned that he wore gloves when removing his condoms.

In all of this we should consider three factors, two of which were deliberate ploys by the defence and one which emerged unexpectedly from the testimony Wright provided. First, it is clear that Mr Langdale had prepared Wright carefully in terms of the evidence that the prosecution was relying on, so that he was able to answer allegations concerning the DNA, the fibres, the ANPR and CCTV evidence. (Later, Mr Wright prosecuting would claim that Wright had 'tailored' his evidence to fit the facts of the case, and reminded the jury that he had answered 'No comment' to questions put to him by the police.) In short, Wright had answers to everything.

Second, what also emerges from Wright's testimony is that he realised he was trying to 'explain' these things to a jury who might not be sympathetic to a man who cheated on his partner and bought sexual services. So, we hear a great deal about why Wright started to use prostitutes while in the merchant navy, and an almost bizarre insistence about how it was always 'normal' sex that he paid for. But there is a cruelty here, too, for poor Pam is also diminished by these explanations – she emerges as an older partner no longer interested in sex, and who is therefore presented as a reason why Wright chooses to buy sex from younger women.

Finally – and unexpectedly – we can also glimpse something of the distaste that Wright feels about having to give this evidence and to account for himself. And although we should not rule out the fact that this might have been specifically constructed so as to portray himself as sympathetically as possible, there were just too many clues in what he said that showed he still hoped to maintain his reputation and 'good name' even when accused of murder, and believed that others – specifically the jury – would warm to his plight and to his circumstances. For example, he was at pains to point out that he found the used condoms that he had worn during sex so 'distasteful' that he had to wear gloves to remove them (even if he then put those same gloves back in his pocket or in his car for use at a later date). And he refused to have sex, or so he claims, with Tania because of her acne, which he suggested 'put him off'. Finally, he was worried that Pam might 'smell' the women he brought back to their flat.

At this point we might ask why such an apparently sensitive man would want, or be able, to buy sexual services at all, but that misses the point. In reality Wright is both socially conservative – he really does worry about what Pam might think – *and* a serial killer. Yet he knows that he wanted to overcome his conservatism and his distaste for the condoms and the sleazy sex in his car, because when he had been able to do so in the past it had been to his advantage. Specifically, he had gained power – something he felt had been denied him in virtually every other sphere of his life – and it was this powerlessness which had over time hurt and humiliated him. Of course when he had had power over the five young women that he murdered he exercised it in the most despicable way, and in many respects we should also see his willingness to take the stand – as big a gamble as he would ever make – as simply the last hurrah of that despicable power, too. No matter that others would suffer by his testimony – the families of his victims, Pam, his father, his siblings. If they were hurt, so what? This was about *him* and it always had been. Wright wanted his day in court and his time in the witness box. He believed he deserved it, and was entitled to it.

One Coincidence After Another?

But Wright hadn't quite bargained on how he would appear to others – or if he had, he severely miscalculated – when he was being cross-examined by a skilful prosecutor. He must have expected to be given a hard time, but perhaps he didn't fully appreciate that three days in the witness box would undo most people – especially if they were lying. Over the three days of Mr Wright's patient, careful and forensic cross-examination Wright had to develop a series of stock replies to each of the questions that were put to him. These answers included:

'I don't know.'
'If you say so.'
'I can't recall.'

'No, it was not.'
'I don't understand the question.'
'I don't know how I can possibly say.'
'No way.'
'No, I did not.'
'I would say it was a coincidence.'
'I don't remember.'
'I cannot say.'
'I can't see how I am expected to answer these questions.
I'm not a forensic expert.'

This last answer was Wright at his most tetchy and irritable on the third day of his cross-examination on 12 February – the eighteenth day of the trial, when Mr Wright was nearing the end of detailing the forensic evidence that linked Wright to the five dead girls. On the first day of his cross-examination Wright had been keener to suggest that everything had simply been a 'coincidence' when Mr Wright had put matters to him, and the following exchange was typical of many hours of cross-examination:

> *Mr Wright QC*: You solicited five women from the streets of Ipswich, amongst others, and each of them is dead. Is that a coincidence?
> *Wright*: I would say it is a coincidence.
> *Mr Wright QC*: You solicited five girls from the streets of Ipswich in the order in which they died. Is that a coincidence?
> *Wright*: It seems so, yes.

Mr Wright also asked if it was a coincidence that Wright had used the road to get to his work and that the bodies of Tania and Gemma might well have been deposited from that road into Belstead Brook. Wright agreed that it was. So, too, according to Wright, it was a coincidence that he was familiar with the areas where the bodies of Anneli, Annette and Paula had been found, and that there was a 'correspondence' between the disappearances of the women and Wright's car being spotted on the ANPR. In all, Wright was asked twelve questions to which he suggested that it was merely coincidence that his DNA was on the bodies of three of the dead women; that fibres were found on his clothes, his house or in his car that linked him to them; and that they disappeared in exactly the same order that Wright bought sexual services from them. Again he claimed it was a coincidence that his movements and car number plate had been recognised at the time that the girls had disappeared, and that Tania had been killed shortly after accepting a lift in his car. He rather cheekily agreed with Mr Wright that in all of this he had simply been 'singularly unfortunate'.

Of course the prosecution did not accept that any of these factors were coincidences at all, which was when Mr Wright suggested that Wright's explanations had been tailored to fit the forensic evidence. As such they were 'an act of desperation'. Mr Wright finished his cross-examination by suggesting: 'The sad truth is, Mr Wright, you were engaged in a campaign of murder for a little over six weeks. That's the truth – you were selecting women with which to have sex with and kill', and with that he sat down.

At this point in the trial Mr Langdale read out an agreed statement from the defence and the prosecution relating to the evidence that would have been presented by 'Miss L' and 'Miss M', who claimed that Tom Stephens had threatened to kill them both in 2005. Miss L – who had had an affair with Stephens – also suggested that he wanted to hold her down while they had sex and that they should have a 'safe word'. Here was a clue as to why Wright kept emphasising that he simply wanted 'normal sex'. In any event Miss L and Miss M reported all of this to the police and this had resulted in Stephens being issued with a harassment order. Once again, what Mr Langdale was trying to do was to deflect blame from Wright on to someone else, in the hope that this would create reasonable doubt as to Wright's guilt. Yet, while this was clearly a dramatic rabbit that was being pulled out of the defence's hat, it hardly seemed dramatic enough after three days of 'I don't remember', 'If you say so', 'I can't recall', 'I don't know' and one 'coincidence' after another. The defence itself formally ended on the nineteenth day of the trial, on 13 February, after further details about Tom Stephens had been read out in court.

Closing Arguments

Mr Wright began his closing argument on Valentine's Day, and suggested to the jury that there were 'five key issues' that they had to consider. First, they had to decide whether or not the five women had died as a result of 'misadventure' – by which he meant misfortune or mishap related to their drug addiction – or if they were in fact murdered. Second, if they had indeed been murdered, whether these murders were connected, and so fitted a pattern. Third, if one or more person was involved in these murders. Fourth, if they thought that more than one person was involved, whether or not they were acting independently, or as part of a team. Finally, the jury had to decide if Wright was responsible for each of these murders.

Of course Mr Wright was trying to lead the jury to convict Steve Wright, and so he was also about to put to them an answer to each of these five key issues. He suggested to the jury that these deaths were not the result of unrelated misadventure, but the consequence of a 'pattern of murder' by a man or men, so that the murders of each of these women were linked and entirely deliberate. All five had been found naked, and their bodies discovered in rural or semi-rural locations. None of the women, argued Mr Wright, had died as a result of a drugs overdose – even if their drug addiction had made them vulnerable – but as a result of having being strangled, or, as it was put in court, 'the normal mechanics of breathing' being interfered with, so that all five had hyper-inflation of the lungs, or injuries consistent with compression of the neck. Mr Wright also suggested that it was simply 'a matter of conjecture' as to whether Tom Stephens had been involved and accepted that the Crown could not rule him out as a suspect because there was no evidence that could provide him with an alibi. However, he argued that 'the absence of evidence proving innocence is rather different to the presence of evidence proving guilt'. He further suggested that the involvement of Stephens was 'not central to the issues in this case', especially as Stephens had been arrested, samples of his DNA had been taken and his home and his car had been searched, but he was never charged with any offence. In other words, it was Wright who 'was the common denominator in the disappearance and murder of the women'.

Mr Wright also put forward some tentative reasons as to why Wright might have turned to murder, although the prosecution did not have to prove a motive to gain a conviction. He explained to the jury, for example, that merely having sex with the five murdered women was 'not enough for the defendant', but that he 'needed more', and had achieved that at the dead women's expense. 'The reality is,' continued Mr Wright, 'Steve Wright couldn't restrain himself . . . he embarked on a course of conduct that deprived these women of their lives', and his silence when questioned by the police was not the result of legal advice, 'but of a man without explanation'. Indeed, Mr Wright suggested that the explanation when it did come had been tailored to suit the forensic evidence, but even then Wright couldn't explain why the blood of some of the women was on his jacket, and why his DNA was on their bodies. Nor could he explain the 'nocturnal' cleaning of his car, or the 'innumerable series of coincidences linking Wright to the murder of each of the women'. Mr Wright finished his closing speech by concluding:

> 'The sad fact is – and for reasons known only to himself – as we said at the outset of the case, Steve Wright embarked on a deadly campaign in late 2006 that ended in the murder of these five women of which he is guilty.'

Timothy Langdale for the defence suggested to the jury that the body of evidence presented at the trial did not prove 'beyond reasonable doubt' that Wright was the person responsible for the women's deaths. Indeed, he suggested that while the prosecution evidence against Wright was suspicious 'there's no smoking gun', and all that the Crown's case therefore added up to was that Wright had had a close association with these women in the hours before they died. Mr Langdale also used the prosecution's willingness to admit that there might have been another person involved to suggest that 'something doesn't quite add up', and queried how Wright could have done what he was accused of by himself. 'There was,' according to Mr Langdale, 'a perfectly sensible possibility' that Wright was not the person responsible for these murders and that they had been committed by someone else. Mr Langdale, as he had done throughout the case, even suggested to the jury that Tom Stephens was a 'real, live candidate', and asked them to consider whether it was just coincidence 'that Tom Stephens cannot be excluded'.

Turning to the forensic evidence, Mr Langdale put it to the jury that the real killer might simply not have left any trace of his DNA, and that the DNA of an unknown man had also been found on Anneli Alderton. So, too, there had been 'hundreds' of fibres which had been found, but no one knew where they came from, or who they belonged to. However, Mr Langdale closed his defence by returning to the possibility that these murders had been committed by someone else – specifically Tom Stephens – who had openly admitted that he had given lifts to all five women, had threatened to kill an ex-girlfriend and did not have an alibi for the days in question. He suggested that there was a 'reasonable possibility' that someone other than Wright had committed the murders, and 'if these points make sense the proper verdict is not guilty'.

Summing Up

The Honourable Mr Justice Gross had presided over the trial in an almost benign manner, in his sometimes barely audible soft South African accent regularly commending the defence and prosecution teams for their 'good sense', and on one occasion teasing the defence's junior for some slight mishap. At times he appeared almost avuncular as he dispensed wisdom and judgement, offering a sense of perspective if things looked as if they might be getting out of hand, not at all the stern, distant, no-nonsense judge so beloved by the media. Above all, Mr Justice Gross seemed to like things to be measured – he was scrupulously fair throughout the trial – and that sense of fairness characterised his summing up, which began on Monday 18 February, the twenty-second day of the trial, and continued until noon on Wednesday, when the jury finally retired. By the time he had finished the judge was coughing regularly, and constantly sipping from a glass of water.

The judge started his summing up by advising the jury that they should not be swayed by sympathy for the five victims or for their families, and reminding them that they should 'try the case on the evidence which has been presented before you', which he characterised as coming from 'a bleak landscape' of drugs, prostitution and murder. He then carefully and at some length went through the fibre, DNA and other forensic evidence, and also reminded the jury that Tom Stephens was not on trial, and that if they were convinced that Wright killed the women and intended to kill the women, then the issue of 'joint responsibility . . . was neither here or there'. Indeed, even if they thought that Wright had acted with another person and that they were 'in it together' as part of a joint plan to kill the women, but they could not determine if Wright himself had done the killing, they should still find him guilty.

Then, again reflecting his desire for balance, Mr Justice Gross suggested that there were nine points that the jury should consider from both the defence and the prosecution cases. For the defence, these nine points concerned the fact that Wright had admitted that some of the girls had been to his home address; he knew all five of the victims; had used the sexual services of four of them; he regularly used prostitutes; all of the five women had been in his car; some of the women had taken off their clothes at his house; he drove late at night because of his insomnia; he had connections with Nacton and Hintlesham, knew something of Levington but nothing of Copdock; and that he had an innocent explanation for the DNA findings. The judge also revealed that Wright had only a previous conviction for theft – something for which 'he should be given credit' – but asked the jury to consider his 'No comment' answers after his arrest. Mr Justice Gross suggested that all the nine points that Wright relied on were matters he could have mentioned in his police interviews, but chose not to because of legal advice, and that it was for the jury to decide if this was true, or whether Wright simply did not have a reliable excuse, as was suggested by the prosecution.

As for the prosecution's case, the judge suggested that the nine points the jury should consider were that the defendant picked up the women in the order that they went missing and at times around their disappearance; that Wright had the opportunity to commit these offences because his partner was at work; they should bear in mind the CCTV and ANPR evidence; the DNA links between three of the women and Wright; the fibres that linked the defendant to all five of the victims; the 'coincidences' suggested by Mr Wright; the fact that the victims started to disappear after Wright had started to use prostitutes, and that the murders ended after his arrest; the traces of blood that were found on Wright's clothing from the two women who shed blood; and the fact that the locations of the deposition sites were familiar to Wright. Even so the judge also reminded the jury that according to Wright's defence all of this 'fell well short' of proving him guilty of murder, and it was for them to determine if that was or was not the case. With a final cough from the judge and the clock standing just after noon, the jury retired to consider its verdict.

Life, Meaning Life

The hiatus experienced once the jury is sent out affects people in different way. For the two legal teams locked in battle for weeks on end, their job is largely over, and the pressure is off. They have done all they can to ensure that the jury has been provided with the best evidence on which to base its decision in the interests of justice, one way or the other. For senior investigators, this is the time to reflect on the evidence they've gathered for the prosecution. Have they done enough to secure a conviction? Was their case water-tight? The victims' families – who in this case had not met before the trial but who had now begun to bond during this most upsetting of periods – crossed their fingers in hope that the man they were sure had murdered their daughters would indeed be found guilty.

There was no such bonding within the Wright family. Despite pleas from Steve Wright for them to unite and stop 'point scoring', sons and daughters who shared the same father but not the same mother would continue to pass each other in the corridors or on the staircase without talking, without even making eye contact. Had family bickering overshadowed the fact that down below in the cells of the court their brother sat wondering whether he would spend the rest of his life behind bars?

For journalists this was a time to gauge the opinions of others to help predict the outcome of the case, and then fine-tune their pre-prepared background reports. There's a prediction, too, on how long the jury will take to reach its decision. One day? One day per victim? More than a week? Crosswords are nervously filled in outside the courtroom, and there are sharp intakes of breath every time an announce-ment is made asking for all parties involved in such-and-such a case to go to a particular court.

It was Thursday 21 February 2008 and the jury had only two hours left to deliberate before being sent home for the day. Pulses started to race when we were told that the nine men and three women appeared to be coming back to court. Was it a verdict or a question? Prosecution and defence teams who'd gone out for a well-earned break hurried back to court leaving their lunch half eaten. This time it was just a question about count one – Tania Nicol – the first victim. This perhaps suggested that if the jury was stuck on an issue regarding conviction for the first count it might not even have begun discussing the rest of the evidence. Some thought that it might be several days before the jurors reached a verdict. How wrong they were.

Those of us lucky enough to have dedicated seats were sitting rather more at ease outside court number one, when from the speaker above our heads came the words: 'All parties in the case of Steve Wright to court number one, please.' Another question from the jury, surely? A shake of the head from one of Wright's defence team suggested otherwise. In just over six hours, the jury had reached a verdict. It was exactly fourteen months to the day that Steve Wright was charged with murdering five women in Ipswich, and his fate would be known in minutes.

Court One had never been so full. The victims' families clutched each other for support as they sat waiting for the judge to appear. Mr Justice Gross explained to Steve Wright that he needn't stand to hear the verdicts read out, perhaps an indication he knew what was coming. Wright had been told by one of his legal team to 'keep it together', but before the jury had even entered the room Steve Wright's sister, Jeanette, began sobbing in the row behind the family of the fourth victim, Annette Nicholls. A moment of compassion came from a relation of one of the other victims, who acknowledged the respect the Wright family had shown them all throughout the trial. Then, as pens were poised and people held their breath, the jury came in.

'Have you reached a verdict upon which you are all agreed?'

'Yes,' replied the foreman of the jury.

'On count one, how do you find the defendant? Guilty or not guilty?'

'Guilty.'

Barely audible through the sound of sobbing and comments of 'Thank God' could be heard four more 'Guilty' verdicts. But the families of Tania, Gemma, Anneli, Annette and Paula knew that once one guilty verdict was delivered, another four would follow. For a split second, Steve Wright showed for the first time a flicker of emotion, a look almost of disappointment that the jury hadn't believed his version of events – that it was all just 'a coincidence' that he'd picked up all five victims in the order they vanished, and at the time they were murdered. And then his face adopted once more its customary blank, cold expression.

By 10.30 the next morning, the forty-nine-year-old was back in the dock awaiting sentencing. Despite knowing full well it wasn't a possibility, the relations of some of his victims had called for the judge to hand down the death penalty. The options open to Mr Justice Gross were either a minimum tariff of thirty years in jail or a life sentence, where life literally meant life. The families had made it very clear they felt neither alternative would see justice done. Good enough for them might have been death through interference with 'the normal mechanics of breathing'. Now a threat to himself, Wright appeared in the dock this time in an open-neck shirt, having been relieved of his tie. Mr Justice Gross addressed Wright directly:

'Steve Gerald James Wright. Yesterday you were convicted of five counts of murder. Between late October and December 2006 you set out to select five vulnerable prostitutes and you murdered them. I should make one thing clear. The women were all addicted to drugs and turned to prostitution to fund that addiction. But neither killed them. You did. Why you did it, may never be known. The deaths of these young women have given rise to much sorrow for their families. This was an extraordinary episode during which you showed signs you wanted to be caught. Upon reflection, and without hesitation, there is a case for a "whole life" order. You should spend the rest of your life in jail.'

As soon as the judge had finished speaking Wright was taken down to spend the rest of his life behind bars. And as we watched the prison van speed away from the court it was hard not to reflect that these were the very same roads that Wright had once cruised in search of his victims.

Suicide Watch

In an exclusive television interview within hours of the verdicts, Steve Wright's partner, Pam, told Sky News how she didn't recognise the man who'd sat in the dock for six weeks at Ipswich Crown Court. 'I hate him for what he's done. I didn't know him at all. It's like a death, like someone has died.' But Wright was far from dead, although he'd already phoned Pam from HMP Belmarsh to say that he couldn't live without knowing she was there for him. That hardly seems likely and Pam was now planning a future not only away from Wright, but away from Ipswich and England. When he spoke Pam said that she had found him strangely calm and laid back. He'd also stopped protesting his innocence, and instead told her that he would never be able to cope with a life sentence. As ever, it was all about him, and Pam wondered if he would ever tell her the truth about Tania, Gemma, Anneli, Annette and Paula, and the other girls he might also have murdered.

Knowing that he would die in jail has made Wright hysterical, and following his two suicide attempts in the past, prison service officials quickly put Wright on an F2052SH, which means that he is checked every fifteen minutes and will remain so until prison staff are convinced he won't take his own life. This system doesn't necessarily always work: in 2007 ninety-two prisoners took their own lives in jails in England and Wales, an increase of 37 per cent on the figure from the previous year. And as one of only thirty or so 'whole life tariff' prisoners, Wright has joined a depressingly awful group of humanity that includes Ian Brady – one of the Moors Murderers (who has attempted to starve himself to death) – Ian Huntley and the serial killers Robert Black, Peter Moore, Dennis Nilsen and Rose West. Rose West's husband Fred was once in that group, too, as was Harold Shipman, but both took their own lives rather than face the prospect of living the rest of their days banged up in the high-security estate of the prison service. Their suicides caused a scandal, and so prison officials will be doing everything in their power to prevent Wright from following in their footsteps, and cutting short what is likely to be a long and lonely journey to the grave.

Chapter Nine

Paying the Price?

'We want this paper to inform the development of a clear view of the brutal realities of prostitution so that its impact can be properly considered in the context of wider policy making – promoting civil renewal and community safety by addressing practical approaches to violence and exploitation, to problematic drug use, to a reduction in serious crime and in people trafficking. We welcome views.'

Former Home Secretary David Blunkett, writing in *Paying the Price: A Consultation Paper on Prostitution*, July 2004

With Wright's arrest, trial and conviction there is a danger that the Ipswich murders will be allowed to drift into our collective memories, to join that increasingly long list of other dreadful murders that are now preserved in true crime accounts of British serial killing, or perhaps rolled out for discussion on the anniversary of the death of one of the victims. After all, has public policy in relation to the management of doctors with access to the elderly changed as a result of the murders committed by Harold Shipman? Have we really done anything tangible to try to prevent, or even reduce, the numbers of children who run away from home or care each year, and who were one of the prime tar-gets of the Wests? So will public policy in relation to street prostitution develop in the wake of these five murders, or will we miss a golden opportunity to learn some valuable les-sons from what happened in Ipswich – lessons which, if we are not careful, will only resurface the next time a young woman working in the sex industry is murdered?

These dreadful, tragic murders offer us an opportunity not only to consider carefully how we should respond to the 'brutal realities' of prostitution in our towns and cities, and how our drugs policies contribute to that reality, but also to think more generally about the phenomenon of serial killing in Britain and how that is likely to change in the future. Most immediately, the murders in Ipswich should also put pressure on the local police to review a series of unsolved murders of other young women working in the sex industry in Suffolk and Norfolk, and which seem to us to be inextricably linked to Steve Wright.

These are important issues, and, while we do not pretend to be able to offer an answer to every question that we pose, it is vital to try to sketch out how we believe we should respond more broadly to the Ipswich murders. These are complex matters, but some of the issues are obvious. The first point to consider relates to prostitution, both in relation to how it should be policed and managed, and then, more generally, as to whether there might come a day when young women no longer feel that they have to sell sexual services as a 'survival strategy'. Do we prevent prostitution by concen-trating on the 'demand' – on the punters, dodgy or otherwise – or should we still try to tackle these matters by looking at the 'supply'?

So, too, it would be helpful to know how and why some young women enter prostitution, if only to see if there are common factors in their backgrounds which might help to prevent other young women going on the streets. This might also help us to consider how to help women selling sex to escape that world, although it is clear that to do so many of them would also have to overcome drug problems. None of these issues is straightforward. Just as we don't know why some young women (and some young men) self-harm, or become anorexic, so we must not pretend that we can fully understand what makes some young people use crack or heroin. Nor should we simply believe that 'Government' holds all the answers.

Other issues emerge from the murders of these five young women, and pose equally interesting questions. Specifically, their murders suggest something about the type of society that Britain is fast becoming, where the gap between the haves and have-nots is becoming wider and where the minimum wage finds it difficult to keep pace with the outsourcing of low-skilled jobs to the developing world. In such a global economy what is the role of young working-class British school leavers with few qualifications and even fewer marketable skills? How are they to make their way in the world and find status, power and autonomy? Do we actually care? Are the lives of these young men and women connected to our own and to the lives of others in our community, or are we just as happy to dismiss them as 'hoodies' or 'chavs' who deserve all they get?

Then there is the whole phenomenon of serial murder. What do the murders of Gemma, Tania, Anneli, Paula and Annette tell us about the activities of serial killers in this country, and where they might be concentrating their attention? Have they changed the focus of their murderous intentions, or are serial killers still targeting the same groups on which they have always concentrated?

While we may not have all the answers, we can at least try to sketch out the territory in which we might find some. At the very least we want to begin a discussion that might take us further down the road to thinking about how best to respond to the reality of street prostitution in this country. After all, before he had to resign in the midst of a sex scandal, Mr Blunkett was keen to 'welcome views' on these matters, and that is what we offer in this concluding chapter.

Prostitution: Supply and Demand

Is prostitution inevitable? There are two ways of answering this question by looking at both sides of the coin – supply and demand. In other words, are there always going to be a small number of young women and some men who, in the right circumstances, will find it easier to sell sex than find employment in more legitimate lines of business? And would these young people have anything to sell if there was no demand for the thing they were selling? Looking at the question from this perspective also allows us to consider ways of responding to prostitution in terms of our public policy and our policing. For example, if we concentrate on the 'supply' side we might consider the various local, regional and international initiatives that have been employed to deter young people from entering this world, or consider the routes that could be developed to help people selling sex get out of prostitution. Looking at the supply side also takes us into issues related to legalised brothels, registration schemes and 'managed zones'.

If we were to consider this question from the 'demand' side of the coin we might think about how public policy and policing could target the men who use, exploit and live off the earnings of those who sell sex. We would criminalise the punters and the pimps rather than the prostitutes (and that seems to have been the direction being taken in Ipswich), and target our policing so that those who wanted to buy sexual services would stop kerb-crawling or grooming young people to enter the sex industry.

Different countries have tried to answer this question by concentrating either on supply or demand. For example, Sweden has no offences equivalent to loitering or soliciting, but instead has made it a criminal offence to pay, or offer to pay, for sexual services – on or off the street. Sweden's public policy and its policing targets the punters, and this, coupled with government-funded outreach programmes to support women who want to leave prostitution, has resulted in a decline in the numbers of prostitutes on the streets. This seems like a successful route to take, but we also have to remember that there are only about 1500 women involved in prostitution in Sweden, compared with some 80,000 in Britain. Nor do Swedish prostitutes seem to have the same levels of problematic drug use either. Sweden is one of the few countries in the developed world with a robust and functioning welfare state which protects its citizens – to a greater extent than most – from the ravages of the global economy.

Should 'off-street' brothels be made legal, as they have been in three states in Australia – Victoria, Queensland and New South Wales – and, if so, would this reduce the number of women working as prostitutes? In these states brothels have been licensed so as to develop a safer environment for both staff and clients, and also to provide access for health services to monitor safe sex practices. All prostitutes must be registered in the Victoria scheme and undertake regular health checks, and licensing requires the promotion of safe sex and use of condoms. As well as constant monitoring to prevent the involvement of underage girls, the scheme also defines the meaning of 'brothel' and does not allow the use of more than six rooms. Finally, it is against the law for a licensee to own more than one brothel. With a few refinements such a scheme has recently been adopted in New Zealand.

There have been considerable difficulties, however, with the licensing model. Licensing brothels seems to suggest that the commercial provision of sexual services is acceptable, as a result of which the level of prostitution has grown – both licensed and unlicensed. Those who have drug problems, and who would fail to pass the mandatory health checks, have continued to work on the streets, while those who are able to meet the requirements have moved indoors. The much hoped-for improvements in the safety of prostitutes have not materialised, with some licensed brothel owners still encouraging sex without a condom, and sacking any women unwilling to satisfy their clients' specific needs. Organised crime is still very much involved with the running of licensed brothels.

Perhaps a more pragmatic approach is simply to register prostitutes and encourage or require them to use a 'managed zone' in a specified part of a city. For example, registration schemes exist in Greece, Germany and Austria, where prostitutes must be at least nineteen years old, register with the police and undergo regular health checks. There are also a number of managed areas in several cities in the Netherlands, which are regularly patrolled by the police and where problematic drug use by those selling sex is tolerated. These managed zones have areas for soliciting and for 'working', as well as a drop-in shelter where health services are provided.

We describe this approach as pragmatic, but even so there are a number of problems with it because, in essence, it has merely semi-formalised prostitution. Women are still selling sexual services, and are still doing so because they have drug problems. Managed areas still need to be patrolled by the police, but the most difficult issue seems to be deciding where a managed area should be located. Where 'traditional' red-light districts have been chosen the managed area works well; where new areas have been created these have not worked so well. So, for example, in Ipswich the managed area would merely formalise existing conditions in and around Portman Road; the prostitutes, and everyone else who lives in the area, would still have to face the same problems. Dirty needles and used condoms would still be found on the pavements and in front gardens; children would still be afraid to play in the local park; and women and men who lived locally would still have to deal with the embarrassment of being mistaken as punters or prostitutes. This hardly seems like progress.

Responding to Paying the Price

In total the Government received 861 responses to *Paying the Price*, ranging from those of the Fawcett Society and the Family Planning Association to those received from the English Collective of Prostitutes and the Metropolitan Police – Clubs & Vice Unit (CO14). These responses form the basis of the Government's new paper, *A Coordinated Prostitution Strategy*. Notably, only five Members of Parliament responded to *Paying the Price* – Stuart Bell, Julie Down, Lynne Jones, Gisela Stuart and Joan Walley – and by January 2006 David Blunkett had been replaced as Home

Secretary by Charles Clarke, who has since moved on himself. For whatever reason, Mr Clarke did not choose to write a foreword to the Home Office's *Coordinated Prostitution Strategy*, as might have been expected, and the background and explanation to what was being proposed was left instead to an unspecified 'Prostitution Review Team'. In summary, this strategy claimed that it would:

> focus on disrupting sex markets by preventing individuals, and particularly children and young people, from being drawn into prostitution; by providing appropriate protection and routes out for those already involved; by protecting communities from nuisance associated with prostitution; and by ensuring that those who control, coerce or abuse those in prostitution are brought to justice.

The Prostitution Review Team was clear that the key element to delivering on all this was to 'change attitudes', and to move away from the view that prostitution, as the 'oldest profession', has simply to be accepted. The premise of the strategy is that prostitution is neither inevitable nor acceptable in our towns and cities – whether in the form of street prostitution or off-street in saunas and brothels. The strategy proposes measures to prevent young people becoming involved in prostitution; initiatives to tackle demand and ways out of prostitution for those selling sexual services; suggests ways to tackle off-street prostitution; and, finally, emphasises the need to prosecute those who exploit individuals through prostitution.

Within this new strategy, therefore, there are to be no new 'managed areas' where prostitution is tolerated; there is to be no registration scheme for prostitutes; and nor are brothels to be licensed. Loitering and soliciting are still deemed criminal offences (although there will be a new 'staged' approach to enforcement), and there will be greater focus on policing kerb-crawlers. The strategy also acknowledges that a high proportion of those involved in street prostitution are Class A drug users, and so stresses that women involved in it should have better access to drug treatment. It has to be said that much of what appears in the strategy is concerned more with tackling the supply of drugs within our communities rather than with treatment initiatives, or how these can be accessed. Class A drugs such as heroin will not be made available on prescription and nor will their possession be decriminalised.

While overall *A Coordinated Prostitution Strategy* appears to have its heart in the right place, it also seems to be missing the opportunity to push the debate further forward. It is long on talk but short on action.

Evidence as to just why this opportunity might have been missed was provided by Katherine Raymond, a former special adviser to David Blunkett who helped to draw up *Paying the Price*. Writing in the *Observer* on 17 December 2006, as the murders in Ipswich were unfolding, Raymond described how the new coordinated strategy's proposals were 'watered-down', and even then not acted upon. She claimed that 'prostitution policy in Britain is a disgrace created by the interlinking scandals of political cowardice and public indifference', that 'sex workers lead difficult and dangerous lives and the truth is that most people, including politicians, don't care what happens to them'. She further claimed that only a 'handful' of politicians and Home Office officials had actually wanted *Paying the Price* to see the light of day, and specifically that the Prime Minister's Office had been 'terrified of a hostile media response'.

Perhaps this explains why Charles Clarke did not write a foreword, and why so few politicians seem to have responded to the consultation exercise. If Katherine Raymond is to be believed, we must take with a pinch of salt the idea that there is any political will whatsoever to change public attitudes on these matters.

Raymond is not an impartial observer and we do not necessarily have to accept her preferred solutions of piloted 'managed areas' for prostitution in several cities, brothels legalised along the lines of the Victoria scheme, and prostitution decriminalised. But we can at least accept that the new coordinated strategy does indeed appear to have been 'watered-down', even if we simply have Raymond's word for it that this was as a result of political cowardice and indifference.

A Coordinated Prostitution Strategy has this to say about the use of CCTV to tackle demand: 'the use of CCTV to identify cars regularly cruising red-light areas is a cost-effective way to deter kerb crawling'. This is not how CCTV was described in *Paying the Price*, which acknowledged that 'there are differing anecdotal accounts as to the impact of CCTV in red-light areas. Some argue that the presence of cameras improves the safety of women working on the streets as areas are necessarily well-lit and the women are able to assess their clients more easily. Others suggest that the "trade" is displaced as those involved fear being caught on camera'. We now have evidence from Ipswich which suggests that such displacement does indeed take place, and that mobile phones are much more commonly used to make contact between punters and prostitutes. Prostitution has reacted to the introduction of CCTV in red-light areas and found new ways of keeping this 'trade' secret and hidden, and therefore just as – if not more – dangerous than it has ever been.

Does all this mean that the Home Office's *Coordinated Prostitution Strategy* will be able fundamentally to tackle the problem of the 'brutal realities' of prostitution in our towns and cities? Or will young, vulnerable women still be drawn into prostitution, with problematic drug use the context in which they will continue to live and work? Will our courts still be clogged with women arrested for selling sex on the streets, and will the historical tension between the police and those involved in selling sexual services continue? Can the coordinated strategy do anything to counter the violence that some prostitutes will face from dodgy punters, and will some of these same dodgy punters want to kill and kill again? We try to answers these questions below, but first we consider what the Ipswich murders might tell us about serial killing in this country.

The Future of the Serial Killer in Britain

As Steve Wright begins his life sentence – with no prospect of parole – we should also consider what his activities in Ipswich might tell us about the phenomenon of serial killing. Specifically, is it increasing and, if so, why? Who is being targeted? Are these targets changing? And what can be done to prevent other young vulnerable women (or men) from becoming the victims of future serial killers?

As we have established, by and large serial killers have historically targeted five distinct groups in this country: the elderly; gay men; young children running away from or being thrown out of their homes; babies and infants; and young women (and some young men) who sell sexual services. On average between 1960 and 2006 the number of people murdered by a serial killer each year was seven, and on average there are two serial killers active at any one time in Britain. Such averages hide peaks and troughs, and some years can produce more serial killers, and more victims, than others. However, the overall trend seems to be that the numbers of both serial killers and their victims are increasing, and that their targets are subtly changing, although there is still a certain continuity. For example, apart from those who sell sexual services, serial killers regularly target young runaways. We know that more than 77,000 young people – most between the ages of thirteen and fifteen – run away from home for the first time every year in Britain, and these large numbers suggest they will remain a prime target group for serial killers in years to come. But are there other groups, too, that might become vulnerable?

One additional group could be young people between eighteen and twenty-five who socialise regularly at night, part of what we might call 'the night-time economy'. Such people are experiencing increased levels of interpersonal violence in towns and cities all over the country and are themselves of interest. Like young people who turn to prostitution as a survival strategy, individuals within this age group are having to respond to changes in Britain's traditional economic manufacturing base. People no longer stay in the same job, in the same place, for life; they are faced with greater job insecurity, the outsourcing of once traditional jobs and increased consumption. In addition, there is a demand for greater geographical mobility, with young people changing jobs more often.

Our former manufacturing towns and cities have, therefore, had to reinvent themselves as places where young people go to socialise, reflecting an economic base that has moved from production to consumption. One by-product of this has been a spectacular increase in social division and interpersonal violence.

The violence now being seen on the streets of towns and cities all over the country is different from that in the past, which was more often than not contained within groups of friends out drinking together. Criminologists have noted that unpredictable violence from outside such groups is becoming more commonplace, and that failure to police our cities at night is a consequence of the insatiable demand for continued economic growth. This failure to control the streets and the increase of alcohol-fuelled violence means that the night-time streets of Britain's cities and towns have become the primary sites for random violence.

All this gives us a glimpse of the future of Britain, and it is not a pretty sight. Specifically, the reality that violence from strangers is becoming more common, and that violence is taking place on the streets of night-time Britain, suggests an emerging problem that needs addressing. We have an identifiable group of possible vulnerable young people in areas where policing is often inadequate, and it seems only a matter of time before somebody decides to turn this to their advantage.

All this might be seen as the product of Britain having become a '40/30/30' society as described by Will Hutton, the journalist and chief executive of the Work Foundation, in his book *The State We're In*, one in which only 40 per cent of the workforce enjoy tenured, full-time employment; the next 30 per cent is insecurely self-employed, involuntarily working part-time, or working casually; while the bottom 30 per cent, the marginalised, are idle or working for poverty wages. Perhaps an 'us and them' society would be a better description, where since 1979 the rich have grown richer and the poor have been left behind, unable to fit into the new Britain of consumption rather than production.

Hutton was writing before New Labour came to power in 1997, but its period in office does not seem to have altered particularly the economic course that was being pursued by the Tories. If anything, New Labour has continued the social and economic policies of the Tories – albeit that these have been characterised as a 'Third Way' – bringing together social justice and a dynamic economy. Nonetheless, New Labour has drawn directly from neo-liberal discourses in its analysis of the global economy. 'Globalisation' has become a favourite justification of the New Labour 'project', and thus the British economy, it is argued, has to continue to make itself as attractive to investors as possible by maintaining an unrestrained free market economy. All of this helps to explain why we suggest that serial killing will continue to rise. But when might this rise first be detected?

In a recent analysis of murder in Britain since 1981 by Professor Danny Dorling of Sheffield University, it was noted that the murder rate is increasing with regard to one specific group – those men born in or after 1964. This gives us some clues about how our society is changing, and what might make one community more dangerous than another. The overriding factor seems to be poverty, and it's also worth remembering that many men born in or after 1964 would have left school in 1980–81, depending on their birthdays. Dorling suggests that this is significant:

The summer of 1981 was the first summer for over 40 years that a young man living in a poor area would find work or training very scarce, and it got worse in the years that followed. When the recession of the early 1980s hit, mass unemployment was concentrated on the young, they were simply not recruited.

The argument here is that, by 1981, the first generation that had reached maturity in a Britain that was rapidly changing its economic base would have quickly become aware that the way their grandfathers, fathers or elder brothers had moved from school into work had changed. That change would bring with it other changes, too, in relation to how this generation could put meaning into their lives, and was predicated upon 'new right' thinking which wanted a deregulated economy, and no 'welfare dependency'. One of the by-products of this change was an increase in the murder rate in this specific group, and, while murder is different from serial killing, this insight might also help us understand why the rate of serial killing would seem to be on the rise, and why these broad social and economic forces create the conditions in which those who wanted to kill and kill again were given the opportunities to do so.

We are not trying to suggest some crude economic cause and effect, but rather a more nuanced observation that in the same way young men in 1981 first became aware that their world had changed, so too those killers who were active found it easier to kill their elderly, gay or child victims, or those vulnerable young women who worked selling sexual services.

The dominant theme in any analysis of the majority of those who have been murdered by serial killers in Britain between 1960 and 2006 is their poverty. They are 'the left behind' in an economy that has moved inexorably from production to consumption. This is significant, for it begs the question as to what role and function the poor have in a society characterised by the economic imperative to consume.

After all, while the labour of the poor was once needed and valued in an economy that produced manufactured goods to sell to the world, in the outsourced, deregulated, lean economy that emerged after 1979, the ability of the poor to work no longer seems to guarantee them the protection of the state that their labour once commanded. As such they became a burden – through their inability to consume in the same way, or to the same extent as those who have power, status and money. As the sociologist Zygmunt Bauman has recently put it, the poor in these changed economic circumstances 'are totally useless'. He continues:

> No one – no one who truly counts, speaks up and is heard – needs them [the poor]. For them, zero tolerance. Society would be much better off if the poor just burnt their tents and left. The world would be much more pleasant without them. The poor are not needed, and so they are unwanted. And because they are unwanted, they can be, without much regret and compunction, forsaken.

Of course, if no one who 'truly counts' speaks up when someone is murdered, and if the world is seen as much more 'pleasant' without the existence of that person – because of their age, gender, sexuality or the fact that they work in prostitution – then no one is either going to notice or care if more and more of the same type of person get killed. The poor have not so much 'burnt their tents and left', as had them burned for them. In this respect serial killing emerges as the ultimate form of 'forsaking'; the ultimate form of abandoning and deserting the poor, in a culture that has increasingly come to place its primary value on consumption. In doing so it has left in its wake fractured communities, where individuals are now more and more cut off from each other, while all the time living precarious and anxious lives that no longer seem to be connected to the lives of anyone else.

Doing It for Themselves?

But there is a small glimmer of hope. The police investigation of the Ipswich murders, for example, did at least demonstrate that, after a slow start and when they had access to the right resources, police forces can bring prostitute-killers to justice. There also seemed to be considerable public support for the police in their investigations, and some evidence of a greater public understanding about the issues that surround young women who work in the sex industry. It's unlikely that this will herald a fundamental change of public attitudes about prostitution, but at least it's a start.

We also believe that *Paying the Price* is an accurate summary of what we know about street prostitution in this country, and that even a 'watered-down' *Coordinated Prostitution Strategy* can offer some workable suggestions as to how to stop the sale of sexual services on our streets, and to make the lives of prostitutes much safer. This coordinated strategy needs greater support and wider promotion to help it succeed. Above all, we have to accept that there are solutions to the problems associated with prostitution, and that we do not have to accept things as they are at the moment.

It is no surprise that, given the Government's lack of action, charities and voluntary organisations working with prostitutes have started to take matters into their own hands. St Mungo's, for example, a charity that was founded in 1969 when it opened its first house run by volunteers for people sleeping rough in Battersea, south-west London, has since established a range of hostels that now help more than ten thousand homeless and vulnerable people each year. The charity runs a housing service for drug-dependent women involved in prostitution in Lambeth, and offers them a safe place to live as part of a strategy to help them out of selling sexual services. One such woman was Jo (not her real name), who spent thirty years working the streets to finance her drug habit, and, given her chaotic lifestyle, found herself sleeping mostly on the floors of crack houses, which merely exacerbated the problem, and made it much more difficult for her to escape prostitution. She was given a place in the hostel, and described this to the *South London Press*:

> The project has really helped me. A few years ago, nobody wanted to know us. Things have changed a hell of a lot. A few years ago, we had no help and no support at all. This has got me on the straight line and I was out there for 30 years.

Another charity, The Magdalene Group, based in Norwich, has for a number of years offered women involved in prostitution, or at risk of becoming involved in prostitution, support and advice to help change their lives. Indeed, the cover of *Paying the Price* shows a picture drawn by one such woman, Ruth, a former prostitute who is now a freelance artist. Another is Tracey, and her story, taken from the group's website, resonates dreadfully with what we know of events in Ipswich. This is what she describes:

> I first came into contact with The Magdalene Group in 1998, when I was homeless with a 5 year old child and a nine month old baby.

They were able to offer a 'listening ear' and support throughout this time of need, until I moved away from Norwich (the reason for moving was due to my best friend being murdered and my fear that I would be next).*

I began taking amphetamines when I was 23 and I soon moved onto Heroin which led me to working as a prostitute to support my habit. My addiction grew so bad that I couldn't continue to look after my children.

I ended up in prison for 3 weeks, during which time my husband left me, this gave me the prompt I needed to sort my life out.

I eventually managed to get 'clean' and moved in with my parents in a bid to beat my six year addiction, but one final lapse just before midnight Christmas 2002 proved almost fatal.

I was found unconscious by my Mum at 7.30 the following morning, eight hours after injecting, I was then taken to hospital, where doctors had no choice but to amputate part of one leg.

I recently highlighted the horrors of drug and alcohol addiction, by being involved in an anti-drugs campaign.

I have a daily reminder of just how destructive drugs can be, I was addicted and ultimately nearly paid with my life.

I have now been clean for almost 3 years and it's getting easier day by day. My children now live with my Mum (my choice), and I see them every single day. I would urge anyone who wants to kick their habit to make full use of their local services.

Use it before its too late – I wish I had!

---

* Tracey does not name the friend who was murdered.

Our final example is Safe Exit Tower Hamlets (SETH), an umbrella group which represents all local voluntary and statutory agencies which work with prostitutes in the East End of London. They produced a self-help handbook designed to assist women to leave prostitution by providing them with advice about a range of issues that they might face – such as violence from pimps or punters, homelessness, drug addiction, physical and mental health – and where they could get help for such issues. The advice the handbook gives is often graphic and to the point. For example, in a section entitled 'Self-Defence' the estimated 250–300 women involved in prostitution on the streets of Tower Hamlets – many around Commercial Street, where Jack the Ripper struck in 1888 – are advised to 'carry a rape alarm if you can', and 'if you must fight, attack soft areas such as the throat, eyes, Adam's apple, underside of nose, groin and shins'.

Women involved in street prostitution are further advised that if they are approached by a punter in a car they should note the registration plates, and make certain that no one is hiding in the back of the car. The handbook continues: 'try to arrange the price, service and location before you get into the car and get the money first. Put it in a different place to your other money so that if he does try to rob you, at least you can save some of your money.' However, in light of events in Ipswich in December 2006, perhaps the most telling advice relates to drugs:

Try not to let customers know about your drug use as they may use this to play money or power games. Insist on getting paid in cash, not drugs. You will look more professional and in control. Remember that heroin doesn't make you warm. It only makes you feel warm. It masks the effect of the cold, but doesn't prevent the harm that the cold can do. Wrap up or, better still, wear layers when working outdoors at night.

Chillingly, the phrase 'power games' takes us back to Wright and how he behaved towards his drug-addicted victims in Ipswich, and also how these victims in turn through their heroin use failed to appreciate the difference between actually being warm and simply feeling warm. They misjudged the circumstances in which they found themselves by no longer being able to differentiate between reality and fantasy. We can only speculate if they would have survived had the handbook's advice been more widely disseminated.

SETH is chaired by Louise Alexander, the local Liberal Democrat councillor for Weavers Ward, which is dominated by Brick Lane and borders Spitalfields. In her online blog she described the launch of *The Safe Exit Handbook* on 10 November 2005 and endorsed the view that it would be better for the laws related to prostitution to target kerb-crawlers, rather than the women who sold sexual services on the street and who were much easier targets for the police to arrest. Councillor Alexander was speaking before the publication of the 'watered-down', Home Office coordinated strategy.

The relationship between SETH, street prostitution, kerb-crawlers in the East End of London and wider Government policy all became bizarrely entangled on a Monday night in June 2006, only some six months after the launch of *The Safe Exit Handbook*, when, half an hour before midnight, Khalique Miah, a plumber, was kerb-crawling in his blue Mitsubishi Space Wagon along Commercial Street in Spitalfields. He stopped one young woman and asked her for

a blow job. Unfortunately for him he had in fact propositioned an undercover police officer, and was promptly
arrested. He was taken to the local police station where he
was charged and then released on bail. Undeterred, less than
an hour later he returned to Commercial Street where he
was again arrested after propositioning another undercover
police officer. Two months later Miah pleaded guilty on two
charges of soliciting and then became only the third man in
England to receive an ASBO for kerb-crawling.* Perhaps we
know about Miah because his story seems so ludicrous, but
it seems to us to highlight the continued reluctance of our
courts to target, as Councillor Alexander suggested, the
punter rather than the prostitute.

Based on what we heard and saw in Ipswich, we would
like to see more attention being devoted to disrupting the
demand for street prostitution by targeting more men like
Miah who kerb-crawl, and much greater emphasis being
placed on drug treatment so as to help women out of prostitution. But neither of these is as easy as it sounds, and we
believe that there are three further issues to be considered.

At the End of it All

First, we have to decide if there is any benefit from continuing to fill our courts with women who have been arrested for
prostitution. It is a waste of both the courts' time and the
police's, but it is also looking at the wrong side of the prostitution coin, failing to deal with the underlying problem

* The first two men served with ASBOs for kerb-crawling were Colin Grist
in September 2004, and then Royston Morgan in February 2006. Both
received ASBOs for kerb-crawling in Fishponds, the red-light area of Bristol.

being presented by these women. We know that 95 per cent of street prostitutes are addicted to Class A drugs and that neither the police nor the courts seem capable of dealing with that reality. Going to court does not create access to health or other outreach services; it merely further stigmatises and socially excludes an already marginalised group.

We would also suggest that both the police and the courts should become much more culturally and temperamentally attuned to enforcing the laws against kerb-crawling, and it is there that we believe that they should concentrate their attention – as they have done in Sweden. The numbers nationally involved in prostitution might be smaller in Sweden, but if every British city or large town concentrated its policing and court activity along Swedish lines we believe there would be a decline in the demand for the sale of sexual services. Some cities, such as Southampton and Bradford, *have* taken a much stronger line on kerb-crawlers. In Southampton, for example, the Change Programme, which was set up in 2002, requires that those arrested for kerb-crawling either go to court or attend a one-day course aimed at changing their behaviour by exploring the issues that surround prostitution, for which they are charged £200 – the average fine for kerb-crawling imposed by a magistrate's court. The last published figures state that of the 406 kerb-crawlers arrested since the programme has been running, 317 men have enrolled on the course and only three appear to have reoffended. There is no knowing if they have simply gone elsewhere, but schemes such as these demonstrate that things can change – if there is the will. Regardless of what individual cities are doing, the fact remains that, nationally, only three men have been given ASBOs for kerb-crawling. This sends out all the wrong messages about what we should be doing to cut the demand for sexual services being sold on the streets of Britain's towns and cities.

Second, we accept that the solutions to drug dependency will always need to be tailored to an individual's circumstances, and therefore in some cases will involve, for example, education, the development of employment skills and the provision of somewhere to stay – as Jo's example from St Mungo's demonstrates. For others it will involve the provision of counselling and mental health support, which is perhaps the 'listening ear' that Tracey refers to at The Magdalene Group. These examples demonstrate that weaning someone off drugs is a complex process, but it is also only the first step to recovery. Even so, we have to take that first step, and so we could also look to schemes that exist elsewhere which try and manage the problems associated with Class A drugs in very different ways to the approach typically adopted in this country.

For example, in Switzerland the Class A drug heroin (rather than methadone) is available on prescription from a doctor, and at a stroke the addict is able to get drugs legally (rather than through a pimp or a dealer), and is also offered a route to medical support to manage (and then reduce) that addiction thereafter. More than a thousand heroin addicts are currently on the Swiss Heroin Assisted Treatment programme – around 75 per cent of the country's addicted population – and they can access heroin at twenty-two injection centres across the country.

One result of this policy has been a dramatic drop in crime, with 70 per cent of those who enter the scheme in Switzerland admitting that they had been involved in criminal activity. That figure dropped to around 10 per cent after eighteen months of receiving their drugs in this way. If a similar scheme was introduced in Britain, the cost benefits in relation to crime would be obvious. For example, a typical heroin addict needs about £15,000 of heroin a year to maintain the habit. Some will turn to crime to maintain that addiction. However, because they cannot sell the goods that they have stolen at their real value they might have to steal as much as £45,000 worth of people's belongings to buy the heroin they need. Of course treating addicts with heroin costs money, too, and the cost of that treatment is calculated at about £12,000 per person. However, schemes such as the one in Switzerland aren't designed simply to allow addicts access to free heroin for the rest of their lives; rather, they are treatment-based and aim ultimately to help the addict first to manage and then lead a drug-free life.

Support for an overhaul of the drugs laws in Britain came as recently as March 2007, when the Royal Society of Arts' Commission on Illegal Drugs, chaired by Professor Anthony King of the University of Essex, concluded that the law in relation to drugs was driven by 'moral panic' and that it was not 'fit for purpose'. The RSA's report – *Illegal Drugs, Communities and Public Policy*, wants the current Misuse of Drugs Act replaced by a Misuse of Substances Act, with the abolition of the existing ABC classification system and its replacement with an 'index of harms'. Overall the report suggests that our drugs policy should be based on reducing harm rather than criminalising people who use drugs; that there should be much wider access to prescription heroin; finally it calls for the introduction of 'shooting galleries' where users can inject drugs. It has yet to be seen how the Government will respond to the RSA's report, and whether it will become the tipping point in our approach to drug use in public policy, although there is to be a major Government review of our drugs strategy in 2008.

Finally, and perhaps most difficult of all, we need to

acknowledge that the Ipswich murders revealed the yawning and increasing gulf in this country between the haves and the have-nots. Weaning young people off drugs and then providing them with training and employment skills merely begs the question 'training for what?' In the lean and mean global economy of Britain, which has also seen welfare benefits cut and much more difficult to access, what would our young, vulnerable former sex workers actually do? Would any legitimate job earn them more money than they were getting on the streets or would they have to settle for less, with all that suggests in our consumer-led society? Would weaning them off drugs and preparing them for work merely confirm their status on the bottom rung of Will Hutton's '40/30/30' ladder, insecurely self-employed or working for poverty wages? Would you choose this option for yourself, or for your own son or daughter?

Ultimately the deaths of Tania, Gemma, Anneli, Paula and Annette are not so much a story of Ipswich or Suffolk, or of prostitution, drug addiction and serial murder – although clearly their murders are also about all of these things – but rather their stories tell us much more about what it means to be young, poor and working-class in Britain in the twenty-first century. Our response to their murder should be on many different levels – from policing and drug initiatives to reconsidering and having the courage to implement much of what appears in *Paying the Price* and the new national coordinated strategy. However, their deaths should also remind us that we cannot abandon the poor, or regard them as a burden on society, but instead we ought to see their lives as inextricably linked to our own, and therefore fight injustices committed against them in exactly the same way that we would if they were committed against ourselves or members of our own families.

What these awful murders reveal is that those who want to kill and kill again can only do this when the social structure in which they operate allows them to do so by placing value on one group or groups to the detriment of others. For when this happens and when communities are fractured and anxious, when people feel isolated and cut off from each other, and when the bonds of mutual support have been all but destroyed as each individual believes he or she has to struggle simply to survive, it is then – and only then – that those who want to kill large numbers of their fellow human beings are able to achieve their deadly purpose.

A Guide to Further Reading and a Note on Secondary Sources

Two issues have dominated this book – prostitution and serial killing. In relation to the latter there are surprisingly few books related to the history of serial killing in Britain that provide a comprehensive overview, although Martin Fido's *British Serial Killing* (2001) and David Wilson's *Serial Killers: Hunting Britons and their Victims, 1960–2006* (2007) are good starting points. In relation to serial killer typologies, the standard introduction remains that by Ronald Holmes and James Deburger titled simply *Serial Murder* (1988), which is referred to throughout Chapter Three. So, too, Ronald Holmes and Stephen Holmes' book, also called *Serial Murder* (1988), and their *Murder in America* (2001) both provide good introductions to the subject, although from an American perspective. Of the many 'true crime' books on this subject, those written by ex-FBI staff are of particular interest and would include Robert Ressler's *Whoever Fights Monsters: My Twenty Years Tracking Serial Killers for the FBI* (1992).

While there are few good overviews of British serial killing, there are a number of excellent case studies of particular serial killers. Of these Gordon Burn's *Somebody's Husband, Somebody's Son: The Story of the Yorkshire Ripper* (1984), and *Happy Like Murderers: The True Story of Fred and Rosemary West* (1998), are both excellent, as is Howard Sounes's *Fred & Rose* (1995). Less well known and more difficult to get hold of, but just as interesting, is the account by the campaigning journalist Nick Davies about Beverly Allitt called *Murder on Ward Four: The Story of Bev Allitt and the Most Terrifying Crime since the Moors Murders* (1993). However, by far the best case history of a British serial killer – largely because of the author's unique access to the killer and to his letters and other papers – remains Brian Masters' *Killing for Company: The Case of Dennis Nilsen* (1985). Masters has also written about Rose West in *She Must Have Known: The Trial of Rosemary West* (1996), although this is more polemical, but does throw interesting light on the media's influence in how Rosemary West was portrayed to the public.

As a bridge between serial killing and prostitution Nick Davies's *Dark Heart: The Shocking Truth About Hidden Britain* (1997) is particularly useful. Davies visits the slums, ghettoes and red-light districts of a number of British cities and tries to make sense of what he finds there – including the growing number of children who sell sexual services. As part of his journey Davies interviews Lin Pearman, the mother of Natalie Pearman who was murdered while working as a prostitute in Norwich, and who is mentioned several times in this book. Those interested in an earlier famous serial killer who attacked prostitutes in Whitechapel in 1888 should consult Stewart Evans and Keith Skinner's *The Ultimate Jack the Ripper Sourcebook: An Illustrated Encyclopedia* (2000). In relation to the current situation about prostitution in this country two Home Office reports are excellent starting points – *Paying the Price: A Consultation Paper on Prostitution* (2004) and *A Coordinated Prostitution Strategy and a Summary of Responses to Paying the Price* (2006) –

and we refer to both in our conclusion. In relation to drugs, the RSA's report *Illegal Drugs, Communities and Public Policy* is a refreshing and new look at this pressing issue and can be downloaded from www.rsadrugscommission.org.

While prostitution and serial killing dominate the narrative of *Hunting Evil*, we have also discussed other issues which some readers might like to investigate further. Chief among these are murder, offender profiling, policing, and the media. In relation to murder in Britain a number of accessible academic books have recently been published. Shani D'Cruze, Sandra Walklate and Samantha Pegg's *Murder* (2006) is a very useful overview, but perhaps Fiona Brookman's *Understanding Homicide* (2005) is the best place to start, as this also provides an excellent guide to how the police investigate murder. We also made use of, and can recommend, Danny Dorling's *Prime Suspect: Murder in Britain* (2005), which appears in a collection of papers called *Criminal Obsessions: Why Harm Matters More Than Crime*, published by the Crime and Society Foundation.

The police have regularly been the subject of scholarly and true crime analyses, and any reader wishing to study the police more fully would do well to consult Robert Reiner's *The Politics of the Police* (2000), which we make use of in Chapter Three. So, too, Clive Elmsley's (1993) *Crime and Society in England, 1750–1900* is very good on the origins and history of the police, and Michael Bilton's *Wicked Beyond Belief: The Hunt for the Yorkshire Ripper* (2003) is an excellent, if very sympathetic account of the many failings of the police in that serial killer investigation, failings which would become the subject of a major inquiry by Lawrence Byford. A more general introduction can be found in David Wilson, John Aston and Douglas Sharp's *What Everyone in Britain Should Know About the Police* (2001).

Offender profiling has only recently become a subject which has been written about outside specialist criminology or psychology journals. However, a good starting point is Peter Ainsworth, *Offender Profiling and Crime Analysis* (2001). So, too, as we argue, it is instructive to compare the differing approaches of Professor David Canter and Paul Britton. Canter's *Criminal Shadows* (1995) and *Mapping Murder: Walking in Killers' Footsteps* (2003) are both of interest. Britton's *The Jigsaw Man: The Remarkable Career of Britain's Foremost Criminal Psychologist* (1998) is widely available.

There are a number of books which describe how the media can shape stories to create a particular social or political agenda, or prompt police action. David Wilson and Jon Silverman, *Innocence Betrayed: Paedophilia, The Media and Society* (2002) is of interest in that it explains how the 'naming and shaming' campaign of a Sunday tabloid created a political agenda to introduce 'Sarah's Law' in relation to community-based paedophiles (although this has been resisted). Paul Mason's *Policing and the Media: Fiction and Faction* (2003) is a helpful starting point, and more details about specific police investigations and their relationship with the media can be found in John Bennett with Graham Gardner, *The Cromwell Street Murders: The Detective's Story* (2005), which complains bitterly about the 'media attention' devoted to the murders of the Wests, but is also of interest because it demonstrates how the media and the police often shaped how the murders were presented. So, too, it describes the operational use of profilers – in this case Paul Britton – and of the HOLMES computer retrieval system.

Finally, we relied on several general books of sociology that we are happy to recommend. Chief among these was

Zygmunt Bauman's *Work, Consumerism and the New Poor* (2005), which describes how the poor come to be poor and the role that they now play in a global economy. Likewise, we were helped by reading Simon Winlow and Steve Hall's *Violent Night: Urban Leisure and Contemporary Culture* (2006), which uses insider accounts to uncover the underlying causes and meanings of violence in the night-time economy of contemporary Britain and which should be a warning to us all about the direction in which our culture is heading.

Acknowledgements

I would like to thank the head of Sky News, John Ryley, and Sky News' managing editor, Simon Cole, for their support and for allowing me unfettered access to Sky News resources. Huge thanks to Nick Peters and his team in the News Library and Andreas Kirchberger in Sky Stills for gathering such powerful images for the book. Thanks also to the Sky News Ipswich trial team and the 'Gobletiers' – among them field news editor Harriet Tolputt, cameraman Dave Prime, editor Emily Dumas, correspondent David Crabtree, producers Victoria Bird and Tim Gallagher, and engineer Chris Britt. Thanks as well to Grant Sherlock from the *Ipswich Evening Star*, whose knowledge of the case proved invaluable. Thanks, of course, to Gordon Wise at Curtis Brown, and to everyone at Little, Brown – particularly Antonia Hodgson, Vivien Redman and Linda Silverman – for their guidance and patience during my first experience in the world of publishing.

On a more personal level I'd like to give special thanks to the following: The Prof – David Wilson – for his wisdom and friendship. My father, John, for having instilled in me the drive and confidence to take on new challenges. My girl-friend, Felicity Barr, whose encouragement and support in everything that I do is so precious. My brother James for showing me if you want something enough, you can make it happen – like being able to retrieve lost documents on my laptop from the other side of the Atlantic.

And finally, thanks to my mum – Penelope. Your infinite strength and love has allowed me to follow my dreams. Thank you.

Paul Harrison

I would like to thank the staff of the Centre for Criminal Justice Policy and Practice at Birmingham City University, the staff and librarians of Cambridge University Library, Birmingham City University and the Radzinowicz Institute in Cambridge; Ross Collins for his book suggestions; Neil and Sue Foster, Anne Maguire, Hugo and Fleur Wilson; the 'Thursday night' group; everyone at Sky News – but especially Harriet Tolputt, Martin Brunt, Dave Prime and Tim Gallagher; can I also thank Harry, who had the patience to teach this old dog the new trick of writing narrative – and who made it enjoyable. Gordon Wise, Jacquie Drewe and Jessica Hanscomb at Curtis Brown; Antonia Hodgson, Kirsteen Astor and Vivien Redman at Little, Brown for their care and dedication to this project; and, finally, all the people in Ipswich who agreed to speak to us about the tragic events that unfolded at the end of December 2006.

David Wilson